MW01519657

Ancient Japanese Rituals and the Revival of Pure Shinto

What is Shinto? is the key question asked by all who seek to understand Japan and the Japanese, answered in this volume by Sir Ernest Satow, the great British scholar and diplomat. Shinto is the unique and little-known religious beliefs that flourished in Japan before the introduction of Buddhism and Confucianism, but there are many versions - which is the pure form? Satow begins with a detailed study of core Shinto rituals as revealed in ancient texts, which embody the deepest and oldest traditions of Shinto belief in divinity, national destiny and, above all, Japan's special favored status as 'the country of the gods', beliefs that endure today behind the facade of Japan Inc. Shinto rites, incantations, sacred objects and symbols are described meticulously, with illustrations and translations by Karl Florenz. Satow then describes how the Ancient Way of Shinto survived centuries of foreign influence to be revived during the Meiji era, when it became the driving force behind the transformation of Japan into a world power. Unrivalled for its scholarship and elegance, this is a classic in Japanese studies.

Sir ERNEST SATOW (1843-1929) was a noted linguist and expert on Japan, where he was long resident and served as British Minister from 1895-1900. The late **Dr. KARL FLORENZ** was a distinguished German Japanologist.

THE KEGAN PAUL JAPAN LIBRARY

Ancient Japanese Rituals
and the Revival of Pure Shinto

Routledge
Taylor & Francis Group

LONDON AND NEW YORK

First published 2002 by
Kegan Paul Limited

This edition published 2012 by Routledge
2 Park Square, Milton Park, Abingdon, Oxon OX14 4RN
Simultaneously published in the USA and Canada by Routledge
711 Third Avenue, New York, NY 10017

Routledge is an imprint of the Taylor & Francis Group, an informa business

© Kegan Paul, 2002

British Library Cataloguing in Publication Data
Satow, Sir Ernest, 1843-1929
Ancient Japanese rituals and the revival of pure Shinto.-
(The Kegan Paul Japan Library)
1.Shinto - Rituals 2.Shinto- Japan - History
I.Title II.Florenz,Karl, 1865-1939
299.5′61'38

ISBN: 9780710307507

Library of Congress Cataloging-in-Publication Data
Applied for.

CONTENTS

ANCIENT JAPANESE RITUALS.—PART I.*

NO. 1.—THE PRAYING FOR HARVEST.

BY

ERNEST SATOW.

*(Read before the Asiatic Society of Japan
on November 12th, 1878.)*

One of the questions most frequently asked by those who take interest in Japanese subjects is, "What is the nature of Shiñtau"? It might seem at first sight that the answer should be easy, but this is not the case. In the first place, there are several kinds of Shiñtau to be distinguished before an answer can be given. There is the Riyaubu Shiñtau, in which the primitive belief has been overlaid and almost hidden by a mass of Buddhist mysticism, and I cannot say that I have had time to study it at all. Then we have the Yuwiitsu Shiñtau, also consisting mainly of a Buddhist superstructure on a Shiñtau foundation; the Deguchi Shiñtau, in which the ancient belief is explained by means of the Chinese Book of Changes, and the Suwiga Shiñtau, which is a combination of Yuwiitsu Shiñtau and the teachings of the Chinese philosopher Choohe. Besides these there is the real Shiñtau, by which I mean the belief actually held and the rites practised by the Japanese people before the introduction of Buddhism and the Chinese philosophy, to which must further be added the Shiñtau of modern writers, such as Motowori and Hirata, whose views I have attempted to summarize in a paper entitled the "Revival of Pure Shiñtau." Of all these kinds, unquestionably the most interesting to students

*Reprinted from the Transaction of the Asiatic Society of Japan, First Series. Vol. VII, Pt. II, pp. 95-126.

of comparative religion is the Shiñtau of the primitive Japanese, because if we can separate it from the spurious counterfeits and adulterations which áre presented to us as Shiñtau, we shall probably arrive at a natural religion in a very early stage of development, which perhaps originated quite independently of any other natural religion known to us, and that would certainly be of value, as showing one way in which a natural religion may spring up. The materials for this study consist of certain books belonging to the earliest period of Japanese literature, some of which are older than the introduction of the Chinese art of writing, but in the absence of any native system of writing, have been preserved first by oral tradition and later through the medium of the Chinese characters. As long as these books remain locked up in the original language they can be accessible, of course, only to the very small number of students who have specially directed their attention to this portion of Japanese literature. There is a wide field for research in Japan, and few if any can hope to find time to explore it thoroughly, because of the difficulties which the language presents. It seems, therefore, most practical to endeavour to remove the principal obstacle which prevents inquirers from learning at first hand what this primitive belief and these early rites were, by making as accurate translations as possible of the most important texts. For thus we shall be contributing towards the stock of material, which must be gathered together for examination by those whose special training fits them to draw the proper inferences from the scattered facts, of which each individual specialist can know only a small portion.

In studying the primitive religion of the Japanese people there are two principal avenues open to us. We may examine the myths which are contained in the Nihoñgi, Kozhiki and other early records of tradition, and by analyzing the names of the gods and other supernatural beings who figure in those legends, discover the real relation in which they stand to each other and the true signification of the stories concerning them. In this way we should gain a general idea of the accepted belief concerning the gods, that was current at the time when those records were compiled, that is to say, if the expression be admissible, of the theory of Shiñtau, and at the same time it would become

possible to show how and in what order these myths were evolved.
But of not less importance than this inquiry would be an investigation into the practical side of Shiñtau, by considering the
attitude which the worshipper assumed towards the objects of
worship, the means which he adopted of conciliating their
favour or of averting their anger, and the language in which he
addressed them. To describe the ceremonies used in the worship
of the gods, the buildings in which it was celebrated, the
organization of the priesthood, such as it still is, or can be shown
to have been in earlier times, would also be of great interest,
but such researches would require more ample leisure than falls
to the lot of most foreign residents in this country. It would
be necessary to visit the chief temples in different parts of the
country, to enter into relations with the priests in charge of
them, and to be present at their principal festivals. Tied to one
spot almost throughout the year, as most of us are, we must
content ourselves with such kinds of information as are to be obtained from books, which, though not entitled to be accepted
as infallible guides, will yield valuable results when studied with
patience.

An important part of every performance of Shiñtau rites,
not less so than the presentation of offerings to the god or
departed human spirit, is the reading or recitation of a sort of
liturgy or ritual addressed for the most part to the object of
worship, in which the grounds of this worship are stated and the
offerings are enumerated. The Japanese word for such a liturgy
or ritual is _norito_*, frequently pronounced _notto_, according to

---

*The etymology of _norito_ is not quite certain. It is evident, however, that
nori is the verb _nori_, to say, which occurs in the modern _na-nori_, to say one's name.
Mabuchi thinks the complete expression should be _norito-goto_, the last element of
which is of course _koto_, word, and he considers to be a phonetic corruption of _ṭe_,
contracted from _tabe_, to give, so that the whole would mean 'words pronounced
and given,' that is, given by the gods to the priests. Motowori disputes this
derivation (K. Zh. K. D. VIII. 48, Ohob. Kot. Gosh. II. 11 verso) and shows that
there is no evidence that the _norito_ were ever supposed to have been taught to the
priests by the gods. He endeavours to prove that the true etymology is _nori-toki-
goto_, and asserts that _toki_ as well as _nori_ means 'to say,' 'to pronounce,' so that it
may be used of speech addressed by an inferior to a superior, as well as vice versa.
A more modern opinion is that _nori-goto_ was the original form into which a redundant syllable _to_ has been introduced for euphony's sake. It is difficult to accept
this last view. Motowori's certainly appears the least open to objection, and the
only point against him is that _toku_ properly means 'to unfold,' 'to explain,' and
that 'say' is a meaning consequent upon the association of _toku_ with the Chinese
character 説 .

a well known law of phonetic corruption. These *norito* may be, and often áre, composed for a single special occasion, as for instance a funeral conducted according to Shiñtau rites, and the Government Gazettes of the years immediately succeeding the Mikado's restoration in 1868 contain a large number of these occasional *norito*. Amongst them are rituals recited to add greater solemnity to the oath by which the sovereign bound himself to govern in accordance with liberal ideas, to celebrate his removal to the eastern metropolis, to obtain military success over his enemies, to give sanctity to the institution of an order of lay-preachers who were intended to spread abroad the teachings of Shiñtau, in honour of the gods of war, and to confirm the bestowal of posthumous titles on certain predecessors of the Mikado who had hitherto not been recognized as legitimate sovereigns. The *norito* used in the celebration of the annual service called Chiñkoñsai (鎮 魂 祭), the object of which is to pacify the Mikado's soul, or, in other words, to ensure to him continuance in bodily health, is also said to have been from the earliest ages composed afresh on each occasion; but it is evident that there would be a tendency for a regularly recurrent ritual to settle down into a nearly constant form, from which the variations would be insignificant and might finally disappear altogether. This apparently happened in the cases of a considerable proportion of the rituals used in the services celebrated in early times at the court of the Mikado, for out of seventy-five such recognized services which are enumerated in the Yeñgishiki, we find that in the tenth century the precise wording of the rituals is prescribed for nearly thirty, and those undoubtedly the most important of the whole number. Whether they had all been committed to writing before the promulgation of the Ceremonial Laws of the year 927 (Yeñgishiki) is not known, but there seems good ground for supposing that some of them at least had assumed their present form much earlier. Mabuchi ascribes the congratulatory address of the chieftains of Idzumo, which is included among the *norito,* to the reign of Zhiyomei Teñwau (舒明天皇, 629-641), the General Purification to that of Teñmu (天 武 ,673-686) and the Praying for Harvest, which is the subject of this paper, to the reign of Kuwauniñ (光 仁, 770-782), but his grounds for assuming these dates as the probable age of the *norito* in question are chiefly peculiarities in the use of certain Chinese characters to represent certain Japanese words (e.g. 尊 for *mikoto,* instead of 命), from which no trustworthy inferences can be drawn, since the scribes of that age were addicted to numerous irregularities in the use of Chinese ideographs. It is more likely that the norito, as we have received them, had been transmitted orally, without any material alteration, for generations before they came to be written down. A principal reason for holding this opinion is that they contain not a few words, the meaning of which had been so far forgotten, that no Chinese equivalents could then be found for them; and instead of being translated into Chinese characters, they were written down phonetically. Of these words some have been ingeniously interpreted by modern native philologists, but there remain a good number that have hitherto defied analysis, and the preservation of such unintelligible words, instead of substituting something that could be readily understood, is a powerful argument in favour of the antiquity of the present text of those *norito* in which they occur.

A few bibliographical notes will be useful to those who wish to study the rituals in the original. The Yeñgishiki, or Ceremonial Law referred to above, had been preceded by two similar codes compiled by authority of the sovereign and published respectively in 820 and 871, which took the titles of Kouniñ-shiki and Jiyauguwañ-shiki from the chronological periods in which they were produced. The former is believed to be no longer extant, and the author of the bibliographical work entitled Guñshiyo-ichirañ condemns as a forgery the twelve sections in MS. which go by its name, but the latter has been preserved, and the first printed edition of it appeared only a few years since. It contains more detailed instructions for the celebration of certain Shiñtau services than even the Yeñgishiki which superseded it, and is on that account esteemed of great value; but the rituals do not seem to have been included in it, probably because there was still sufficient vitality in the Shiñtau religion to preserve the tradition without the special sanction of an authoritative publication. In 905 a commission of twelve functionaries and scholars, to whom others were afterwards added, was appointed to revise the ceremonial law, and the result of their labours was a collection of regulations in fifty books, to which the title of Yeñgishiki was given from the chronological period in which it was begun (901-23), though it was not promulgated until the year 927. Of these fifty books the first ten are exclusively occupied with matters concerning the practice of the Shiñtau religion, such as the ceremonies observed and the offerirgs made at the fixed annual, and at the occasional, services (bks. 1-3), the organization of the priesthood at the temples of Watarahi in Ise, the ordering of the services at those temples and the ceremonies connected with their maintenance and reconstruction every twenty years (bk. 4), the consecration of two virgin princesses of the Mikado's family, one as priestess of the temples of Watarahi, the other for the temples of Kamo in Yamashiro, with the regulations for the management for their households and the services in which they took part (bks. 5 and 6), the ceremonies which were performed to celebrate the accession of the sovereign (bk. 7), a catalogue of the chief Shiñtau temples recognized as entitled to state support (bks. 9 and 10), while in one book, the 8th, were collected together the *norito* or rituals to be used at the chief services.

The first printed edition saw the light in 1647 under the editorship of Nakahara Mototada. It was complete all but book 13, a copy of which was known to be in the possession of the noble family of Kudeu, but Nakahara was unable to gain access to it. A transcript of this copy was discovered by the well known scholar Hayashi Daushiyuñ in the library of the prince of Wohari in the following year, and the whole work was eventually published by a Kiyauto bookseller named Idzumozhi in 1657. Ten years later the text was revised by Matsushita Keñriñ, and new blocks were cut. In 1723, a copy having been ordered by the government, it was found that the blocks were much worn and worm-eaten, so that a fresh set had to be engraved. Advantage was taken of the opportunity to correct the text again, and an edition was produced which satisfied everybody's wants for the next hundred years. This is the edition commonly found in the booksellers' shops.

A much better edition is that known as the Deha-boñ, for which the text has been carefully emended, and supplemented by a collection of various readings. The credit of this is due to

Matsudaira Deha no kami Naritsune, the daimiyau of Matsuye in Idzumo. It was published in 1828, in sixty-one volumes, and is a splendid example of good Japanese block-cutting and printing. There is also a printed edition of the first ten books only, omitting the prefatory matter and list of contents usually given. At the end of volume 10 is the date 1503 and the signature at full-length of Yoshida Kanetomo, the originator of the heretical form of the native religion called Yuwiitsu (唯 --) Shiñtau, from which it is supposed that he is responsible for the *kana* readings given by the side of the Chinese text.

The well-known scholar Mabuchi wrote a commentary in five books on the whole of the rituals contained in the Yeñgishiki, to which he gave the name of Norito Kai, but this work has never been published. Just before his death he completed a revised commentary, under the title of Norito Kau, which was printed in 1800 by one of his pupils. It is still the chief guide to the understanding of the Rituals.

Commentaries on the ritual of the General Purification (*Ohobarahi*) under its more popular name of Nakatomi no Harahi, are very numerous, and a list of them is to be found in the Guñshiyo Ichirañ (群書一覽), vol. ii. p. 73. Motowori's commentary on this ritual, entitled Ohobarahi no Kotoba no Goshiyaku (大祓詞後釋), which is an admirable work, has been followed by the Ohobarahi no Kotoba Gogo Shiyaku (大祓詞後々釋) of Fujiwi Takanaho, the Ohobarahi Shifuchiuseu 大祓執中抄) of Koñdau Yoshiki and the Ohobarahi no Kotoba Sañdeubeñ (大祓詞三條辨) of Nemoto Manahe. Motowori also composed a commentary on the "congratulatory address of the chieftains of Idzumo," entitled Idzumo no kuni no miyatsuko no kamu yo-goto goshiyaku (出雲國造神賀詞後釋). Finally, Hirata Atsutane edited a very good text of all the rituals, which has been published by his son under the title of Norito Shiyaukuñ, or Correct Reading of the Rituals (祝詞正訓), and prepared a commentary on the Ohobarahi, which has not yet seen the light. The same scholar published, under the title of Amatsu-norito Kau (天神祝詞考), the texts of several copies of an ancient ritual not contained in the Yeñgishiki, which he had discovered.

The rituals are written entirely with Chinese characters, used for the most part as ideographs (*mana*), which are to be read into the corresponding Japanese words. No internal evidence of the exact manner in which these ideographs are to be read is afforded by the text, the Japanese syllabic characters at the side having been added in modern times, and disputes have consequently arisen concerning the proper reading of several phrases, the discussion of which may be left until we come to the passages where they occur. The terminations of verbs and particles, called *teniwoha* by the native grammarians, are written with whole Chinese characters used phonetically, and belong therefore to the kind of signs known as Mañyefu-gana. Further, the Mañyefu-gana not infrequently occur in the bodies of words, of which, as stated already, the meaning had been forgotten or could not be adequately expressed by any combination of ideographs. In several places a note is attached to ideographs showing how they are to be read, which was an alternative expedient for avoiding the difficulties of inadequate expression.

The order in which the ideographs are generally arranged is in accordance with Japanese syntax; and inversion, or following the Chinese order of words, is very rare. The following are all the cases of inversion which I have been able to discover. In writing the negative in *zu,* 不 is placed before the character which represents the negative base, as *ochizu* 不 落, *arazu* 不 在, *ahasetamawazu* 不相賜, *nasazu* 不 成, *hosazu* 不 干, *mawosazu* 不申. The causative termination *shime* is often represented by 令 before the base, but is also expressed in *kana* after it, as *sasage-motashime* 令 棒 持, *masashime* 令 在 or 令 座, *sarashime* 令 避 and *sakayeshime* 令 榮, but *tsutomeshimete,* 勤 之 米 氏, *sakayeshime* 佐 加 叡 志 米 and *masashime* 座 志 米. Negatives of such causatives are written with 不 above, as *nasashimezu* 不令爲, *arashimezu* 不 令 在. Honorific derivative verbs whose bases end in *s* are frequently written with 所 prefixed, as *shiroshi* 所 知, *kikoshi* 所 聞, *omohoshi* 所 思, *sonahashi* 所 行, and the causatives with their base in *s* are written in the same manner, as *tarahashi* 足所, *yosashi* 所依. In passive forms like *yakayete,* 被, which denotes the passive, precedes the base *yaku* 燒. Certain prepositions are placed before the substantives to which they belong, as *kuchi yori* 自口, *shita yori* 自下, *ima yori* 自今.

Gotoku 如 is as often placed at the end of the phrase as at the beginning. The adverb *kaku*, 'thus,' is always represented by 如此, and *kakaru*, 'to be thus,' by 如是. But *mochite* 以 always appears after the noun which it governs, with the exception of a single instance, and the same is true of *ni yori* 依 , 'in consequence.' In one place we find the words *tsuki hi*, 'moon sun,' which is the Japanese order of naming the two luminaries, written 日 月 , 'sun moon,' according to the Chinese practice. These rare departures from the Japanese syntactical sequence are for the most part mere devices for saving time in representing certain grammatical forms and inflections, and as they do not affect the general character of the compositions in which they occur, it cannot be inferred from their use that the rituals are in any way formed upon a foreign model. In all other cases the usual order of words peculiar to the Japanese language is strictly preserved. It may in fact be fairly claimed for the greater number of the *norito* that they are the oldest specimens of indigenous Japanese literature extant, excepting only perhaps the poetry contained in the Kozhiki and Nihoñgi, and this alone would render them of the highest value to students of the language, even apart from the light which they throw upon the practice and origin of Shiñtau religion.

The following is a list of the Norito contained in the Yeñgishiki.

1. Toshigohi no Matsuri, service of the Praying for Harvest.
2. Kasuga no Matsuri, service of the gods of Kasuga.
3. Hirose oho-imi no Matsuri, service of the goddess of food.
4. Tatsuta kaze no kami no Matsuri, service of the gods of wind.
5. Hiranu no Matsuri, service of the temple of Imaki (dedicated to Yamato-dake no mikoto).
6. Kudo Furuaki. Ritual for the service of the temples of Kudo and Furuaki (dedicated to Chiuai Teñwau and Niñtoku Teñwau respectively).
7. Minadzuki no Tsukinami no Matsuri. Half-yearly service performed in the sixth month (originally a monthly service, the ritual almost identical with that of the Praying for Harvest).
8. Ohotono Hogahi, or Luck-wishing of the Great Palace.
9. Mikado Matsuri, service of the GATES.

10. Minadzuki Tsugomori no Ohobarahi, General Purification celebrated on the last day of the sixth month.

11. Yamato no Fumi-no-imikibe ga tachi wo tatematsuru toki no Zhiyu, or invocation pronounced by the hereditary scholars of Yamato, in presenting a golden sword to the Mikado before the reading of the Ohobarahi.

12. Ho-shidzume no Matsuri, service of the Quieting of Fire.

13. Michiahe no Matsuri, service to propitiate the gods of pestilence. (More probably this is in reality the service of the Road Gods).

14. Ohonihe no Matsuri, or Harvest Festival.

15. Mitama wo ihahido ni shidzumuru Matsuri, the service of settling the SPIRITS in the sanctuary.

16-24. Services at the Temples of Ise.

16. Kisaragi no Toshigohi, minadzuki shihasu tsukinami no Matsuri, or form used at the Praying for Harvest in the 2nd month, and at the monthly services in the 6th and 12th months at the sun goddess' temple.

17. Toyuke no miya. The same form, slightly varied, to be used on these three occasions at the temple of the goddess of food. Both were read by the Mikado's envoy.

18. Udzuki no kamu miso Matsuri, or presentation of sacred CLOTHING at the temple of the sun-goddess in the 4th month.

19. Minadzuki no tsukinami no Matsuri, or form used by the chief priest at the temple of the sun-goddess at the monthly service in the 6th month.

20. Nagatsuki no kamu name no Matsuri, or service of the Divine Tasting (Harvest festival) in the 9th month, at the temple of the sun-goddess.

21. Toyuke no miya no onazhi Matsuri, or, same service at the temple of the goddess of food. This and No. 20 were read by the Mikado's envoy.

22. Onazhiku kamu name no Matsuri, service read on the same occasion by the Chief Priest of the Temples of Ise.

23. Itsuki no hime-miko tatematsuri-iruru koto, read on the induction of a Princess of the Blood as Priestess.

24. Ohomikami no miya wo utsushi-matsuru norito, ritual for the removal of the goddess to her new temple.

25. Tatari-gami wo utsushi-yarafu Matsuri, service for the

removal and dismissal of avenging deities. (Considered to be really the Michiahe ritual).

26. Morokoshi ni tsukahi wo tsukahasu toki ni mitegura tate-matsuru, offerings made on the occasion of the despatch of envoys to China.

27. Idzumo no kuni no miyatsuko no kamu Yogoto, or Congratulatory address of the Chieftains of Idzumo.

The Praying for Harvest, or Toshigohi no Matsuri, was celebrated on the 4th day of the 2nd month of each year, at the capital in the Zhiñgikuwañ or office for the Worship of the Shiñtau gods, and in the provinces by the chiefs of the local administrations. At the Zhiñgikuwañ there were assembled the ministers of state, the functionaries of that office, the priests and priestesses of 573 temples, containing 737 shrines, which were kept up at the expense of the Mikado's treasury, while the governors of the provinces superintended in the districts under their administration the performance of rites in honour of 2,395 other shrines. It would not be easy to state the exact number of deities to whom these 3,132 shrines were dedicated. A glance over the list in the 9th and 10th books of the Yeñgishiki shows at once that there were many gods who were worshipped in more than half-a-dozen different localities at the same time, but exact calculation is impossible, because in many cases only the names of the temples are given, and we are left quite in the dark as to the individuality of the gods to whom they were sacred. Besides these 3,132 shrines, which are distinguished as Shikidai, that is contained in the catalogue of the Yeñgishiki, there were a large number of unenumerated shrines in temples scattered all over the country, in every village or hamlet, of which it was impossible to take any account, just as at the present day there are temples of Hachimañ, Koñpira, Teñzhiñ sama, Sañwau sama and Señgeñ sama, as they are popularly called, wherever twenty or thirty houses are collected together. The shrines are classed as great and small, the respective numbers being 492 and 2,640, the distinction being two-fold, firstly in the proportionately larger quantity of offerings made at the great shrines, and secondly that the offerings in the one case were arranged upon tables or altars, while in the other they were placed on mats spread upon the earth. In the Yeñgishiki the amounts and nature of the

offerings are stated with great minuteness, but it will be sufficient
if the kinds of articles offered are alone mentioned here. It will
be seen, by comparison with the text of the *norito,* that they had
varied somewhat since the date when the ritual was composed.
The offerings to a greater shrine consisted of coarse woven silk
(*ashiginu*), thin silk of five different colours, a kind of stuff called *shidori* or *shidzu,* which is supposed by some to have been a
striped silk, cloth of broussonetia bark or hemp, and a small
quantity of the raw materials of which the cloth was made,
models of swords, a pair of tables or altars (called *yo-kura-oki*
and *ya-kura-oki*), a shield or mantlet, a spear-head, a bow, a
quiver, a pair of stag's horns, a hoe, a few measures of *sake* or
rice-beer, some haliotis and bonito, two measures of *kitahi*
(supposed to be salt roe), various kinds of edible seaweed, a
measure of salt, a *sake* jar and a few feet of matting for packing.
To each of the temples of Watarahi in Ise was presented in
addition a horse; to the temple of the harvest god, Mitoshi no
kami, a white horse, cock and pig, and a horse to each of nineteen others.

During the fortnight which preceded the celebration of the
service, two smiths and their journeymen and two carpenters,
together with eight *inbe,** were employed in preparing the ap-
paratus and getting ready the offerings. It was usual to employ
for the Praying for Harvest members of this tribe who held
office in the Zhiñgikuwañ, but if the number could not be made
up in that office, it was supplied from other departments of
state. To the tribe of quiver-makers was entrusted the special
duty of weaving the quivers of wistaria tendrils. The service
began at twenty minutes to seven in the morning by our reckon-
ing of time. After the governor of the province of Yamashiro
had ascertained that everything was in readiness, the officials of
the Zhiñgikuwañ arranged the offerings on the tables and below
them, according to the rank of the shrines for which they were
intended. The large court of the Zhiñgikuwañ, where the service
was held, called the Sai-iñ, measured 230 ft. by 370. At one end
were the offices and on the west side were the shrines of the
eight Protective Deities in a row, surrounded by a fence, to the
interior of which three sacred archways (*toriwi*) gave access.

*See Note 44 to the translation of the Ritual, infra.

In the centre of the court a temporary shed was erected for the occasion, in which the tables or altars were placed. The final preparations being now complete, the ministers of state, the virgin priestesses and the priests of the temples to which offerings were sent by the Mikado entered in succession, and took the places severally assigned to them. The horses which formed a part of the offerings were next brought in from the Mikado's stable, and all the congregation drew near, while the reader recited or read the *norito*. This reader was a member of the priestly family or tribe of Nakatomi, who traced their descent back to Amenokoyane, one of the principal advisers attached to the sun-goddess' grandchild when he first descended on earth. It is a remarkable evidence of the persistence of certain ideas, that up to the year 1868 the nominal prime-minister of the Mikado after he came of age, and the regent during his minority, if he had succeeded young to the throne, always belonged to this tribe, which changed its name from Nakatomi to Fujihara in the 7th century, and was subsequently split up into the Five Setsuke or governing families. At the end of each section the priests all responded 'O!' which was no doubt the equivalent of 'Yes' in use in those days. As soon as he had finished, the Nakatomi retired, and the offerings were distributed to the priests for conveyance and presentation to the gods, to whose service they were attached. But a special messenger was despatched with the offerings destined to the temples at Watarahi. This formality having been completed, the President of the Zhiñgikuwañ gave the signal for breaking up the assembly.

The earliest account of the proceedings on these occasions is contained in the Jiyauguwañ Gishiki (貞 觀 儀 式), of the year 871, and repeated with a few alterations in the Yeñgishiki (927). We find it also almost unchanged in the Hokuzañseu (比 山 抄) of the Dainagoñ Kiñtafu (b. 966, d. 1041), and in the Gouka no Shidai (江 家 次 弟) of Ohoye no Masafusa (b. 1041, d. 1111). It may perhaps seem curious that the ceremonies should have been directed by officials organized on a Chinese model, but it can hardly be doubted that the functions which they discharged were older than the introduction of the Chinese system of administration, which merely furnished a convenient means of classifying and arranging what already existed, just as it is evident that even under the Tokugaha Shiyauguñ there were organs of government which the new power has merely coördinated and defined with greater clearness. The priestly families of Nakatomi and Iñbe, and the four tribes of Urabe or diviners certainly date from a prehistoric period, and that the sanctity which antiquity confers attached to the functions with which they were clothed, is clear from their being taken up into the new religious hierarchy instituted in the ninth century, while still preserving their hereditary character.

At some remote period it was the practice to hold a monthly service at every temple or shrine of importance, at which offerings were presented either in recognition of blessings already enjoyed, or as inducements to the gods to confer the favours which were besought from them. These monthly services were afterwards curtailed to two half-yearly services, but still retained their original name of the *Tsukinami no Matsuri*, or monthly services. Mabuchi thought that they were celebrated in honour of all the 3,132 shrines mentioned in the Yeñgishiki, but Motowori's opinion is that only the 304 greater shrines, the charges for whose services were defrayed by the Zhñigikuwañ, were concerned, and this was probably the case when the most recent ceremonial laws were drawn up, although it seems likely that in the beginning the services were performed at all the recognized shrines. One reason for this view is that the liturgy of the half-yearly (so-called monthly) services is identical, word for word, with that of the Praying for Harvest, with the exception of the passage in which the harvest god is directly addressed, and it is more likely that this part was inserted in a general liturgy which already existed for use on other occasions, than that the liturgy of the Tsukinami no Matsuri was borrowed from the Toshigohi, with the omission of the passage from which it was named. It will be seen that in the Praying for Harvest many gods are addressed who have nothing at all to do with the success or failure of the farmer's toil. It seems to follow, therefore, that the Toshigohi was the less ancient of the two services. Mabuchi is of opinion that the Praying for Harvest dates back to the reign of the Mikado to whom many hundred years later the posthumous title of Suuzhiñ Teñwau, or God-honouring Heavenly Sovereign, was given, and whom the fabulous early chronology assigns to the first century B. C. He gives as his grounds for this opinion the received tradition that in the reign of this sovereign all the gods received their due meed of honour, and that the wind and rain consequently came in good season, so that the seed of the field flourished; but his motive probably was the occurrence, in the first paragraph, of the phrase, "heavenly temples and country temples," for it is recorded of Suuzhiñ Teñwau that he divided the shrines of the gods into these two categories. Neither Mabuchi's alleged reason, nor that which I suppose to have guided him, is satisfactory; but whether this ritual dates from the extremely vague epoch to which he ascribes it, there seems sufficient internal evidence that it owes its origin to a very remote period of antiquity.

The offerings intended for the Temples of Watarahi in Ise were sent by the hands of a special envoy, and the short rituals used in presenting them at the shrines of the sun-goddess and the goddess of food are Nos. 16, 17 and 19 of the preceding list.

In the following translation I have endeavoured to be as literal as possible; that is to say, to use English words which exactly express in their original and etymological meaning the sense of the Japanese. I have also been careful to use the same English equivalents for the same Japanese words wherever they occur. Words in italics have been supplied in order to complete the meaning.

RITUAL.

[TRANSLATION]

He[1] says: "Hear all of you, assembled KANNUSHI[2] and HAFURI."[3]

He says: "I declare in the presence of the sovran[4] gods, whose praises by the WORD[5] of the sovran's dear progenitor's[6,3] augustness[7] and progenitrix, who divinely remain in the plain of high heaven, are fulfilled as heavenly[9] temples[10] and country temples. I fulfil your praises *by setting-up*[11] the great OFFERINGS of the sovran GRANDCHILD'S[12] augustness, *made* with the intention of deigning[13] to begin the HARVEST[14] in the second month of this year, as the morning-sun rises in glory."[15]

He says: "I declare in the presence of the sovran gods[16] of
the HARVEST. If the sovrán gods will bestow in many-bundled
ears and in luxuriant ears[17] the late-ripening harvest which they
will bestow, the late-ripening harvest which will be produced by
the dripping of foam from the arms and by drawing the mud
together between the opposing thighs,[18] then I will fulfil their
praises by setting-up the first fruits in a thousand ears and
many hundred ears,[19] raising-high the beer-jars,[20] filling and ranging-in-rows the bellies of the beer-jars, *I will present them* [*i.e.
the first-fruits*] in juice and in ear. As to things which grow
in the great-field-plain[21]—sweet herbs and bitter herbs: as to
things which dwell in the blue-sea-plain[22]—things wide of fin and
things narrow of fin, down to the weeds of the offing and weeds
of the shore: and as to CLOTHES—with bright cloth, glittering
cloth, soft cloth and coarse cloth[23] will I fulfil praises. And
having furnished a white horse, a white boar and a white cock,[24]
and the various kinds of things in the presence of the sovran
god[25] of the HARVEST, I fulfil his praises *by setting up* the great
OFFERINGS of the sovran GRANDCHILD'S augustness."

He says: "I declare in the presence of the sovran gods whose
praises the chief PRIESTESS[26] fulfils. I fulfil your praises, declaring your NAMES:—Divine PRODUCER, Lofty PRODUCER, Vivifying
Producer, Fulfilling Producer, Soul-lodging Producer, Woman of
the Great HOUSE, Great Goddess of FOOD and Events-symbol-lord,[27]
thus: Because you praise the AGE of the sovran GRANDCHILD'S
augustness as a long AGE eternally and unchangingly, and bless
it as a luxuriant AGE, I fufil your praises as our sovran's dear
progenitor's augustness and progenitrix's augustness *by setting
up* the great OFFERINGS of the sovran GRANDCHILD'S augustness."

He says: "I declare in the presence of the sovran gods whose
praises the PRIESTESS of Wigasuri[28] fulfils. I fulfil your praises,
declaring your NAMES, Vivifying Well, Blessing Well, Long-rope
Well, Foot-place and Entrance-limit, thus: Because *the builders*
have made stout the HOUSE[29] pillars on the bottom-most rocks,
which the soveran god*s* command(s), have made high the cross-
beams to the plain-of-high-heaven, and have constructed the fresh
ABODE of the sovran GRANDCHILD'S augustness, and *he* hiding
therein as a SHADE[30] from the heavens and as a SHADE from the
sun, tranquilly possesses the countries of the four quarters as a

peaceful country, I fulfil your praises *by setting-up* the great
OFFERINGS of the sovran GRANDCHILD'S augustness."

He says: "I declare in the presence of the sovran gods whose
praises the PRIESTESS of the GATE fulfils.   I fulfil your praises,
declaring your NAMES, Wonderful-rock-gate's augustness and
Powerful-rock-gate's augustness,[31] thus: Because you obstruct
like innumerable piles of rock in the GATES of the four quarters,
in the morning open the GATES, in the evening shut the GATES,
guard the bottom if unfriendly things come from the bottom,
guard the top if they come from the top, and guard by nightly
guarding and daily guarding, I fulfil your praises *by setting-up*
the great OFFERINGS of the sovran GRANDCHILD'S augustness."

He says: "I declare in the presence of the sovran gods whose
praises the PRIESTESS of Ikushima fulfils: I fulfil your praises,
declaring your NAMES, Country-vivifier,[32] thus: Because the
sovran gods confer *on him* the many tens of islands which the
sovran gods[33] command, the many tens of islands of islands,
without *any* falling-short, *as far as* the limit of the taniguku[34]'s
passing, *as far as* the bound where the salt-foam[35] stops, *making*
the narrow countries wide and the hilly countries plane—I fulfil
your praises *by setting-up* the great OFFERINGS of the sovran
GRANDCHILD'S augustness."

He says: "Parting the words,[36] I declare in the presence of
the From-heaven-shining-great-DEITY who sits in Ise.   Because
the sovran great DEITY bestows *on him* the countries of the four
quarters over which her[37] glance extends, *as far as* the limit
where heaven stands-up like a wall, *as far as* the bound where
the blue clouds lie flat, *as far as* the bounds where the white
clouds lie away fallen:—the blue-sea-plain *as far as* the limit
whither come the prows of the ships without letting their poles
or paddles be dry, the ships which continuously crowd on the
great-sea-plain:—the road which *men* go by land, *as far as* the
limit whither come the horses' hoofs, with the baggage-cord tied
tightly, treading the uneven rocks and tree-roots and standing-
up continuously in a long path without a break:—*making* the
narrow countries wide and the hilly countries plane, and as it
were drawing together the distant countries by throwing many
tens of ropes over them, *because she does all this,* he will pile-up
the first-fruits like a range of hills in the great presence of the

sovran great DEITY, and will tranquilly take to himself the remainder."

"Again, because you praise the AGE of the sovran GRAND-CHILD'S augustness as a long AGE, eternally and unchangingly, and bless it as a luxuriant AGE, I plunge down the root of the neck cormorant-wise[38] *before you* as our sovran's dear progenitor and progenitrix's augustness, and fulfil your praises by *setting-up* the great OFFERINGS of the sovran GRANDCHILD'S augustness."

He says: "I declare in the presence of the sovran gods who sit in the FARMS.[39] Declaring your NAMES, Takechi, Kadzuraki, Tohochi, Shiki, Yamanobe and Sofu. Because the sweet herbs and bitter herbs which grow in these six FARMS have been brought, and the sovran GRANDCHILD'S augustness takes them as his long FOOD and distant FOOD,[40] I fulfil your praises *by setting-up* the great OFFERINGS of the sovran GRANDCHILD'S augustness."

He says: "I declare in the presence of the sovran gods who sit in the mouths of the mountains. Declaring your NAMES, Asuka, Ihari, Osaka, Hatsuse, Unebi and Miminashi.[41] Because *the builders,* having cut the bases and ends of the big trees and little trees which have grown-up in the distant mountains and the near mountains, brought them and constructed the fresh ABODE of the sovran GRANDCHILD'S augustness and *he,* hiding *therein* as a SHADE from the heavens and as a SHADE from the sun, tranquilly possesses the countries of the four quarters as a peaceful country, I fulfil your praises *by setting-up* the great OFFERINGS of the sovran GRANDCHILD'S augustness."

He says: "I declare in the presence of the sovran gods who dwell in the partings of the waters.[42] I fulfil your praises, declaring your NAMES, Yoshinu, Uda, Tsuge and Kadzuraki, thus: If you will bestow in many-bundled ears and luxuriant ears the late-ripening harvest which the sovran gods[43] will bestow, I will fulfil your praises *by setting-up* the first-fruits in ear and in juice, raising-high the beer-jars, filling and ranging-in-rows the bellies of the beer-jars, and the remainder the sovran GRAND-CHILD'S augustness takes with ruddy countenance as the divine grains of morning FOOD and evening FOOD, as his long FOOD and distant FOOD. Therefore, hear all of you, the fulfilling of praises *by the setting-up* of the great OFFERINGS of the sovran GRAND-CHILD'S augustness."

He says: "Parting the words, let the *Kannushi* and the *Hafuri* receive the OFFERINGS which the *Imibe*,⁴ hanging thick sashes to their weak shoulders have reverently prepared, and lifting, bring and set them up without erring."

NOTES.

¹ 'He' is the reader of the ritual, one of the Nakatomi tribe, and the word rendered by 'says' signifies that the speaker is supposed to be speaking the words of the Mikado. Mabuchi reads *nori-tamafu*, and supposes this word to issue from the mouth of the Nakatomi, but his successors Motowori and Hirata read *noru*, according to which 'He says' are a rubric, and the ritual actually begins with 'Hear all of you.' I think it probable, however, that in later times, after the rituals were committed to writing, and were read instead of being recited from memory, the word *noru* was also read, as if it were an integral part of the *norito*.

² *Kañ-nushi* is the general term for all Shiñtau priests in the modern language, but it is more correctly restricted to the chief priest in charge of a temple. The priesthood was for the most part hereditary, and in many cases the priests could trace their descent from the chief god to whom the temple was dedicated, a fact which is easily understood when we find that a large number of gods were simply deified ancestors. From this sense of property in the temple sprang the term *Kami-nushi*, owner of the god, corrupted into *Kamu-nushi* and *Kañ-nushi*.

³ The *Hafuri* (pronounced *hôri*) were an inferior class of priests, whose chief functions were to present the offerings and read the prayers. We might translate the word by 'deacon,' but for the associations which this rendering would call up. *Hafuri* is said by some to be derived from *ha*, wings, and *furu*, to wave or shake, and to represent the waving of the sleeves in performing sacred dances; but another derivation is from *hafuru* (pron. *hôru*), to throw away, which is explained by saying that their special function was originally to bury the dead and to read the funeral service over them. *Hafuru* is the same as *haufuru*, modern *haumuru*, to bury, which suggests the conjecture that in the earliest times the dead were simply exposed to natural decay in the middle of a forest or moor. The Chinese characters 祝部 with which *hafuri* is written mean literally felicitating section or body, and refer to the recital of the glorious deeds of the dead which formed a part of the ritual or address spoken over his grave.

⁴ 'Sovran' as an adjective or substantive is a translation of *sume* (adj.) or *sumera* (subst.) both written 皇. Most scholars, with the exception of Motowori, consider *sume* to be the same as *sube-*, root of *suberu*, to have power over, to rule, which survives in the spoken language as *sube-kukuru*, to have the chief control of and *subete*, all (adv.), the interchange of *b* and *m* being one of the commonest phenomena in Japanese etymology. I have not been able to discover what origin Motowori attributes to the word, but in one place he asserts, without offering any proof, that it is merely an honorific. This is hardly satisfactory, for a word which is now merely honorific must evidently have had some more specific meaning previously. *Sumera* is the ancient term used to denote the ruler of the nation, derived from *sumeru* (perh. like *naha*, rope, from *nafu*, to twist), and 'sovran' appears to me to be the fittest equivalent in English, on account both of its close correspondence in meaning, and of its double applicability as a substantive and adjective, thus resembling the employment of *sumera* and *sume*. By adopting the spelling 'sovran,' for which Milton is a sufficient authority, all the secondary associations connected with the ordinary spelling 'sovereign' are avoided, while the meaning here intended is made clearer.

⁵ WORD is a literal rendering of *mikoto*, compounded of the honorific *mi*, identified with *ma*, which is constantly used as an honorific prefix in the old language, and appears in such words as *ma-koto*, truth (real-words), *ma-sugu*, perfectly straight, also in the root *maru*, round, perfect. *Mi* is prefixed to the names of

things which derive their origin from the gods or the Mikado or princes of the royal house, and conveys much the same sense as 'august,' but the perpetual recurrence of this word in translation would be tedious and sometimes even ludicrous, and the purpose which it serves can be equally attained by printing the English of the word to which it is prefixed in capital letters. *Mikoto* is employed in another sense to form titles of gods and princes, where its fittest rendering would be 'august-ness,' used like 'majesty' or 'highness,' as titles of European sovereigns and their children. Thus a son of the Mikado was anciently styled *miko no mikoto,* literally 'august-child's augustness.' In the names of many gods it was used alternately with *kami;* thus Izanami no mikoto and Izanami no kami are equally correct as appellations of the All-mother. It must, however, not be supposed that it can be employed by itself as a convertible term for *kami,* or that, as Kaempfer has erroneously stated, it was used alone as a designation of the Japanese sovereign, in the same way that Mikado, Teñwau, Teñshi and so forth are applied to him.

   [6] Progenitor and Progenitrix are the most convenient renderings of *kamurogi* and *kamuromi,* which are written partly with Chinese characters used as ideographs, partly as syllabic signs (神漏伎 and 神漏彌 ; in the Ohobarahi 岐 and 美 are used for the terminal syllables). *Kamu* evidently means 'divine,' but the etymology of *rogi* and *romi* is by no means so clear. Motowori derives the one from *are-oya-gimi* (生祖君) begetting-parent-prince, by dropping *a* and *ya,* contracting *re o* into *ro* and cutting off *mi* from the end, the other from *are-oya-me-gimi* (生祖女君) begetting-parent-princess, by the same process varied by the contraction of *me-gi* into *mi.* This is a bold use of the weapons which Japanese philologists claim to have at their command, but is too far-fetched to be admitted for one moment. I am inclined to accept the explanation given by my friend and teacher Hori Hidenari, that *ro* is the second syllable of *iro,* seen in the archaic *iroha,* mother, *iroto,* younger brother, *irose,* husband, and *irone,* elder brother, where *iro* apparently indicates a tie of natural affection, and is identified by him with *iro,* colour, beauty, love, as in the modern *iro-otoko,* lover. *Gi* is *ki* (with the *nigori*), a root which in one of its significations is equivalent to 'male,' while *mi* correspondingly means 'female,' as seen in the pairs *okina* and *omina,* old man and old woman, in the names Izanagi, the male-who-invites, and Izanami, the female-who-invites. It is probable that *ko* and *me,* which appear in *wotoko,* young man, and *wotome,* young woman, in *hiko* and *hime* (*hi* = sun), honorific epithets applied respectively to men and women, are variations of the same pair of roots. If this etymology be correct, then the literal equivalents of *kamurogi* and *kamuromi* are divine-dear-male and divine-dear-female; and as these titles are sometimes written with the Chinese characters 神祖, divine ancestor, and are applied generally to all the ancestors of the Mikado, the terms used in the translation seem to convey their meaning pretty closely. They occur altogether fourteen times in the rituals contained in the Yeñgishiki. In the congratulatory address of the Chieftains of Idzumo they denote the first pair of deities Taka-mi-musubi and Kamimusubi, who, according to the cosmogony of the Kozhiki, came into being next after Ame-no-mi-naka-nushi, 'the lord in the centre of heaven,' who is called the oldest of the gods. In the same ritual we have *kamurogi* used of Susanowo, the ancestor of Ohonamuji. In the Praying for Harvest it will be seen that *kamurogi* and *kamuromi* are used respectively of Taka-mi-musubi and the sun-goddess, are then applied to a larger group of deities, several of whom were never supposed to be ancestors of the Mikado (unless it be admitted that the five Producers are the sun-goddess under other names), and lastly both epithets are employed in speaking of the sun-goddess herself. Much later, a couple of centuries after the beginning of the strictly historical period, Koutoku Teñwau (孝德天皇) speaks of Chiuai Teñwau (仲哀天皇) more than twenty generations earlier, as his 'dear *kamurogi,*' and in a poem presented to Niñmiyau Teñwau on the occasion of his fortieth birthday,* the god Sukunabikona, one of those who took the greatest share in the work of civilizing the country, is called his *kamirogi.* Closely allied to this epithet is the word *sumerogi,* in which the first element is the root already mentioned,

which is rendered by 'sovran.' We find it in the Mañyefushifu applied to Ninigi no mikoto, the grandson of the sun-goddess and first of the Mikado's ancestors to inhabit the earth, and also to other ancestors of the Mikado, whether gods or human beings. In two places it occurs written in *kana* 須賣呂伎 (Riyakuge, v. 18, p. 22 and v. 20, 下, p. 19 verso), where there can be no doubt of the true reading. Other ways of writing it are 皇祖御 (v. 18, p. 23) 皇神祖 (v. 18, p. 34) 皇祖神 (v. 19 上, p. 28 v.; v. 7, p .15 and v. 3 上, p. 15. v.; in the last case *kamirogi* is an alternative reading proposed by the commentators) and 皇祖 (v. 11 上. p. 34 v.; v. 6, 11 v. and v. 3 下, p. 37); in the last two cases *kamirogi* is suggested as an alternative reading. From these examples it seems not unreasonable to infer the former independent existence of a pair of word *irogi* and *iromi*, which were used to denote ancestors or note-worthy personages of previous generations.

[7] The insertion of *mikoto*, rendered 'augustness' after progenitor, is probably the act of an ignorant copyist, who thought it was required to correspond to the second *mikoto*, translated WORD.

[8] Mabuchi takes the terms progenitor and progenitrix to denote in this passage all the gods from Taka-mi-musubi and Kami-musubi down to Izanagi, Izanami and the sun-goddess, while Motowori thinks that only Taka-mi-musubi and the sun-goddess are meant. The passage in the Nihoñgi, which says that the distinction between 'heavenly temples' and 'country temples' was made in the reign of Suuzhiñ Tenwau, represents it as the final act of that Mikado after making a series of arrangements about the worship of certain other gods, but does not give the slightest indication of the 'progenitor and progenitrix' being concerned in the settlement. It is safest to conclude that the phrase is vaguely used without any particular significance being attached to it.

[9] 'Heavenly temples and country temples.' Temple is here a metonymy for god. The only meaning which can possibly be attached to this statement is that some gods were recognized as of heavenly origin, who either remained on high or descended to the earth, and others as of earthly origin, but that any ruler could ever be the arbiter of such a question is inconceivable, and the assertion is only an additional proof of the mythical character of the Mikado concerning whom it is made.

[10] The word *yashiro*, rendered 'temples,' deserves a passing notice. It is compounded of *ya*, house, and *shiro*, which must mean area or enclosure. We find it in *naha-shiro*, area or inclosure for the young rice-plants (*nahe*), in *mushiro*, a mat (*mu* is *mi*, body; *mu-shiro*, area for one body), and the word *shiro*, usually translated 'castle,' is identical with it. Hence *yashiro* does not signify the buildings themselves, but rather the piece of land on which they are built. Metaphorically employed, *shiro* came to mean that which was given in 'place' of something, that is, price, and hence *shiro-mono* signifies price-things, merchandise, goods. The idea that *shiro*, a castle, is the root of the adjective *shiro-ki*, white, because of the white plaster parapets, is untenable, because the use of it in that sense dates from a period when *shiroki* signified 'conspicuous,' of which 'white' is a derivative meaning.

[11] 'Set-up' is the literal translation of *tate-matsuru*, compounded of *tate-*, to stand (t.v.) and *matsuru*, originally to serve, and hence used as an honorific auxiliary verb, just like *haberu* or *hañberu* and *safurafu* or *samurofu* in the later language. *Matsuri*, usually translated 'festival,' is the root of this verb, and properly signifies 'service' of a god, and *matsuri-goto*, government, as we are accustomed to render it, is simply 'service' of the sovereign, corresponding thus in etymology and signification to our word 'administration.' Students of the epistolary style are familiar with the use of *tatematsuru*, written 奉, as an honorific auxiliary, but this character properly means *matsuru*, and 立奉 would be a more exact equivalent of the compound *tate*-matsuru, if any one were to begin over again the labour of assigning correct Chinese equivalents to Japanese words. Words in the translation which are printed in italics have been supplied to complete the sense, but *tate-matsuru* does actually occur in the original a little further on.

[12] GRANDCHILD, i.e. of Amaterasu oho-mi kami, the sun-goddess, meant in the first place Ninigi no mikoto, child of Oshi-ho-mi-mi no mikoto, adopted by her as her son. The latter was really the son of Susanowo, according to the myth, and

consequently her nephew by birth. The Kozhiki (Notice of Ancient Things, 古事記) tells the following story of the miraculous birth of Oshi-ho-mi-mi. Izanagi divided the universe between his three children, assigning the sovereignty of the heavens to the sun-goddess, giving the kingdom of night to the moon and making Susanowo ruler over the sea. Susanowo neglected his royal functions, and gave himself up to such a violent fit of petulant weeping, that the land was laid bare and the rivers dried up. On being rebuked by his father, he excused himself by saying that he wanted to go to his mother in the lower regions, and was consequently expelled from the earth. He then ascended to heaven to pay a farewell visit to his sister, who was frightened by the rumbling of the mountains and streams, and by the earthquakes caused by his passing upwards, and misdoubting the loyalty of his intentions prepared to defend her realm against his attack. Susanowo explained the reasons which led to his visit, and protested that he harboured no evil designs. In order to test his good faith she demanded of him a sign, to which he responded by proposing that they should see which could bring into existence the best children. For this purpose they took up their position on opposite sides of the milky way, and the goddess, first breaking the sword which her brother wore into three pieces, plunged it into a well, and then chewing it into minute fragments, blew them from her mouth. Three goddesses sprang from the cloud of spray. Then Susanowo performed a similar series of operations with the chaplets which the goddess wore in her hair, and produced five male gods, the eldest of whom was Masaka-akatsu-kachi-hayabi Ame no Oshi-ho-mi-mi no mikoto. The sun-goddess claimed the five as her own offspring, and told Susanowo that he might take the three female children born from the fragments of his sword. Susanowo boasted that the purity of his intentions was made clear by the birth of three gentle maidens, and commenced the series of violent actions which ended in the frequently mentioned retirement of the sun-goddess into the 'heavenly rock-cavern.' In this way Oshi-ho-mi-mi was, as it were, adopted by the sun-goddess, and his eldest child was therefore her grandson, the effect of adoption being to place the adopted person in the position which he would have held if he had been legitimately begotten by the adopter. The epithet 'sovran grandchild' having been first applied to the founder on earth of the Mikado's dynasty, came in time to be applied to each and all of his successors on the throne.

[13] 'Deigning' is used of the Mikado, who by this service deigns, as it were, to begin harvest.

[14] 'Beginning the harvest' means soaking the seed and preparing the ground for its reception. It has been suggested that the Chinese character 初, commencement, may be a copyist's error for 祈, praying-for. *Toshi*, which exclusively signifies year in its modern acceptation, seems originally to have meant harvest, and is probably from the same root as *toru*, to take. The ancient Japanese counted time by harvests, moons and suns; the first term entirely lost its earlier meaning, that of the second was obscured, and a Chinese equivalent being substituted for the third, the real nature of the units of measurement was forgotten.

[15] 'As the morning-sun rises in glory,' seems at first sight an allusion to the time of day at which the service was held, i.e. between six and seven o'clock in the morning, but from the use of this phrase it appears to be adverbial to *tatahe-goto tatematsuraku*, I fulfil your praises.

[16] Who the gods of the Harvest were is unknown. Several temples dedicated to such gods appear in the catalogue of the Yengishiki, but the names of the gods themselves are not mentioned. According to the Kozhiki, Susanowo begot the Great Harvest god, Ohotoshi no kami, who begot the HARVEST god, Mi-toshi no kami, and several other names of deities supposed to provide the human race with the grain which formed their chief food, occur in various myths. The most famous of these are the goddess worshipped at the Outer Temple (Gekuu) at Watarahi in Ise, and the deity, Uka no mitama or SPIRIT of Food, to whom is dedicated the temple of Inari on the road between Kiyauto and Fushimi. All other temples of Inari, of which there are thousands, are erected in honour of this SPIRIT of Food, and those worshipped with it, but although common speech uses the term Inari sama, as

if Inari were the name of a god, it must be remembered that it is merely the name of a place.

[17] The original is *yatsuka ho no ikashi ho ni*, 八束穗能伊加志穗爾. *Ya* originally signified 'many,' and is no doubt connected with the old word *iya*, still more, which I believe to be merely an interjection of astonishment, also used as a negative=No, identical with *iya*, hateful, and the root of such words as *iyashiki*, hateful, contemptible, *iyashimu*, to despise, and *iyagaru* (=*iya ge aru*), to dislike. *Ya* settled down afterwards as the numeral 'eight' (the ordinary *yatsu* is *ya* with the generic particle *tsu*), and at the moment when the *norito* were committed to writing, its original meaning had no doubt been forgotten. *Tsuka* is the same as *tsuka*, hilt, and is the root of *tsukamu*, to grasp with the hand. *Ho* denotes anything which prominently attracts the attention, as an ear of corn, the spike at the end of a spear, a flame (*honoho* for *hi no ho*), in *iha-ho*, a big rock, also *ho*, a sail, *nami no ho*, the crest of a wave, in *akani ho*, ruddiness of (countenance), perhaps also in *hou*, cheek. The so-called genitive particle *no* is the most interesting portion of this phrase, which is unintelligible if we translate *no* by 'of.' Students of the Mañyefushifu (萬葉集 will have observed that it has a dozen other uses besides this 'of.' In the present case it is most easily interpreted if we look upon it as identical with the verb *ni*, to be, the existence of which at an early stage of the language has been conjectured, with great appearance of truth, by Mr. Aston. The phrase would then be literally rendered by, 'the luxuriant ears which are many-bundled ears,' which is the same thing as saying 'many bundled and luxuriant ears.' It is not necessary, in order to support this view, to maintain that *no* was any longer understood to be a variation of the attributive form of a verb *ni*, to be, at the moment when this phrase was woven into the present *norito;* on the contrary, the infinitely varied uses of *no* and also of *ni*, which is many cases is held by Mr. Aston to be the root of *nu*, in the earliest extant specimens of Japanese literature, show that the original meaning of these syllables had long been forgotten.

[18] The process of preparing the half-liquid soil of the rice fields for the reception of the young plants is thus described. An early variety of rice called *wase* is sown in nurseries in the beginning of April, planted out early in May and harvested about the middle of September. In the west of Japan these several operations are probably carried out a fortnight earlier respectively.

[19] *Kahi*, here rendered by 'ear,' is more exactly the seed of rice enclosed between the paleæ. The same word originally applied to bivalves, which enfold the mollusc just as the paleæ do the grain of corn, and it is also supposed that *kahi*, in tht sense of a 'deep valley,' the sides of which appear to open out like the two halves of a bivalve, is identical with *kahi*, a grain and *kahi*, a shell.

[20] *Mika no he takashiri.* Mabuchi explains *mika* to be an earthernware jar in which *sake* is brewed, and afterwards offered up to the gods, and *he* to be the same as *uhe*, top. There are plenty of cases of the omission of an initial *u* after *o* in the old literature; e. g. *sakadzuki no he ni*, on the top of the cup (Mañyefu v. 5, p. 27 v., 1. 1.). But by others *mika* is said to have signified the liquor itself, *mi* being the honorific prefix, and *ka* the same as *ke* or *ki*, used to denote the grain in either its solid form as boiled rice, or its liquid form as rice-beer, and *he* a flat-bottomed vessel. If Mabuchi's explanation were adopted, the phrase would have to be rendered, 'raising-high the tops of the (beer) jars.'

Taka-shiri and its alternative expression *taka-shiki*, must not be understood literally; the secondary meaning of both *shiru*, to know, and *shiku*, to spread, is 'to govern,' 'to command;' but in the compounds which they form with adjective roots they have merely the force of the English verbal termination 'en' in such words as heighten, widen. A similar change is presented by *nafu* (or *namu*), to spin, which forms the ending of a large number of derivative verbs, such as *tomo-nafu*, to accompany, *azhinafu* to taste, *otonafu*, to make sound, *ni-nafu*, to carry as a burden. In *ito-nafu*, to spin thread, it preserves its original value, which was lost when, with the change of *f* into *m*, this word came to be employed solely in a figurative sense.

[21] *Oho-nu-hara.* Both *nu* (which is the archaic form of the modern *no*, on the authority of Mañyefu, v. 5, p. 26 v., 1. 9, where 'we find *haru no nu ni* written in *kana*) and *hara* are applied to uncultivated ground, not occupied by trees, but not necessarily flat, as might be inferred from the use of the word 'plain' in the translation. *Hara,* belly, is no doubt identical. Still, the term *no-hara* is very frequently applied to wide tracts of uncultivated level ground.

[22] *Awomi no hara,* the blue sea plain. Awo is evidently connected with *awi,* the name of the plant (polygonum tinctorium) from which the Japanese obtain a dye resembling indigo, and blue is therefore a fair rendering for it, especially when applied to the sea. In the Mañyefushifu, however, it is used as an epithet of horses (in the sense of black, that also being a colour afforded by the *awi* plant), also to clouds (white), to willow-trees (green), and to mountains (green). *Mi* for *umi,* sea, is another example of the elition of an initial *u* after a terminal *o.* Some Japanese etymologists derive *umi,* the sea, from *umu,* to give birth to, thus attributing to it the meaning of 'producer,' on account of its furnishing the inhabitants of these islands with a large proportion of their daliy food in the shape of fish, shell-fish, and seaweed. Another derivation from *awo,* blue, and *mi,* water, has also been proposed, but is not supported by any good authority in such matters.

[23] On the word *tahe,* here rendered by cloth, Mabuchi has the following note: "As five kinds of silk cloth were offered up, and the terms 'bright' and 'glittering' "express their colour, so 'coarse' and 'soft' express the coarseness and fineness of "the textures. 妙 is a *karizhi* (借字 a character of which the *yomi* or *kuñ* is used "as a *kana*), and in the Mañyefu we find 栲, which is the proper character to use. "Cloth, whether of *tahe* or of hemp, when fine was called *nigo-tahe,* soft cloth, "and when coarse was named *ara-tahe,* coarse cloth, but after the date of the founda- "tion of the present capital silk was called 'soft cloth,' and hemp 'rough,' and it is "in this sense that the terms are used jin the Yeñgishiki." In the earliest ages the materials used were the bark of the paper-mulberry (broussonetia papyrifera), wistaria tendrils and hemp, but when the silkworm was introduced the finer fabric naturally took the place of the humbler in the offerings to the gods. The use of *aratahe* as a makura-kotoba or 'pillow-word,' to Fujihara, proves that the wistaria was used in making coarse cloth· The wands adorned with strips of white paper which are seen in modern Shiñtau temples are the survivals of the offerings of cloth fastened to the branches of the sacred tree (*masakaki*) in ancient times. *Yufu,* which seems to have strictly meant paper-mulberry bark, also appears in some passages to include the cloth woven from it, and even hemp cloth besides.

[24] The horse for the god to ride on, the cock to tell the time, and the boar (a domesticated animal,—not the wild boar) for the god's food. Why white was the colour prescribed is unknown, but perhaps its rarity was a sufficient reason.

[25] In the preceding sentence the plural *kami tachi* occurs and is probably to be understood here also, but as the original has simply *kami,* deity, I have not considered it justifiable to translate 'gods.' Motowori is of opinion that only one deity is here meant.

[26] *Oho mi kamu no ko* is the reading given to 大御巫, which is rendered here by 'chief priestess.' There were virgins taken for a time to serve the gods, but there was nothing to prevent their being married after they had quitted the priest-hood. There were apparently four such priestesses consecrated to the service of the twenty-three gods worshipped in the chapel of the Zhiñgi-kuwañ, and the chief of them was distinguished from the others by the prefix *oho,* great.

[27] The Japanese names of these deities are Kami-musubi, Taka-mi-musubi, Iku-musubi, Taru-musubi, Tama-tsume-musubi, Oho-miya-no-me, Oho-mi-ke-tsu-kami and Koto-shiro-nushi. Whether *musubi* in the first five be compounded of *musu,* to grow, and *hi,* applied to everything that is great and glorious, as the sun for instance, according to Motowori's view, or whether it be simply the root of *musubu,* to tie together, matters very litle as far as the signification is concerned. All agree in giving to it a meaning which is best rendered by 'Producer.' The Kozhiki calls the god who existed before the heavens and earth and before all other gods, Ame-no-mi-

naka-nushi, or the Lord-in-the-very-centre-of-heaven, and the next gods who came
into existence were the pair Taka-mi-musubi and Kami-musubi. The first part of
each of these appellations is simply honorific, and does not denote any special function;
nor is either god to be regarded as superior to the other, for the order in which they
are named is a matter of indifference. The other three, Iku-musubi, Taru-musubi,
and Tama-tsume-musubi are not mentioned in the Nihoñgi or Kozhiki, and in the
Kogo-shiui they are only enumerated together with the others of the eight deities
whose worship is performed by the chief priestess. Mabuchi points out that their
names closely resemble those of certain precious stones brought from Heaven by one
of the gods (Nigihayahi), which in conjunction with several other treasures, had the
virtue of healing pain and recalling the dead to life. These stones were called *iku
tama, taru tama, magaru-gaheshi tama* and *chi-gaheshi tama*. In such compounds as
these, *iku*, which signifies 'to live,' 'breathe,' is to be taken in the sense of 'that by
which one lives,' as Motowori explains in the case of *iku-dachi, iku-yumi* and *iku-ya*,
sword, bow and arrows which have the property of giving life to the person who
possesses them. So *iku-tama* is 'precious stone by which life is ensured,' and *iku-
musubi* is literally 'the producer by whom life is ensured,' which may be rendered more
freely by 'vivifying producer.' *Taru tama* is the precious stone by which completeness,
sufficiency, fulfilment of all requirements are assured, and *Taru-musubi* is the producer through whose influence perfection is attained. By perfection is here meant
the perfection of bodliy strength and beauty. It is possible, too, that as Motowori
thinks, these two gods may have been identical with the Ikuguhi and Omodaru of
the Kozhiki, but the point is of minor importance, and the only argument in favour
of his view is the occurrence of *iku* and *taru* in the names of the two pairs respectively. Tamatsume I take to be a compound of tama, soul (the character 玉 is a
karizhi), and *tsume-* or *tome-*, to stop, detain, which is the interpretation hinted at by
Mabuchi, when he compares the efficient virtue of this god with that of the stones
which 'turn-back from death' and 'from the road' to the region of the dead. These
etymological interpretations do not necessarily conflict with a conjecture of mine
that the five names are merely epithets of a single deity, probably the sun-goddess,
whose modes of action may have thus been distinguished.

In the Yamashiro survey quoted by Motowori we find the name of a deity
天照高彌牟須比命, which must be read Amaterasu (or Amateru) taka mi-musubi
no mikoto, and means the 'From-Heaven-Shining-Lofty-PRODUCER's augustness,' a
combination of the ordinary epithet of the sun, From-Heaven-Shining, and the title
of one of the pair of creator gods. Mi-musubi, PRODUCER, is often written,御魂, and,
wherever these two characters are found in the name of a god it seems legitimate
to give them that reading. Hence 天照御魂 found in three places in the Catalogue
of Temples (Zhiñmeichiyau) in vol. 9, pp. 7 v., 14 v. and 15 v. of the Yeñgishiki,
Deha-boñ, where the *kana* of the editor is Amateru mitama, may fairly be read
Amateru (or Amaterasu) mi-musubi, From-heaven-shining PRODUCER. This, however,
is not the only argument for identifying the sun with Taka-mi-musubi. We have
seen already that the terms progenitor and progenitrix of the Mikado are sometimes
taken to mean both the Divine PRODUCER and the Lofty PRODUCER; that in some
places the sun-goddess is substituted for the Divine PRODUCER and in one place both
terms art applied to the sun-goddess, who was thus both mother and father of the
race. It would almost seem to have been a matter of indifference what epithets were
used in speaking of the Mikado's progenitors, which is easily accounted for if we
suppose those epithets to have been synonymous and therefore interchangeable. It
is also worthy of notice that, with perhaps the exception of the Soul-lodging PRODUCER,
these names of deities do not indicate distinctly separate functions (being combinations
of laudatory epithets prefixed to the word 'producer'), but rather the different effects
which the beneficent workings of a single great and powerful deity would produce.

There is still another point that deserves notice. We should naturally expect
to find that the first god of all, the Lord-in-the-very-centre-of-heaven, and perhaps
the pair which followed him, the Lofty-PRODUCER and Divine-PRODUCER, would
play a great part in the early legends of the Japanese, and also that Izanagi, the

parent of the sun and moon, would take an important share in ordering events; but as a matter of fact we find that these deities have very little to do, with the exception of the Lofty-PRODUCER, who is usually represented as ruling the world in conjunction with the sun-goddess. Izanagi and his consort disappear from the scene after they have given birth to the land, sea, rivers and the elements, and it is the child of Izanagi who becomes the centre of the mythology and worship of the ancient Japanese. It is difficult to resist the suggestion that the sun was the earliest among the powers of nature to be deified, and that the long series of gods who precede her in the cosmogony of the Kozhiki and Nihoñgi, most of whom are shown by their names to have been mere abstractions, were invented to give her a Temple at Watarahi in Ise.

Oho-mi-ya-no-me is probably, as the meaning of the name suggests, the personi-fication of the successive generations of female attendants of the Mikado. From the earliest times of which we have any record, whether legendary or historical, the sovereign appears to have been surrounded by a large number of women, and during the most recent period, that is down to the reign of the last Mikado, none but women were admitted to his presence. The statement in the Kogo-Shiui that Oho-mi-ya-no-me was appointed to serve before the sun-goddess, when she issued forth from the cave, simply indicates the great antiquity of the practice. Faithful service was rewarded eventually by the erection of an altar to the memory of the mythical personage who was invented to be the type of all these female attendants.

Oho-mi-ke-tsu-kami, the deity of the great FOOD, where 'great' is merely an honorific term like *mi,* applied to anything belonging to a god or to the sovereign, is no doubt the same as the goddess of Food worshipped at the Gekuu, or Outer Temple at Watarahi in Ise.

Koto-shiro-nushi was a son of Oho-kuni-nushi (who is identical with Oho-na-muji), and his name contains a reference to the act by which he symbolized his surrender of the sovereignty over Japan to the descendant of the sun-goddess. When it had been determined by the council of the gods that possession should be taken of the earth in the name of the sun-goddess' grandson, several messengers were sent in succession to claim the land from its ruler, but as no tidings were received from them it was finally resolved to despatch Takemikadzuchi, to whom was joined in the mission Ame-no-tori-fune. "These two gods descended upon the shore of the province of Idzumo. They drew their sword, ten-hand-breaths' long, and planting it on the crest of a wave, hilt downwards, took their seat cross-legged on its point. They then made inquiry of Oho-kuni-nushi, saying: The From-heaven-shining great GODDESS and Takagi no kami (another form of the name Takami-musubi) have sent us to ask saying, I have charged my CHILD to rule over the central region of reed-plains which you possess as chieftain. What is your feeling concerning this matter? He replied: I am unable to say. My child Yahe-koto-shiro-nushi no kami will be able to speak, but he has gone to Cape Miho pursuing birds and taking fish, nor has he yet returned. So Takemikadzuchi sent Ame-no-tori-fune no kami to summon Koto-shiro-nushi no kami, and when the question was put to him, he said to the great god his father, I submit. Deliver up this region to the CHILD of the heavenly god. He then trod upon the edge of his boat so as to overturn it, and with his hands crossed back to back (in token of consent), transformed his boat into a green fence of branches, and disappeared."

The daughter of the god who thus surrendered the land to its new ruler married Iharehiko, who was canonized as Zhiñmu-Teñwau, and Koto-shiro-nushi is therefore an ancestor of the Mikado by the female side; but it is doubtful whether any consideration of that kind led to his being included among the eight gods who were supposed to be in a special sense the protectors of the Mikado. The eight may be classified as follows, five synonyms of the sun-goddess, ancestress of the Mikado and bestower of the Kingdom, one deity representing the female influence that surrounded the sovereign and imparted a gentle smoothness to his relations with his subjects, the goddess of food, and lastly one of the chief gods of the conquered race, who represented the compromise of antagonistic interests.

[28] Wi-ga-suri is held to be a corruption of *Wi-ga-shiri*, behind or by the well, and of the five gods enumerated in the Zhiñmeichiyau as being served by the priestess of Wi-ga-suri, viz., Iku-wi no kami, Saku-wi no kami, Tsunagu-wi no kami, Hahigi no kami and Asuha no kami, the first three are the gods of the 'vivifying well,' the 'blessing-well,' and the 'long-rope-well,' which are probably synonymous epithets of some well, highly esteemed for the quality of its water and the cool depths where it lay. Asuha is explained to be *ashi-ba*, foot-place, that is, the first place where the foot is set down after issuing from the house, and *hahi-gi* to be derived from *hahiri-giha*, entrance limit. Motowori has an elaborate and learned note on the subject of these two names which is worth consulting, in the Kozhiki-deñ, vol. 12, p. 47. It appears from a verse in the Mañyefushifu, XX, pt. 1, p. 24, that Asuha no kami was in ancient times worshipped in the court-yard of every house, which would be easily understood if he was supposed to be the guardian deity of court-yards.

[29] HOUSE is *mi-ya*, composed of the honorific *mi* and *ya* house. It was used indiscriminately for the house of a chieftain, the tombs of the dead and the temples of the gods.

[30] This means that the house protects the Mikado from the weather and the heat of the sun.

[31] Kushi-iha-mado no mikoto and Toyo-iha-mado no mikoto are the names of these two gods. In the Kogo-Shiui they are called by these names in one place, while in another *kami* is used instead of *mikoto*, a common alternation, as I have already observed. The Kozhiki says distinctly that these are simply synonyms of the single god Ihato-wake no kami, who is the 'god of the GATE,' so that we have here another case of alternative titles of a god coming to be looked on as separate gods. In the Kozhiki there is the statement that the three are one, while at the Mikado's court, a century or two later, we find that two separate gods of the gates are worshipped. The Catalogue of Temples says that there were eight shrines to the two gods named in the ritual, one to each at each gate in the four sides of the palace enclosure. Motowori's explanation of the names used in the ritual seems indisputable. *Kushi* and *Toyo*, wonderful and powerful, are honorific epithets; *mado* is not 'window,' but 'gate,' *ma* being the honorific prefix, so that 眞門 would be the correct equivalent in Chinese characters, and *iha* is rock, used in the sense of strong, enduring, eternal. The genealogy of Ihato-wake is another instance of the confusion between Taka-mi-musubi and Kami-musubi, for while the Kogo-Shiui makes him the grandchild of the former through Futo-dama, the Shiyau-zhiroku (姓氏錄) speaks of a family of Tame no Murazhi descended from Ihatsu-wake (evidently the same as Ihato-wake) the child of the latter. The Catalogue of Temples contains the names of eight, in Yamato, Afumi, Mutsu, Tsu, Mimasaka, Bizeñ (2) and Tosa, dedicated to Ihato-wake, besides the original temple in Tañba, with two shrines, sacred to Kushi-iha-mado. Besides the address to these gods, or to this god, which forms a part of this ritual, there is another whole ritual, called *Mikado Matsuri*, the service of the GATES, which is entirely dedicated to them, or to him.

[32] The Japanese equivalents of these two names are *Iku-kuni* and *Taru-kuni*, the origin of which is not very clear. Perhaps they are synonyms of a single deity. From the Catalogue of Temples we learn of a temple in Yamato called Iku-kuni no Zhiñzhiya, of another in Shinano called Ikushima Tarushima no Zhiñzhiya, and of a temple to Ikukuni Mitama, with two altars to a pair of gods. The last of these is probably the full title. It means the 'spirit by which the country, or region, lives.' In old Japanese, *shima* can scarcely have differed in meaning from *kuni*, and the signification common to both was more nearly that of the words 'region,' or 'country,' in such expressions as the 'Black country,' 'the west country' amongst ourselves. It is found frequently forming part of the names of places which are far inland, as for instance Hiruko-jima in Idzu. This explains the occurrence of both *shima* and *kuni* in the names of these gods and temples. The god or 'spirit who vivifies' or 'completes,' 'fulfils' the country, is the principal god of the locality, and is represented in later times by the Ichi-no-

miya, or chief Shiñtau temple, in each of the provinces into which the country came to be formally divided for administrative convenience.

[33] In the original the expression here rendered by 'Sovran gods' is in the singular number, while just above (below in the Japanese) it is plural. But every student knows how commonly the singular number is used when plurality is intended.

[34] I have not been able to learn what species is meant by *taniguku*, but it is certainly a large kind of frog, which, as its name 'valley-creeper' indicates is found in damp shady places.

[35] 'Salt' is probably not the primary meaning of *shiho*, but rather sea-water, from which salt, properly *yaki-shiho*, is obtained by desiccation.

[36] *Koto wakete*, parting the words, i.e. taking up a fresh and special theme.

[37] As already pointed out, the Japanese language generally makes no difference between god and goddess, but we know that Amaterasu is a goddess. Hence the use of the feminine pronoun here, which, it must be noted, has no representative in the original. Like the articles, relative and nearly all other pronouns, it has to be supplied by the translator.

[38] This is a simile descriptive of bowing the head. In the Mañyefu (vol. 3 下 p. 12, v.) we have a similar expression *shishi zhi mono hiza wori fuse*, bending the knees like the deer.

[39] *Agata* originally meant 'upper fields' (*ageta*), that is to say, arable land, such as is now called *hata*. *Mi agata* were therefore the 'august fields' of the 'sovereign. The Nihoñgi speaks of officials having to be sent to the six FARMS in the province of Yamato to take a census and to measure the rice-fields and arable lands. When the country was parcelled out into provinces (*kuni*) and departments (*kohori*), what had previously been called *agata* were renamed *kohori*. The six farms here spoken of are the modern departments of the same name, Kadzuraki, Shiki and Sofu having been each divided into two, so that there are nine instead of six. These were no doubt selected to form the household domain of the Mikado at an early period, when the capital was still in Yamato. It will be seen by looking at the map of Yamato that they form nearly the whole of the northern half of the province, with the exception of Heguri, Hirose and Oshinomi. For further details see the long note in the Kozhiki-deñ, vol. 29, p.p. 59 et infra.

[40] *Naga mi ke no toho mi ke* in the Japanese. Here *no* places the two terms of the phrase in apposition, and has the force of 'which is,' i.e. literally rendered, distant FOOD which is (at the same time) long FOOD. Both words, *toho* and *naga*, have reference here to time. In the Mañyefu they are thus employed over and over again; e.g.

> *hafu kuzu no*
> *iya toho nagaku*
> *yorodzu yo ni*
> *tayezhi to omohite;*

"thinking that it would last for a myriad ages, ever longer and more distant, like the creeping pueraria." The idea is that the Mikado is to partake of this food during a long life, and the whole phrase might more freely be rendered 'perpetual FOOD' without its meaning being at all sacrificed.

[41] We know nothing more about these gods than that they were supposed to inhabit the mountains here named, whence timber was brought for the palace buildings. All six are situated within three departments of the province of Yamato, where most of the ancient Mikado had their capitals, and the expression 'distant mountains' is consequently not to be taken literally, but rather coupled with 'near mountains,' as a poetical way of speaking of mountains in general, just like the *taka yama and hiki yama,* high mountains and low mountains, of hte *Ohobarahi no Kotoba.*

[42] *Mikumari* is the reading of the two characters 水分, translated 'parting of the waters.' This rests on the authority of the text of the Kozhiki Deñ. (vol. 5. p.

38), where Ame no mikumari no kami and Kuni no mikumari no kami are enumerated amongst the children of Izanagi and Izanami. *Kumari* is the same as the more familiar *kubari*, 'to part' or 'apportion.' The four names in the text are those of localities where temples to such gods of streams were raised. Several others are enumerated in the Catalogue of Temples. They were supposed to be able to control the supply of water for irrigation; and it was necessary to propitiate them lest they should withhold it altogether or send such floods as would destroy the crops. 'Parting of the waters' might be rendered by 'watershed,' if that expression were not slightly technical.

⁴³ i.e. the gods who are here addressed.

⁴⁴ *Imibe*, corrupted later into *Imube* and *Iñbe*, were a class of hereditary priests, belonging to several families, whose duties were to prepare the more durable articles offered to the gods at the principal services, to cut down timber required for building the temples, and further, to construct the temples. This appears from several passages in the Kogo-Shiui. There were families of Imibe in Awa, Sanuki, Kii, Tsukushi (i.e. Chikuzen and Chikugo) and Ise. We learn from the few lines of introduction to the Rituals in vol. VIII of the Yeñgishiki, that the Imibe, besides these functions, were allowed to read the liturgies at the two services of the Luck-wishing of the Great Palace (*Ohotono hogahi*) and GATES (*mikado matsuri*). It is not easy to see why this was the case. Perhaps the fact of their being the builders of the palace was considered a reason for their being allowed to recite the ritual in which the Wood Spirit and Spirit of Rice are besought to watch over the building and to protect its occupant. Mabuchi observes that Oho-mi-ya-no-me, who is also addressed by name in the Luck-wishing of the Great Palace, and Kushi-iha-ma-do and Toyo-iha-ma-do, to whom the ritual of the GATES is addressed, were children of Futodama no mikoto, from whom the Imibe were also supposed to be descended, and he suggests that the collateral relationship between them and these three gods entitled them to perform the services in which these gods were concerned. It was Futodama who held the *mitegura* or tree adorned with beads, the famous mirror and the offerings of cloth before the door of the cavern into which the sun-goddess had retired, on that great occasion which has so often to be recalled in speaking of the myths, and his descendants naturally performed a similar function, says Mabuchi. *Imibe* is compounded of *imi-*, to dislike or avoid, because it was particularly necessary that these priests should avoid all uncleanness, especially when performing their duties, and *be* is said to be identical with *me*, a contraction of *mure*, flock or body of persons, with which are connected *mura*, village, and *muragaru*, to flock together.

ANCIENT JAPANESE RITUALS.—PART II.*

(Nos. 2, 3 AND 4.)

BY ERNEST SATOW.

(Read before the Asiatic Society of Japan on June 30th, 1879.)'

No. 2.—KASUGA MATSURI, OR SERVICE OF THE GODS OF KASUGA.

This ritual is comparatively modern, having been composed for use at a service which we are told was first celebrated in the year 859, A.D., and it contains, in fact, certain internal indications from which we should naturally be led to conclude that it was not of ancient origin. The earliest book which professes to give any information concerning the foundation of the Temple of Kasuga and of the services performed in honour of the gods to which it is dedicated is the *Kuzhi Kongen* (公事根源), written about the year 1422 by a noble named Ichideu Kaneyoshi, entirely from memory, and perhaps we can hardly be expected to place implicit belief in everything that it tells us. Its account of the foundation of the temple of Kasuga at Nara, one of the ancient capitals of Japan, is as follows:—

'In the year 767 (A.D.) Take-mika-dzuchi no mikoto, one of the four gods to whom this temple is consecrated, set out from Kashima in Hitachi, a province in the extreme east of Japan, in search of a dwelling-place. He rode a white deer, and carried in his hand a branch of willow, which he used as a whip. In this style he arrived in the department of Nabari in Iga, accompanied by the Nakatomi no murazhi Tokikaze and Hidetsura. From Nabari he shortly afterwards crossed over to Abe yama in

*Reprinted from the Transactions of the Asiatic Society of Japan, First Series, Vol. VII, Part IV, pp. 393-434.

Yamato, and finally arrived at Mikasa yama, close to the city of
Nara (which, if the date given by Kaneyoshi be accepted as his-
torically correct, was then the capital of the country). Having
found a resting-place that pleased him, he announced the fact to
the other three gods, of whom Ihahi-nushi came from Kadori
in the province of Shimofusa, Ama-no-koya-ne no mikoto from
Hirawoka in the province of Kahachi, and the goddess, who is
named last of all, came from the great temple of the sun-goddess
in Ise. In the autumn of the same year, in accordance with a
divine command, the Mikado sent an envoy to Mikasa-yama, to
plant the foundations of the stout pillars of the temple on the
· rocks which lay deep in the earth, and so manifested due
reverence towards the four gods.'

This story, which the author of the *Kuzhi Kongen* professes
to have derived from the account given by the priests of the
temple, explains the goddess to be an emanation from the per-
sonality of the sun-goddess, but Motowori argues with reason
that she was in reality the wife of Ama-no-koya-ne, or as we
should put it, of the ancient chieftain deified under that title, and
that her worship, like his, was derived from the temple of
Hirawoka in Kahachi. The whole legend is of course a fiction
invented by the priests of the temple, at a date long posterior
to its foundation in the ordinary way by the heads of the Fujihara family in the name of the Mikado, in order to produce an
effect upon the imagination of credulous worshippers, for it does
not bear traces of being a genuine myth. It moreover appears
to contain some anachronisms. Such names as Tokikaze and
Hidetsura, formed by combining two separate words, had not
come into vogue in Keiuñ, to which period the migration of
Takemikadzuchi is referred. The real name of the man who, in
767, founded the temple of these gods at Kasuga was Uweguri
Kuhimaro, a member of the Nakatomi tribe, who simply established at this spot the worship of his family gods. Tokikaze and
Hidetsura were descendants of his who lived about the middle
of the 9th century, when the Fujihara, who were extremely
powerful, chiefly through the marriage ties which bound successive Mikado to their family, took advantage of their position to
introduce an innovation by which the Mikado was made to
worship the ancestral gods of his mother as well as his own.

I.

Take-mika-dzuchi, also called Take-ika-dzuchi, is one of three gods .who, according to the version of the myth given in the *Kozhiki,* sprang from the blood of Kagutsuchi, the god of Summer-heat, as it dropped from the hilt of Izanagi's sword on to the stones in the bed of the River of Heaven (as the Milky Way is called in Japanese). According to the *Shiyauzhiroku* (姓氏錄) he was the ancestor in the 15th generation of a family called Yamato no Kahara no Imiki, who belonged to the province of Kahachi. It seems at first sight strange that the only persons who claimed descent from this god should be settled in a part of the country so remote from the original seat of his worship, and it would have been natural to suppose that the guardians of the temple of Kashima traced their lineage from him, as is the case with many other families of hereditary priests. This is not the case, however, for according to the *Kashima Meishiyo Dzuwe,* the Daiguu-zhi, or Chief Warden, is decended from Ama-no-koya-ne, who here appears in subordinate position as one of the *ahidono* gods or secondary deities of the temple.

A passage in the *Hitachi Fudoki* (常陸風土記), although somewhat obscure, appears to afford an explanation of the manner in which the Nakatomi tribe and the branch of it called the Fujihara family came to worship Take-mika-dzuchi as one of their ancestral gods. The legend says that 'in the reign of the sovereign Mimaki (usually known as Shuuzhiñ Teñwau), a spirit clad in white garments and armed with a white spear appeared on the top of a mountain and pronounced the following words: "If thou wilt order things aright before me, I will make the country which thou rulest tranquil, Oh Kikikatsu, and will grant unto thee large countries and small countries." Hereupon the sovereign summoned his followers and laid the matter before them. Kamu Kikikatsu of the Nakatomi tribe replied:—"This information has been given by the great GOD who dwells in the Kashima country, and promises thee the Great Many-island country to rule over." The heavenly sovereign on hearing this was startled, and presented the above mentioned offerings at the temple of the god.' It is inferred from this extract, which purports to record the legend existing among the inhabitants of Hitachi in the beginning of the 8th century, that the temple of

Kashima was founded in the reign of Suuzhiñ Teñwau, Kikikatsu being appointed the first high priest and bearer of the offerings spoken of, which are very nearly the same as those enumerated in the ritual. It would be natural for the peasant who repeated this legend to the official appointed to compile the Fudoki, to make Kikikatsu seem to say that the spirit who appeared was 'the god of Kashima,' that being the expression which he was himself in the habit of using, while Kikikatsu simply said that the spirit was Take-mika-dzuchi. This sort of confusion in the report of another person's words easily happens in Japanese, owing to the absence of any means of distinguishing direct from indirect speech. For example, in Japanese the phrases 'he said that it was too late' and 'he said: "It is too late"' would be expressed in exactly the same manner, so that it is impossible to know without special inquiry whether the speaker is repeating the exact words of another person or is merely giving the sense of what he said. Another difficulty in connection with this passage is that the spirit apparently promises dominion over the country not to the Mikado but to Kikikatsu, but the explanation of this is that supernatural utterances are always essentially of an enigmatical character, and resemble rather the incoherent mutterings of a dreamer than the sayings of a person wide awake, and if the revelation made on this occasion had been clear there would have been no necessity for calling a council together to declare its meaning. In the present case, Kamu Kikikatsu is the only one who understands the oracle, and he expounds it to mean that if he performs due rites in honour of the god Take-mika-dzuchi, the god will maintain the Mikado Mimaki as ruler over the 'Great Many-Island Country.' Perhaps the foundation in the east of Japan, as yet not completely cleared of its aboriginal inhabitants, of a temple dedicated to the conquering sword which, in the hands of the founder of the dynasty, had subjugated the western and central parts of the country, was emblematic of the assumption of sovereignty in that region by this Mikado. The people of later times, in repeating the explanation given by Kikikatsu, would then represent him as speaking of the 'god of Kashima,' and so the idea that the foundation of the temple was anterior to the legendary period, *i.e.* that it dated from the 'age of the gods,' would inevitably spring up. It became the hereditary function of the descendants of Kikikatsu, who succeeded him as high priests of Kashima, to worship Take-mika-dzuchi, and it is not difficult to see how they would come to look upon rites the performance of which had come down to them from their ancestor as a family duty. Hence, when a member of the Nakatomi tribe founded, in 767, the little temple of Kasuga in honour of his family gods, he naturally included among them the god of Kashima.

The Yamato no Kahara no Imiki were no doubt a tribe of sword-cutlers, settled on the banks of the Yamato-gaha, which flows through the province of Kahachi. There is no evidence to decide whether they regarded Take-mika-dzuchi as a famous sword or as the warrior who wielded it, but they no doubt found it convenient to adopt the fiction that they were descended from him.

In the *Kozhiki* version of the myth, Take-mika-dzuchi is celebrated as the god who descended from heaven to subdue the chieftain whom he found ruling in the province of Idzumo, and thus prepared the way for the advent of the Sun-goddess' grandchild. According to other versions of the story he was accompanied and assisted by a god named Futsu-nushi, but doubt is entertained by the commentators as to the reality of Futsu-nushi's existence as a separate deity. Some think that Futsu-nushi is merely another title for Take-mika-dzuchi himself; others take Futsu-nushi to be the name of the sword which he carried. It seems more reasonable to regard Futsu-nushi as the epithet of the warrior and Take-mika-dzuchi as one of the names of his sword. The *Kozhiki* in one passage represents Take-mika-dzuchi to have been the son of a god named Ame no Wo-habari no Kami, and in another place it says that Ame no Wo-habari was the name of the sword with which Izanagi slew the god of Summer-heat, so that Take-mika-dzuchi must also have been a sword. Wo-habari seems to mean broad blade; that is, a double-edged sword, and Take-mika-dzuchi was probably a single-edged weapon. In the *Kahachi Meisho Dzuwe*, vol. 3, p. 20, there is a wood-cut representing a pair of old swords, one of which is two-edged, the other single-edged, both called Futsu no mitama, and smilar swords are figured on the back of two curious discs of pottery under the name of 'treasures of Futsu no Kami,' and dated 730 (天平 , 2nd year). It is clear that in that age Futsu-nushi was looked upon as the owner of the sword, and not as a sword himself. The name Take-mika-dzuchi is merely a title compounded of various honorific words, if we accept Motowori's interpretation. *Take* is of course the root of the adjective *takeki*, bold, and is perhaps merely a secondary form of *taka*, tall. The double meaning of 'stout' in our own language is an illustration of how a single root may signify both size and warrior-like qualities. *Mika* and its alternative both mean 'big'; the first form occurs in the word *mikado*, which originally meant 'big place,' and the second has survived to this day in some parts of the country as the adjective *ikai*, big, numerous. Motowori explains *tsu* to be the archaic generic particle, and *chi* to be an honorific word found in the names of several other gods, in the word *woji*, an old man, and reduplicated in *chichi*, father.

A much easier explanation is that *ikadzuchi* is the same as the modern word for thunderbolt, and is compounded of *ika*, great, and *tsuchi*, mallet or hammer, so that Take-ika-dzuchi or Take-mika-dzuchi would simply be the god of thunder. And as a matter of fact the name is sometimes written 御雷之男 (Mi-kadzuchi no wo, august thunder man, in the *Kozhiki*) and 甕槌神 (Mika-dzuchi no kami or Great Hammer god, in the *Nihongi*, where 甕 is evidently used as a sort of *kana* and the second character means 'mallet' or 'hammer'). Further, the names of the gods who, according to the form of the myth in the *Kozhiki*, were produced at the same moment as Take-mika-dzuchi, are Hi-haya-bi and Mika-haya-bi, epithets the most obvious inter-pretation of which would lead us to conclude that they were gods of fire, the sort of brethren that the god of thunder would be naturally supposed to have. Motowori, and Hirata following him, warn us against accepting any such easy common-sense derivations, which are of course contrary to the spirit of ortho-dox Shiñtau and opposed to the general preference of these and other modern writers for far-fetched supernatural interpreta-tions. It seems on the whole most reasonable to suppose that this name of the Thunder god, who sprang from the blood of the god of Summer-heat, was also applied metaphorically to the famous sword which had subdued the foes of the Mikado's ancestor.

The date of the foundation of the temple of Kashima is unknown, and in 1act it is usually referred back to the 'Age of the Gods,' which precedes even the legendary period of Zhiñmu Teñwau and his immediate successors. We have, however, seen reason to suppose that it took place in the reign of Suuzhiñ Teñwau, and we may fairly conclude that it is one of the most ancient temples in Japan. In fact only five Shiñtau temples are supposed to have existed before the time of that Mikado, namely, the Oho-yashiro in Idzumo and the four temples of Asuka, Kadzuraki, Unada and Ohomiwa in Yamato, mentioned in the Ritual of the Miyadzuko of Idzumo, all of which were dedicated to Ohonamuji and his children, who ruled Japan before it was taken possession of by the founder of the present dynasty.

The second of the four gods of Kasuga, Ihahi-nushi of Kadori, in the province of Shimofusa, is identical with Futsunushi, as is clear from a passage in the *Nihongi*.[1] But the meaning of either name is not so evident.[2] In the *Kozhiki* we find mention made of a sword which had once done great service in subjugating Japan in the time of the sun-goddess' grandchild. When Ihare hiko (Zhiñmu Teñwau) was afterwards engaged in conquering the country for himself, in the course of an adventure in Kii, near Kumano, he met with a man who presented him with this very sword, in accordance with the command of Take-mika-dzuchi, delivered to him in a dream.[3] This sword was variously called Sazhi-futsu no kami, Mika-futsu no kami and Futsu no mitama, and was evidently supposed to be a god in itself. Hirata boldly supposes the god Futsu-nushi to be identical with this sword, but it is better to regard him as its owner. Both he and Motowori before him explain *futsu* to be an onomatopœia denoting cutting off in a trenchant manner, without leaving anything behind, and compare it with the modern colloquial *puttsuri to kiru*,[4] to cut clean off, so that *futsu no mi tama* would mean the "SOUL of Sharpness." Futsu-nushi is then the name of the owner of this sword, and Ihahi-nushi is that given to him to denote the fact of his worshipping the miraculous

---

[1] 日本紀集註, vol. ii. p. 19.

[2] *Ihahi* means 'to talk together' (*ihi-ahi*), and therefore to rejoice in company, to celebrate a festival, to worship; so that *Ihahi-nushi* means 'the master who celebrates' or 'who worships.'

[3] *Kozhiki Deñ*, vol. xviii. p. 45.   [4] Spelt phonetically.

blade. Like Kashima, the temple of Kadori is said to date from
the 'Age of the Gods,' and a family of hereditary arrow-makers
who claimed descent from Futsu-nushi is recorded in the
Shiyauzhiroku as settled in Kahachi, like the descendants of
Take-mika-dzuchi. In the *Hitachi Fudoki* (常 陸 風 土 記   p. 5,
verso) occurs a curious passage with reference to this god Futsu-
nushi, to the effect that after subduing the violent gods of the
mountains and rivers, he felt a longing to return to heaven, and
so, leaving behind him his magic staff, armour, spear, shield,
sword and precious stones, he mounted on a white cloud and
ascended to the skies. What clearer proof than this legend can
we have of his being simply a deified warrior chief? It is worthy
of note that both these gods are worshipped in the form of
swords.

The meaning of the name Ama-no-koya-ne or Ama-tsu-koya-
ne is even more obscure.[5] *Ama* is of course the same as *Ame*,
heaven, but there all certainty ends. Motowori suggests that
koya is a corruption of *woki-oya*, the beckoning elder, which
contains an allusion to the constantly recalled incident of the sun-
goddess' retirement into a cave in consequence of Susanowo's
misconduct, on which occasion it fell to the part of this god to
invite her forth from her seclusion by reciting the "great ritual."
Ne is considered by both Motowori and Hirata[6] as a merely
honorific suffix to names of gods. Hirata takes *koya* to be an
inversion of *ya-ko*, much heart or understanding, *ko* being the
radical part of *kokoro*, which in old Japanese is used for mind,
heart, intelligence, will and every other form or faculty of the
immaterial part of man. Both of these derivations are extremely
far-fetched, and it is much more likely that the god or hero from
whom the Nakatomi were descended took his name from a place
called Koya in the province of Tsu, in the department of Kaha-
nobe, which belonged to the chief branch of the tribe even down
to the time of Kamatari (b. 620, d. 675) in the 7th century. It
was Kamatari who took the surname of Fujihara, the other
members of the tribe retaining that of Nakatomi. His youngest
brother was the ancestor of the *Kannushi* of Kasuga. Oho-
Nakatomi was adopted as a surname by Omi-maro, a son of a

---

[5] Motowori and Hirata call this god-hero Ame-no-koya-ne.

[6] 古史傳 vol. xiii. p. 2.

first cousin of Kamatari. The Fujihara family gave up the service of the gods, and devoted themselves entirely to politics, while the Nakatomi still remained in the priesthood, which explains the fact that so many of them were officials of the Zhiñgi Kuwañ, or Ministry of Shiñtau religion.

II.

The temple of Hirawoka, whence the worship of Ama-no-koya-ne was brought to Kashima, is situated in the department of Kahachi in the province of the same name. To judge by the wood-cut at page 23, vol. v., of the *Kahachi Meishiyo Dzuwe*, the buildings cannot be very magnificent, but a noteworthy peculiarity of the temple is the absence of a *haiden* or oratory, and the worshippers appear to prostrate themselves on the bare ground below a raised terrace on which the chapels are ranged in line. According to the book just quoted, the other three deities are Oho-hiru-me (the sun-goddess), Futsu-nushi and Mika-dzuchi. Himegami, or Lady-god, is the official designation of the goddess in the national records, where she is frequently mentioned, together with Ama-no-koya-ne, as receiving some accession of rank and dignity in the divine hierarchy, but always two or three grades below him in rank, which is incomprehensible if we believe her to have been the Sun-goddess; and the explanation that the Hime-gami is the wife of Ama-no-koya-ne is the one which must be accepted.

A curious custom used formerly to be practised at this temple, called *Mi kayu ura*, or "DIVINATION by gruel." On the 15th day of the 1st moon, a quantity of beans of the species called *adzuki* (phaseolus radiatus) having been boiled in the presence of the gods, a roll of 54 tubes of fine bamboo, each inscribed with the name of a kind of seed-crop, was lowered into the semi-fluid mass, and from the way in which the beans entered the tubes, the priests drew inferences as to the probability of the particular crops being successful or the reverse. The peasants then knew what it would be best to sow during the year.

The temple of Kasuga is situated on the flank of a hill, and is surrounded by a wooden arcade, closed on the outside, and pierced by several gateways, the main entrance being on the south. Inside of this first enclosure is a second one, raised on a terrace, which is likewise surrounded by an arcade, with a principal gate in front, to which access is given by flights of steps. The ordinary layman performs his obeisance in front of this gateway, and only priests are allowed to enter further. There is no oratory (*haiden*), but the four chapels of the gods are ranged in a row, beginning with that of Take-mika-dzuchi on the right, and then in the following order to the left, Futsu-nushi, Ama-no-koya-ne and the goddess. The material of which the buildings are constructed is chiefly wood, painted red, and pictorial decoration has been applied very sparingly, as must have been unavoidable in the case of a temple which used to be rebuilt every twenty years.

The temple of Ohoharanu, near Kiyauto, was founded in 850, after the removal of the capital from Nara to its modern site in the province of Yamashiro, and dedicated to the same gods as the temple of Kasuga. The court apparently found it convenient to be able to invoke the gods without having to make a long journey of two days to Nara and back on each occasion. The buildings are on an insignificant scale, which shows that the temple was a mere make-shift.

According to the Ceremonial Regulations (*Jiyauguwan gishiki*) the service was performed twice in each year, namely, on the first day of the monkey in the 2nd and 11th moons.

Before the celebration of the service, orders were given to the Divination Office to fix a day, hour and locality for a "purification" to be performed. On the day preceding the purification a sort of tent was erected near the river (*i.e.* the Kamo-gaha at Kiyauto), and at the hour appointed the priestess who had been selected for the occasion proceeded to the place of purification in a bullock-car. The procession was magnificent and ordered with extreme precision. It consisted of nearly one hundred and forty persons, besides porters. First went two municipal men-at-arms, with white staves, followed by two citizens and eight officials of rank. They were succeeded by the bailiff of the priestess' official residence with four attendants, after whom came ten corporals of the Guard of the Palace Gates and a few men from the other four Imperial Guards. Next came the car of the priestess herself, with eight attendants in brown hempen mantles, two young boys in brown, and four running foot-pages in white dresses with purple skirts. A silk umbrella and a huge long-handled fan were borne on either side of the car by four men in scarlet coats. Ten more servants completed her immediate retinue. Then came a chest full of sacrificial utensils, and two carriages containing a lady who seems to have acted as a sort of dueña to the priestess, and the Mikado's messenger, surrounded by attendants in number suited to their rank. Close behind them were borne two chests full of food-offerings, and four containing gifts from the Mikado intended for those members of the Fujihara family who attended on the occasion. Seven carriages carried the female servants of the priestess, each of them being a lady of rank, and therefore accompanied by half-a-dozen followers of both sexes. Two high officials of the provincial government of Yamashiro awaited the procession at a convenient point, and conducted it to the spot chosen for the ceremony of purification. A member of the Nakatomi tribe presented the *nusa*, consisting of a white wand with hemp-fibre hanging from its upper end, the symbol of the primitive offerings of greater value, and a Diviner[7] read the purification ritual. After the ceremony was over, refreshments were served out, and the Mikado's gifts distributed. The priestess then returned to her official residence.

On her journey to the temple of Kasuga the priestess was preceded by various priests, diviners, musicians, cooks and other functionaries of inferior grade, who set out one day earlier in the charge of an officer of the Minister of Religion. At the boundary of the province of Yamato she was received by officers of the provincial government, who accompanied her to the temporary building erected for her accommodation on the banks of the Saho-gaha. During the day the rite of purification was performed on the western side of the temple, and the offerings placed in readiness for the final ceremony. At dawn on the following

---

[7] *Miyazhi*, the term in the original here rendered "diviner," is a contraction of *miya-nushi*, master of the House, the person who sacrificed to the hearth god in the Mikado's palace. *Tozhi*, the later meaning of which is woman, was originally the person who discharged the same function in the house of a subject. It was evidently the head of the household who at first performed these sacrifices and the office was afterwards delegated to another.

day officials of the Ministry of Religion superintended the clean-
ing of the shrine by a young girl (*mono-imi*), who had been
carefully guarded for some time previous from contracting any
ceremonial uncleanness, while other officials (*kandomo*) decorated
the buildings and set out the sacred treasures close to the shrines
and by the side of the arcade round the innermost enclosure.
Everything being now in readiness, the high officers of state
who had come down from the capital for the service entered by
the gate assigned to them, and took their seats in the outer
court, followed by members of the Fujihara family of the 6th
rank and under. The priestess now arrived in a palanquin, with
a numerous retinue of local functionaries, infantry and cavalry
soldiers, and followed by porters carrying the offerings of the
Mikado, his consort, the heir-apparent and of the priestess herself. Next came race-horses sent by the Mikado's consort, by the
heir-apparent and from the Six Guards of the Palace, the rear
of the procession being brought up by a crowd of lesser officials
and men-at-arms. The palanquin of the priestess was surrounded
by a large body of guards, torch-bearers and running pages,
umbrella- and screen-bearers, and women and girls on horseback.
After them came the chest of sacrificial vessels, a number of
servants, three chests full of food-offerings, six chests of clothing
for the gods, with carriages containing some of the Mikado's
female attendants, the priestess' dueña and some young girls.
On arriving at the north gate on the west side of the temple
enclosure, the men got off their horses and the women descended
from their carriages.   The priestess then alighted from her
palanquin, and passing between curtains, held by her attendants
in such a way as to render her invisible to the crowd, entered
the waiting room prepared for her inside the court-yard, followed by the women of the Mikado's household. The Mikado's
offerings were now brought forward by the Keeper of the Privy
Purse, and laid on a table outside the gate, while the women of
the Household entered the inner enclosure, and took their places
in readiness to inspect the offerings. In a few minutes they
were joined by the priestess, who had changed her travelling
dress for sacrificial robes. The Keeper of the Privy Purse now
brought the Mikado's presents in through the gate, and placing
them on a table in front of the *midzu-gaki* or inner fence,

saluted the chapels by clapping his hands four times, alternately standing upright and bowing down to the ground. On his retiring, the same ceremony was performed by the persons charged with the offerings of the Mikado's consort and heir-apparent, after which the offerings of the Fujihara and other noble families were deposited on lower tables, with similar ceremonies. The *Kandomo*, or subordinate officials of the Ministry of Religion, next carried up the Mikado's offerings and delivered them to the *mono-imi*, who carried them into the chapel. The *Kandomo* then spread matting on the ground in front of each of the four chapels, and members of the Fujihara clan who held a sufficiently high rank carried in and arranged the tables destined to receive the food-offerings. Two barrels of *sake* were then brought in and placed between the first and second and third and fourth chapels, in a line with the tables, a jar of *sake* brewed by the priests being also placed in front of each chapel. This over, every one quitted the enclosure, making way for the women of the household, who uncovered the food-offerings and poured out two cups of *sake* for each deity. The liquor appears to have been of the turbid sort called *nigori-zake*. All the preparations being thus complete, the high officers of state and the messengers sent by the court entered the enclosure and took their seats. Four saddle-horses intended as offerings to the gods and eight race-horses were now led up in front of the temple, preceded by a major-general of the Guards and the Master of the Horse. A superior priest, with his brows bound with a fillet of paper-mulberry fibre (*yufu-kadzura*), then advanced and read the ritual, bowed twice, clapped his hands four times and retired. The congregation afterwards withdrew to the *Nahorahi-den,* or refectory, where the food-offerings were consumed by the participants in the solemn act of worship, and the *sansai,* or thanksgiving service, was conducted by the *Kandomo* of the Ministry of Religion.

The sacred horses were then led eight times round the temple by the grooms of the Mikado's stables, who received a draught of sanctified *sake* as their reward. The general of the body-guard next directed some of his men to perform the dance called *Adzuma-mahi,* and when they had finished, a meal of rice was served to them with much ceremony by the Mikado's cooks. At the command of the Vice-Minister of Religion the harpists and flute-players were summoned to perform a piece of music, called *mi koto fuwe ahase,* the concert of HARP and FLUTE; the flutes played a short movement alone, and were then joined by the harps, whereupon the singers struck in. An officer of the Ministry of Religion sang the first few bars, and the official singers finished the piece. This was followed by one of the dances called *Yamato mahi,* performed in turn by the principal priests of the temple, by members of the Fujihara family and by the Vice-Minister of Religion himself. After the *sake*-cup had been passed round three times, the company clapped their hands once and separated. The priestess changed her robes for a travelling dress and returned to her lodging in stately procession as before. A Secretary of the Council of State then presented to the Minister of State a list of non-official persons of rank who had attended at the service, and the gifts of the Mikado were distributed to them as their names were called out by a clerk, after which everybody adjourned to the race-course and the day was wound up with galloping-matches.

The procedure at the half-yearly festivals of Ohoharanu was almost exactly the same.

III.

The *Yengi Shiki* gives lists of the articles required to be supplied at the two festivals of Kasuga, either as offerings or in their preparation. The cost was defrayed chiefly out of the revenues of the temples of Kashima and Kadori, which contributed between them 500 pieces of tribute-cloth (*tsuki-nuno* 調布), 300 pieces of excise-cloth (*chikara-nuno* 庸布), 600 pieces of commercial-cloth (*aki-nuno* 商布), 600 catties of hemp and 600 sheets of paper. These articles were forwarded to the Ministry of Religion, and deposited in the government store-houses as a fund for the celebration of these services. Other offerings were provided at the expense of the several departments of the government, as for instance, the horses came from the Mikado's stables, and the matting from the *Kamori no tsukasa.*

In the ritual a mirror, sword, bow and spear are enumerated among the presents, but as no provision is made in the regulations for furnishing these articles, it seems probable that the same sword, bow and spear were brought out year after year and used again, while the mirror was no doubt permanently placed in the temple in front of the gods. It must not be forgotten that in the beginning of the 10th century, when these regulations were drawn up, the practice of the Shiñtau religion had become a matter of form, and it seems likely that the mirror seen until a few years back in every Shiñtau temple had then already assumed its place before the shrine. In the regulations for the conduct of the service of the Wind-gods at Tatsuta, the use of the same saddle on the horse-offering year after year, until it became too old and ragged for the purpose, is specially ordered.

The 'bright cloth, glittering cloth, soft cloth and coarse cloth' consisted, according to the Yeñgi regulations, of 7 feet of *ashiginu* (coarse silk), 23 feet of tribute cloth, 46 feet of bleached cloth and 12 pieces (each about 12 yards in length) of commercial cloth, all being fabrics of inferior quality and representing a very small value in money. The 'things wide of fin and things narrow of fin,' *i.e.* large fish and small fish, are represented by bonito, *tahi* (Serranus marginalis), haliotis and cuttle fish (sepia), six catties of each. 'Weeds of the offing and weeds of the shore' are represented by six catties of *me* (Halochlea. sp.). For 'things of the mountains and plains—even to sweet herbs and bitter herbs,' beans of two sorts (*daizu*, Glycine hispida and *adzuki*, Phaseolus radiatus), oranges and miscellaneous fruits were offered. Of ordinary rice and *mochi* rice 3 *to* (about 1½ bushels) each, and of *sake* 1½ *koku* (about 58 gallons) were allowed. Besides these offerings there were provided a large number of coarse earthen-ware dishes and cups of various kinds, the very form of which is now forgotten in most cases, nothing but their names having been preserved.

The principal service was followed by the *sansai*, or thanksgiving for the feast, at which the food-offerings were consumed. The *Yengi Shiki* states the amounts of the various articles supplied for this service, but we have no account of the ceremonies observed. Nor are any details given about the ceremonies of 'purification' (*harahi*), which preceded the brewing of sacred *sake* for use at the festival (properly called *mi ki*), nor of the service of the fire-places where the *mi ki* was manufactured,

although we learn incidentally that such ceremonies were performed in connection with the principal service.

RITUAL.

[TRANSLATION]

The sovran *who is called* "According to his great WORD"[1]
says in the great presence of the four pillars of sovran gods,
namely, dread Mika-dzuchi's augustness who sits in Kashima,
Ihahi-nushi's augustness who sits in Kadori, Ama-no-koya-ne's
augustness and the lady-deity who sit in Hirawoka.

He says: In accordance with the request which the great
gods have deigned to make, *the builders* have widely set-up the
HOUSE-pillars on the bottom-most rocks of Kasuga's Mikasa
yama, and have made-high the cross-beams to the plain-of-high-
heaven, and have humbly[2] fixed *it* as *their* SHADE from the
heavens and *their* SHADE from the sun;—as to the
divine treasures which are set-up, humbly providing a
MIRROR, a SWORD,[3] a BOW, a SPEAR and a HORSE;—as to CLOTH-
ING, taking[4] bright cloth, glittering cloth, soft cloth, coarse cloth,
and ranging-in-rows the first-fruits of the tribute[5] set-up by the
regions of the four quarters; as to things of the blue-sea-plain—
things wide of fin and things narrow of fin, weeds of the offing
and weeds of the shore; as to things of the mountains and wilds
—even to sweet herbs and bitter herbs, as to LIQUOR, raising-
high the beer-jars, filling and ranging-in-rows the bellies of the
beer-jars, and piling up the various things like a range of hills
—namely the great OFFERINGS which *he* sets-up, having fixed
upon such-and-such an officer, named so-and-so, as Kañnushi
(priest), *he* humbly fulfils the praises of the sovran great
DEITIES, *by saying* take *them* tranquilly and peacefully as peaceful and sufficient OFFERINGS.

He says: *I* humbly fulfil your praises, *saying:* in consequence
of *my* having done this, humbly praise the court of the sovran
peacefully and tranquilly, and as a satisfactory and luxuriant

AGE, and humbly bless it unchangingly and eternally, and deign to prosper also the princes and councillors of the *various* places and houses⁶ who share *in the administration* and serve, and cause them to serve tranquilly in the court of the sovran like the perpetual growth of luxuriant trees.

NOTES.

¹ 天皇我大命爾坐世, *sumera ga oho mikoto ni mase*, with which the ritual commences, presents considerable difficulty. Mabuchi got over this by simply changing *mase* into *masu*, so that the altered passage meant 'it is the great WORD of the sovran.' But apart from the apparent want of connection between such a sentence and that which immediately succeeds it, the fact that this phrase *oho mikoto ni mase* occurs several times in the *Sen-miyau* (宣命) or Royal Announcements in the *Shiyoku Nihongi* (續日本紀) and in the *Ruwizhiyuu Kokushi* (類聚國史), and always in such a context that it must be translated as a compound noun, prevents us from accepting his emendation. In an Announcement of Ohowi no Mikado (750-764) occurs the sentence *mata oho mikoto ni mase nori-tamahaku*, again the *oho mikoto ni mase* deigned to say, where the expression under examination is clearly used as a synonym for sovereign. An Announcement of Shiyaumu Tenwau of the year 743 opens with 天皇大命爾坐西奏賜久, *sumera (ga) oho mikoto ni mase mawoshi tamahaku*, the sovereign('s) *oho mikoto ni mase* deigns to report, i.e. to his mother, the ex-Mikado Genshi-yau. Besides these two undoubted cases of the use of this term to denote the Mikado, there are four other passages which are most probably to be read in the same manner. In the Announcement by which the Mikado Genmei Tenwau makes known her accession to the throne on the death of her son and predecessor Monmu, she relates first that in the previous year he had desired to abdicate on account of ill-health, and had addressed her in the following words: *Are mi mi tsukarashiku masu ga yuwe ni itoma yete mi yamahi wosametamahamu to su. Kono ama tsu hitsugi no kurawi ha oho mikoto ni mase oho mashi mashite wosame tamafu beshi*: Because my BODY is fatigued I intend to take leave and order-aright my disease. Thou shalt deign to be *oho mikoto ni mase* and order-aright the seat of the successor of heaven's sun, or more freely, "Thou shall be *oho mikoto ni mase* and occupy the throne of the sun's descendant." In all the copies of the *Shiyoku Nihongi*, MS. or printed, the Chinese characters are 大命爾坐母, but 母 is evidently a mistake, and Motowori is right in reading 世 instead. The phrase occurs again, 1st in a joint Announcement of Shiyaumu Tenwau and his daughter Kauken Tenwau in 749, on the occasion of his resigning the throne to her, 2nd in an Announcement issued by Shiyaumu Tenwau proclaiming his accession in 724, and 3rd in his Announcement of the year 729 by which the chronological style was altered from Zhinki to Tenbiyau. In the first of these the MSS. and printed books have *to* instead of *se*, which is Motowori's emendation; but as the former makes no sense at all, while the correction does, it may fairly be accepted. There is no *kana* in either the second or third of these cases, but in the second 天皇乃大命爾坐, is evidently the subject of the verb *noritamahaku* which follows immediately, and it is therefore necessary to read *sumera mikoto no oho mikoto ni mase*, by comparison with the first three examples concerning which there is no doubt whatever. In the third case we have 大命坐皇朕 without any *kana* at all. It would be possible to read *oho mikoto ni masu sumera ha*, and to translate, "I, the sovran, who am the great augustness," but there is absolutely no evidence in favour of such a reading. I do not know of any passage where the Mikado is called a 'great augustness,' '*oho mikoto*,' and the term *mikoto* is never used except as part of a title or as an abbreviated way of speaking of the person who bears that title, after he has been previously mentioned in the same passage. So that we are driven to read *mase* here, as in the other cases. In the *Ruwizhiyuu Kokushi*, bk. 36, p. 7, there is an undoubted case of the use of this

term 天皇我大命爾坐世石作乃山陵爾申給久, *sumera ga oho mikoto ni mase Iha-tsukuri no yama no misasagi ni mawoshitamahaku*, "the sovran *oho mikoto ni mase* deigns to report to the tomb on mount Ihatsukuri," and it is found also at the beginning of the Hirano Ritual.

It remains to inquire what is the literal meaning of *Oho mikoto ni mase*. The last word is the only one which presents any difficulty. Motowori suggests that 坐 is merely a 'borrowed character,' used to express quite a different *ma* from that which it usually means, and that this *ma* is identical with the root which we find reduplicated in the expression *ma ma ni*, in accordance with, in *ma ni ma ni*, an old form of the same, and also in *makase*, to leave to, to submit to. The whole phrase would then signify 'submitting to' or 'in accordance with the great command,' and he supposes that it may have been so constantly used of the Mikado as to sink finally into the condition of a mere epithet, and so have become a title; just as some of the attributive phrases called *makura-kotoba*, abandoning their original function of epithets, came to denote the substantives to which they had originally been prefixed. This suggestion is not wanting in plausibility, especially as we find the term joined to the preceding word *sumera* (or *sumera mikoto*) as often by *ga* as by *no*. Though there seems good reason to believe that *no* was a particle of apposition (not to say a verb) before it became a possessive particle, *ga* in the early Japanese is almost always a possessive particle, and never became appositive. In the passage quoted from the *Ruwizhiyuu Kokushi*, and in the two rituals where the expression under discussion occurs, the particle *ga* is used, with a sense, as it were, of the original meaning, while in only one place it is preceded by *no*, which might be understood either as possessive or appositive.

[2] *Matsuri* is here rendered by 'humbly,' its real character being that of an auxiliary verb, originally meaning 'to serve.' From being used as a verb expressing humility on the part of the speaker, it became a mere mark of polished speech, like *safurafu* and *haberu* of the written language, and *masu* in the modern colloquial language. (See Aston: Grammar of the Written Language, 2nd edit., p. 174.)

[3] The words for sword and bow in the original are *hakashi* and *tarashi*. The authority for reading 刀 as *hakashi* is firstly the tradition among the Shiñtau priests that it is to be so read in this place, and secondly a passage in the *Nihoñgi* (see 集註 editn. bk. 7, p. 12. verso) in a name 御刀媛 which is followed by the explanatory note 御刀此云彌波迦志, august sword is here called *mikahashi*. *Hakashi* is the root of *hakasu*, a form of *haku*, to wear, and means, therefore, a 'thing worn.' *Tarashi* is probably a corruption of *torashi* (which is adopted by Hirata as the better reading, in spite of the voice of tradition), which in like manner is the root of a 'lengthened form' of *toru*, to take, to grasp, and in the sense of a 'thing to grasp' might very well be used to denote a bow. The term 'lengthened form,' which Japanese grammarians are very fond of using to denote forms ending in *afu* or *asu* redundant syllable *ka*, as in *tsukarakasu* for *tsukarasu*; *fukurakasu* for *fukurasu*; *chirakasu* for *chirasu*; *fuyakasu* for *fuyasu*; *ikarakasu* for *ikarasu*, which seems to be simply due to natural impulse towards the employment of emphasis, of which *matsugu* for *masugu*; *matsuhira* (pronounced *mappira*) for *mahira* are other examples. But the archaic forms in *asu* and *afu* may be explained in another way. In a certain number of verbs this termination in *afu* is due to the suffixing of the verb *afu*, to meet, used as a substitute for the adverb 'mutually'; thus *tatakafu*, to fight, is *tataki-afu*, to beat mutually; *katarafu*, to persuade, is *katari-afu*, to tell to each other; *hakarafu*, to manage, is *hakari-afu* to weigh together, in the metaphorical sense; *mukafu*, to be opposite, is *muki-afu*, to be mutually turned towards; *tsugafu*, to pair is *tsugi-afu*, to be connected together. *Ihafu*, to celebrate, is probably *ihi-afu*, to talk of together, and perhaps *utafu*, to sing, is *uchi-afu*, to beat time together. Just as the root *ahi-*, which originally was prefixed to verbs in the same way as *afu* is suffixed, *i.e.* in the sense of 'mutually,' frequently occurs, sometimes even in the poems of the Mañyefu, with no meaning at all, so it seems not improbable that the practice of adding *-afu* to the root of a verb and dropping the final vowel of the root, came to be pretty general, without the speaker having any consciousness

of its real signification. To prefixes like *ahi-*, *uchi-*, *tori-*, *ma-*, the original meaning of which is patent, and *sa*, *i*, the derivation of which is not yet known, the term ornamental prefix may be applied, and *-afu* in like manner might be called an ornamental suffix. In some cases the ornamental form has been accepted for ordinary use in the modern language, to the exclusion of the simpler, as *negafu*, to pray for, formerly *negu*, and *tamafu*, to deign, formerly *tabu*, while in *sumu* and *sumafu* both are used concurrently. The termination *-asu* seems to have come into use in a similar manner. Just as in the modern spoken tongue causative verbs are often inflected at the choice of the speaker, as if they belonged to both conjugations, so in the old language there was much confusion between verbs of the first and second conjugations (*yo dañ no hataraki* and *ni dañ no hataraki*), of which the confusion between verbs in *-su* and *-seru* is only a particular case. Such forms as

tatasu, to stand, to start;	*nagekasu*, to lament;
karasu, to reap;	*wemasu*, to smile;
watarasu, to cross;	*omohosu*, to think;
kikasu, to hear;	*morasu*, to guard;
tohasu, to ask;	*kumasu*, to draw (water);
shinubasu, to love;	*obasu*, to wear (a girdle);

were probably at first causative verbs used honorifically, and as it is the well-known tendency of all honorific epithets and phrases to descend in the social scale, until they come to be used without distinction of persons, so it became a common practice to use this corrupted causative form in *-su* indifferently, merely for the purpose of ornament. Innumerable examples are to be found in the Mañyefushifu, and because they are so common in the old poetry, it is considered a sufficient explanation to say that they are poetical forms; but it can hardly be supposed that in any language special forms were invented for use in poetry. The most reasonable explanation of 'poetical forms' is the fact that variety of expression is one of the principal means of giving ornament to a composition, and that synonymous and alternative forms were retained in poetic diction, after they had been discarded for the sake of convenience in plain prose and conversation.

[4] *Ni tsukahematsurite*, here freely rendered 'taking,' is the equivalent of the modern conversational '*ni shite*,' which is used in the sense of choosing one out of many things offered or present for selection. *Tsukahe-matsuru* is seen at once to be a compound of *tsukaheru*, to be employed, and *matsuru*, to serve, used as an auxiliary verb, as in the compound *tatematsuru*, to set up humbly, to offer to a superior. In the modern form of this word the syllable *he* has been dropped, and it has become *tsukamatsuru*, used as a polite substitute for *suru*, to do.

[5] The word rendered 'tribute' is *mi-tsugi*, a compound of the usual honorific prefix *mi*, and *tsugi*, root of *tsugu*, to continue (t.v.), used as a substantive, that which is continued in order to supply a constant want, *i.e.* anything supplied without payment) for the support of another. In the modern language there is a verb *mitsugu* derived from *mitsugi*, which means to contribute toward the support of a person whose income is insufficient for his needs. 'Contribution' best renders the etymological signification, but 'tribute' more fitly expresses the portion of produce paid to the sovereign by way of income.

[6] By 'places' is meant departments of the government, and by 'houses' the families to which the princes and the Mikado's councillors belonged.

No. 3.—HIROSE OHO-IMI NO MATSURI, SERVICE OF THE GODDESS OF FOOD.

According to the *Riyau no Gige* (令儀解), or Exposition of Administrative Law, there were two Oho-imi no matsuri, the

object of which was 'to cause the waters of the mountain gorges
to change into sweet waters and to fertilize the young rice-plants,
so that a full harvest might be reaped.' One of these was at
Hirose, dedicated to the goddess Waka-uka-no-me; the other at
Tatsuta, dedicated to the Wind Gods. No satisfactory explanation has yet been given of the name Oho-imi. We learn from the
Yengi Shiki that both services were celebrated twice in each
year, on the 4th days of the 4th and 7th moons, first when the
rice-plant was springing up, and afterward when it was ripe, but
this can only mean the early variety called *wase*. The *Zhinzhiya
Keimou* (神社啓蒙) identifies Waka-uka-no-me with the Food-
goddess of the Gekuu temple in Ise. Other names of this goddess
are Toyo-uke-bime, child of Waku-musubi the Vegetative Producer (*i.e.* the growth of plants personified), who was the offspring of Ho-musubi, god of Summer-heat, and Hani-yama-bi-
me, goddess of earth[1]; Oho-getsu-bime, under which name she
is regarded as the child of Izanagi and Izanami[2]; Uka-no-mi-
tama, child of Susanowo and the daughter of the God of Mountains, Oho-yama-tsu-mi[3]; Oho-mi-ketsu kami in the Praying for
Harvest, Uke-mochi no kami[4]; Toyuke in the 'History of the
Foundation of the temple of the sovran deity Toyuke;' Toyouke
no kami in the *Kozhiki*[5]; Toyo-uka-no-me no mikoto as the goddess of *sake*, which is prepared from rice; Oho-uka no kami in
the Catalogue of Temples and Toyo-woka-hime no kami in the
Kagura-uta. Hirata[6] and Mabuchi[7] agree in identifying the
goddess of Hirose with the Food-goddess of Ise.

The text of this Ritual is probably corrupt, at least the latter
portion of it. The phrase "Sovran gods who dwell in the entrances to the mountains of the six FARMS of Yamato" is nonsense, for the six FARMS were not situated in the same localities
as the temples of the entrances to the mountains, as can be seen
from the passages in the 'Praying for Harvest,' where their
worship is spoken of. The gods of the 'entrances to the mountains' were worshipped for the sake of the timber which grew

[1] K. Zh. K. D. vol. 5, p. 51.
[2] Ib. vol. 5, p. 50.
[3] Ib. vol. 9, p. 50; *Nihoñgi Shifuchiyuu*, vol. 1, p. 14 verso, p. 22 verso.
[4] Ib. p. 26 verso; p. 28.
[6] 古史傳 § 13.
[5] Vol. 15, p. 30 verso.
[7] Norito-kau, vol. 1, p. 28 verso.

under their care, and had nothing to do with the supply of water, for which the 'gods who dwell in the partings of the waters' are worshipped. Nor is it consonant with the functions of either the Farm or Forest gods that they should be besought "not to inflict bad winds and rough waters." It was natural enough in worshipping the goddess of food to offer up prayers also to the gods of the farms where the rice was to be grown under her protection, and likewise to the gods of water, without whose aid irrigation of the growing rice was impossible, and as the goddess of food was at the same time the goddess of trees, we can perhaps see how the worship of the forest gods may have come to be conjoined by mistake with hers. Motowori thinks that the original *norito* of this extremely ancient service must have been lost, and replaced much later with one composed by ignorant priests, who borrowed a piece from the Praying for Harvest and a phrase or two from the service of the gods of wind (*i.e.* about bad winds and rough waters), and mixed the Farms, Forests and Waters together in one petition.

It appears from a passage in the regulations for conducting the regular services that a *harahi* or purification was performed in connection with this service, probably before its celebration, in order to purify the principal persons who were to take part in the ceremony, as we have seen was done before the Kasuga service, where the priestess *ad hoc* underwent lustration. The list of articles to be expended for the Hirose service contains the item "2 *kin* and 5 *riyau* (a little over 3 lbs.) of hemp, of which 5 *riyau* are for this service and the 2 *kin* for the purification." The remaining articles in the list were apparently intended either for offerings, or to be used in some way or other in connection with their presentation. Worship was also celebrated on the same day at the temple of the six imperial domains and at the fourteen temples of the Mikado's timber-forests, the allowance of cloth and other few articles being extremely small, but each god received a spearhead and a mantlet. No account of the ceremonies is to be found in books.

RITUAL.

[TRANSLATION]

He declares the NAME of the sovran god whose praises are fulfilled at Kahahi[1] in Hirose.   Declaring her NAME as the Young food-woman's augustness   (Waka-uka-no-me no mikoto), who rules[2] over the FOOD, he fulfils praises in the PRESENCE of this sovran deity.   *He* says: Hear all ye Kaññushi and Hafuri the fulfilling of praises, by sending the princes and councillors to lift up and bring the great OFFERINGS of the sovran GRANDCHILD'S augustness.

He says: Deign to declare in the presence of the sovran deity that as to the great OFFERINGS which are set-up—*he* deposits in abundance and offers up, as to CLOTHING—bright cloth, glittering cloth, fine cloth and coarse cloth, the five kinds of things,[3] a mantlet, spear and HORSE; and as to LIQUORS, raising-high the beer-jars, filling and ranging-in-rows the bellies of the beer-jars, in soft grain and in coarse grain;[4] as to things which dwell in the mountains—things soft of hair and things rough of ha'r;[5] as to things which grow in the great-field-plain—sweet herbs and bitter herbs, as to things which dwell in the blue-sea-plain, things wide of fin and things narrow of fin, down to weeds of the offing and weeds of the shore.

He says: Declare in the presence of the sovran deity that if the sovran deity with peaceful and tranquil heart accepts as peaceful OFFERINGS and sufficient OFFERINGS the great OFFERINGS thus set-up, and if the sovran deity will deign to perfect and bless in many-bundled ears the sovran deity's harvest-fields in the first place *and also* the late-ripening HARVEST which the CHILDREN,[6] princes, councillors and great PEOPLE[7] of the region-under-heaven shall make by dripping the foam from their arms and drawing the mud together between the opposing thighs, in order that it may be taken by the sovran GRANDCHILD'S august-ness with ruddy countenance as his long FOOD and distant FOOD, *he* will draw hither the first-fruits both in liquor and in husk, *even* to a thousand plants and many thousand plants, and piling them up like a range of hills, will offer them up at the autumn service.[8]

He says: Hear all ye Kaññushi and Hafuri. *He* sets-up the great OFFERINGS of the sovran GRANDCHILD'S augustness, bright cloth, glittering cloth, soft cloth and coarse cloth, the five kinds of things, down to the mantlet and spear, in the presence of the sovran gods also who dwell in the entrances of mountains of the six FARMS⁶ of the province of Yamato. As to the setting *of offerings* in this way, if the water which the sovran gods deign to send boiling down the ravines from the entrances of the mountains which they rule be received as sweet water, and ye¹⁰ will deign to bless the late-ripening harvest which the great PEOPLE of the region under heaven have made, and deign not to inflict on it bad winds and rough waters, the princes, councillors, functionaries, down to the male and female servants of the six FARMS of the province of Yamato, will all come forth on the [number]¹¹ day of the [number] month of this year, to set-up the first fruits in juice and in the husk, raising-high the beer-jars, filling and ranging-in-rows the bellies of the beer-jars, piling-up *the offerings* like a range of hills, and plunging down the root of the neck cormorant-wise in the presence of the sovran gods, will fulfil praises as the morning sun rises in glory.

NOTES.

¹ Kahahi, the name of the village in Hirose department where the temple stands, is evidently a contraction of *kaha-ahi*, the meeting of streams. The Yamato-gaha runs past the back of the grove, and is met by a small brook which flows along the side of the temple.

² *Motasuru*: Motowori objects to the final syllable -*ru*, but if the so-called lengthened forms are primarily honorific, then the regular causative verb belonging to the 2nd conjugation must have been the original form, and *motasu*, for which he contends, a corruption. See note 2 on *hakashi* in the Kasuga Ritual. *Mochi*, to rule over, in the sense of having a certain department committed to one's charge; as Yama-tsu-mi no kami rules over the mountains and Wata-tsu-mi no kami over the sea, so this goddess has charge of the FOOD *i.e.* the Mikado's food.

³ The phrase rendered 'the five kinds of things' might also be 'the things of five colours,' and in the list of articles to be furnished as offerings we find the entry 'thin coarse-silk of five colours, 15 feet of each,' which seems to correspond closely to the language of the Ritual. But it is hardly safe to draw too strict an inference from such a coincidence, for in many cases the *norito* speaks of offerings which are not provided for by the *Yeñgi Shiki*, and omits to mention several of those that are actually presented.

⁴ 'Soft grain' is the grain of rice divested of its husk and ready to be boiled for food; 'coarse grain' is paddy, or rice before it has been hulled.

⁵ Birds and beasts, that is, game of various kinds.

⁶ *Mi-ko*, august child, is the old Japanese designation of a child of the Mikado, and is used as the equivalent of the Chinese *Shiñ wau* (親王), Prince of the Blood.

⁷ The Chinese characters (公民) here translated 'great PEOPLE' are variously read by different editors and commentators. Nobuyoshi and Mabuchi have *oho-*

takara, the Deha-boñ edition of the *Yeñgi Shiki* has *ohomu takara*, while Motowori and Hirata both adopt the reading *oho mi takara*. The solitary passage in support of this last reading, quoted from the Gouka no Shidai, in reality proves nothing at all. This is part of a proclamation of amnesty for ordinary offences, which says: "In consequence whereof he (the Mikado) deigns to pardon. Let each return to his own home, and not repeat his offence, but becoming *oho mi takara* (御財) duly furnish tribute." It is clear, however, that the char. 御財 might be translated literally, 'imperial treasure,' loyal subjects who pay their taxes regularly being naturally regarded as treasures by their sovereign, but we need not infer from this single example that this was the usual term employed to denote the Mikado's people. Hori suggests *oho mi tami*, great PEOPLE, which is a more likely reading.

[8] The original of this passage can only be constructed by omitting, as Motowori suggests, the seven char. 取作奥都御歳者 (in the *Norito Kau,* vol. 1, p. 31, line 3; in the *Norito Shiyaukuñ,* part 1, page 9 verso, line 3).

[9] The gods who dwell in the entrances of the mountains are gods of the forests, to whom altogether fourteen temples were dedicated, named in the Catalogue of Temples, and all situated within the province of Yamato. See note 41 to the Praying for Harvest. They had nothing to do with supplying the rice-fields with water or protecting them from wind storms. This last section is evidently a hash of the three petitions at the end of the Praying for Harvest, made by a priest who was ignorant of their real meaning and purport. This is one reason for thinking that the art of composing *norito* had been quite lost by the time when the *Yeñgi Shiki* was compiled.

[10] *Na ga mikoto,* lit., thy augustness, must be taken as addressed to the gods of the mountains, and therefore rendered by the plural pronoun. The older texts and Mabuchi read *Mimashi mikoto,* which seems hardly so good.

[11] In the original is the char. 某 *sore no,* which is used in Japanese just as we leave a blank to be filled up with the required number.

No. 4.—TATSUTA KAZE NO KAMI NO MATSURI, SERVICE OF THE GODS OF WIND AT TATSUTA.

In the Catalogue of Temples contained in vol. ix. of the *Yengi Shiki* are two entries of temples at Tatsuta, in Heguri department of the province of Yamato; firstly, one containing two shrines to Ame no mi hashira and Kuni no mi hashira, both 名神 or 'famous gods' (*natataru kami*) and ranking as greater shrines (see Praying for Harvest) entitled to take part in the Tsuki-nami, or so-called monthly services, and in the Nihi-name or Harvest Festival; secondly, a smaller temple containing two shrines dedicated to Tatsuta hiko and Tatsuta hime, Youth and Maiden of Tatsuta. The first of these is evidently the temple at which this Ritual was used, and it exists to this day on the same spot, at a village called Tatsumo, marked on most of the maps of the province of Yamato. Other temples to the gods of wind are in Naka department in the province of Idzu, called Kuni no mi-hashira no Zhiñzhiya, at Yamada in

Ishikaha department in the province of Kahachi, called Shinaga
no Zhiñzhiya, and in the grounds of the temple of the Sun-
goddess in Ise there is also a shrine to the god of wind. In the
Kozhiki[1] only a single god of wind is mentioned. Shina-tsu-hiko
no kami, said to have been begotten by Izanagi and Izanami.
The *Nihongi*[2] on the other hand says that "after Izanagi and
Izanami had bogotten the country of many islands, Izanagi said:
"The country which I have begotten is completely beclouded and
filled up with morning-mists." The breath with which he then
blew away *the mists* became a god, called Shinatobe no kami
and also Shinatsu-hiko. This is the god of wind." But the text
of the Ritual shows clearly that there were two wind-deities,
one male and one female, who are first called Ame-no-mi-hashira
and Kuni-no-mi-hashira, Heaven's PILLAR and Country's PILLAR,
and are afterward called the youth-deity and maiden-deity
(*hiko-gami* and *hime-gami*). From this it may safely be con-
cluded that Shinatsu hiko is the name of the male and Shinatobe
that of the female god of wind, *be* being the equivalent of *me*,
woman (b and m being constantly interchanged), and *to=tsu,*
the generic particle. *To* and *tsu* are also interchangeable, as
shown for instance in several passages in the *Manyefushifu,*
where *mato* is written with 松, a pine tree, usually read *matsu.*
Shina is for *shi-naga,* long breath, *shi* being an obsolete word
for breath, seen in *tama-shi-hi,* soul=precious-breath-fire, *shi-
nuru,* to die=*shi inuru,* breath departs, *shinaga-dori,* long-breathed bird, applied to a species of duck.[3] Long-breathed youth and
Long-breathed maiden, as we may most euphoniously render
these names, are very appropriate epithets for gods of wind,
which is always blowing and never seems out of breath, but the
teachers of Shiñtau are not content with such an obvious idea.
They base their explanation of the name upon the assumed verity
of the myth, and say that it was necessary for Izanagi, in blowing away the mists which obscured the land, to continue the
emission of breath for a long time, and hence the appellation
given to the gods who were evolved from his breath. It is more
difficult to explain the names Heaven's PILLAR and Country's
PILLAR. Heaven and Country are more often used as correlatives

[1] K. Zh. K. D. vol. 5, p. 41.   [2] *Nihoñgi Shifuchiyuu*, vol. 1, p. 15.
[3] The 日本紀纂疏 is the original authority for this explanation of *shina*.

in the earliest Japanese literature than Heaven and Earth. The ancient Japanese must have imagined the sky to be extremely light and buoyant by nature if they looked upon the wind as the sole agent which prevented it from falling to the ground, yet this is the explanation given by Motowori, and adopted by his followers. If *hashira* originally meant pillar, then the epithet 'country's pillar' is not easy to understand. The wind might be supposed to support the sky, but not the earth. The only way out of the difficulty is to conjecture that the first idea was to call the wind *ten chi no hashira,* as being a pillar planted on the earth and bearing the heavens on its summit, and that this phrase when translated into *norito* language became *ame no mi-hashira* and *kuni no mi-hashira,* thus bringing the names into harmony with the more ancient recognition of the winds as a pair of gods. It seems clear from the Ritual itself that these names were given to the wind-gods by the Mikado who founded the temple of Tatsuta, and who, there is reason to believe, was Teñmu Teñwau (673-686), so that there would be nothing surprising in the epithets having in reality originated from the Chinese expression *ten-chi,* heaven and earth.

It is true that that the word *hashi* in the sense of 'bridge' and 'ladder' (the ordinary word *hashigo* for staircase or ladder is compounded of this *hashi* and *ko,* an archaic of *ki,* tree or wood), and *hashira* seem to be closely allied, and at first to have signified generally anything which fills up and bridges over a gap. The Japanese do not seem to have held the theory that the sky is shaped like an inverted bowl placed over a flat surface, but rather that it was a flat thing generally equidistant from the earth. Inhabitants of flat countries might naturally adopt the former view, while it would be a fact daily making itself patent to a race of active mountaineers and huntsmen that there was no real limit to the horizon, whenever they climbed a hill and saw lying at their feet localities and objects which were invisible to them before they ascended. Thus they might have conceived of the wind as a something that filled up the gap between earth and heaven, and also as the means of transit from one to the other, by observing the flight of birds for long distances borne by the wind, and the elevation in the air of dust, dead leaves and other objects. For this reason it appeared quite natural to believe that the Sun-goddess, when sent forth from the earth by her father Izanagi to assume her sovereignty over the kingdom of heaven, should travel thither by the *Ame no mi hashira*, the thing that bridged over the distance from heaven, in other words the wind. The interpretation which makes out this *ame no mi hashira* by which she ascended, to have been a solid pillar of earth, which in the early days of the world united it to the sky, but afterwards fell flat on its side and became a sand-spit in the province of Idzumo, is a modern invention for the purpose of the explaining the cosmogony of the teachers of 'pure Shiñtau.'

The institution of the worship of the wind gods is usually attributed by the commentators to Suuzhiñ Teñwau, although no such fact is recorded in either the *Nihongi* or *Kozhiki*. They found this view upon the phrase *Shikishima ni ohoyashima-guni shiroshimeshishi sume mi ma no mikoto* in the Ritual, which they take to mean "the Sovran GRANDCHILD'S augustness who ruled the great-eight-island-country at Shikishima,' and they say that Shikishima is the same as the ancient department or hundred of Shiki in Yamato, where the residence of that Mikado is said have been situated. There was another Mikado, namely Kiñmei Teñwau (540-571), whose palace was called Shikishima no Ohomiya, the great HOUSE of Shikishima, and it would be more reasonable, if the question were to be decided by the mere name, to attribute the foundation of the temple to this sovereign. In the *Manyefushifu* we find Shikishima used as the *makura-kotoba*, or recognized epithet, of *Yamato no kuni*, which in those passages means the whole of Japan, and not the province of Yamato by itself. If we give to this expression its most natural and obvious meaning of 'spread-out islands,' then its employment as an epithet for the whole country is seen to be extremely apt, and its application to Oho-ya-shima-guni, another of the poetical names of Japan, would be perfectly natural. We should of course expect to find the particle *no* after Shikishima in such a case, but there was a certain indefiniteness in the use in early Japanese of the particles *no* and *ni*, which appear to have been more or less interchangeable. The phrase in the original might consequently be used to denote any Mikado who ever sat on the throne of Japan. Mabuchi and Motowori were led to interpret

this passage as referring to a previous Mikado by the verb
shiroshimeshi being put in the past tense, *shiroshimeshishi*, but
this termination *shi* is evidently an error. Even if it were necessary here to denote past time, *shi* would not be correct, and under
any circumstances *shiroshimesu* must have been the original form
used, just as we have *tsukuru mono* and not *tsukurishi mono* just
afterwards. They took the first part of the Ritual to be a recital
of events which had occurred long previously to its composition, but it was clearly composed for the first celebration of the
worship of gods of Tatsuta, and used without alteration ever
afterwards. In the *Nihongi* (*Shifuchiyuu*, bk. 29, p. 8 verso) we
have the positive statement that Teñmu Teñwau in the 4th year of
his reign (676) 'sent two persons from the court to worship the
Wind-gods at Tatsuno in Tatsuta, and two others to worship
Oho-imi no kami (the goddess of Food) at the bend of the river
in Hirose,' the meaning of which is probably that the temples of
the Wind-gods and the goddess of Food were then founded at
those places. Some Japanese scholars think that they recognize
in this Ritual indications of its having been composed about the
time of Teñmu Teñwau, and certainly neither it nor the Hirano
Ritual appears to belong to the oldest of these compositions. The
few archaic words which it contains are to be found in poems of
the *Manyefushifu* fifty or sixty years later.

It is interesting to note that we have in this Ritual a legend
(for it is nothing more) of the way in which the winds first
came to be worshipped. During a succession of years violent
storms, such as even now frequently visit Japan in the autumn
and do considerable damage to the ripening rice, had destroyed
the crops, and after the diviners had in vain endeavoured to
discover by their usual method who were the workers of the
calamity, the gods revealed themselves to the sovereign in a
dream, and directed that temples should be raised in their honour
and certain offerings made to them. The offerings demanded
are of course such as would be acceptable to human beings, it
being beyond the power of insight of the first worshippers of the
unseen to suppose that the beings whom they dreaded and desired to propitiate could wish for anything different from the
articles usually offered at the graves and shrines of departed

ancestors, namely, whatever was most useful to mankind itself in that primitive age.

We know nothing of the ceremonies and forms observed in the worship of the Wind-gods previous to the 10th century, when the rules contained in the *Yengi Shiki* were framed. From them we learn that the envoys sent by the Mikado to represent him at the celebration of the service were a prince and a minister of the 5th rank or upwards, and two officials of the Ministry of Religion, of not above the 6th rank, accompanied each by a diviner and two *Kandomo*. Either the governor of the province or his lieutenant had charge of the arrangements. Each department (*kohori*) in the province of Yamato had to take its turn in furnishing a couple of loads of food-offerings. The cost, as well as that of rice, *sake* and rice in ear, was defrayed out of the taxes of the province, but all the other articles were supplied by different departments of the Mikado's household. The list of articles in the *Shizhi-sai shiki* (四時祭式) corresponds very nearly with the offerings named in the Ritual. The 'bright cloth, glittering cloth,' etc., are represented as in the preceding Ritual, with the addition of China-grass. In addition to the spear and mantlet, for which the iron and deer-skins were needed, it appears that bows and arrows were offered up, and a certain quantity of slender bamboo stalks, feathers for winging them and horn for arrow-tips was therefore supplied. Each deity received a horse and saddle; new saddles were not presented every year, but the old ones were made to last as long as possible on successive occasions. The varnishes mentioned in the directions were intended for the 'golden thread-box, golden *tatari* and golden skein-holder,' which so far from being made of the precious metal were merely painted wood. Lastly, the food-offerings of the produce of mountain, plain and sea are the same as on all other occasions.

RITUAL.

[TRANSLATION.]

He says: "I declare in the presence of the sovran gods whose praises are fulfilled at Tatsuta.

"Because they had not allowed, firstly the five sorts of grain[1] which the sovran GRANDCHILD'S augustness, who rules the spread-out islands[2], the country of many islands[3], takes with ruddy countenance as his long and lasting FOOD, and the things produced by the great[4] PEOPLE, down to the least leaf of the herbs, to ripen, and has spoilt them not for one year, or for two years, but for continuous years, he deigned to command: As to the HEART of the god which shall come forth in the divining[5] of the men who are learned in things, declare what god it is."

"Whereupon the men learned in things divined with their divinings, but they declared that no HEART of a god appears.

"When he had heard this, the sovran GRANDCHILD'S: augustness deigned to conjure them, saying: 'I thought to fulfil their praises as heavenly temples[6], without forgetting and without omitting, but let the gods, whatever gods they be, that have prevented the things produced by the great PEOPLE of the region under heaven from ripening and have spoilt them, make known their HEART.'

"Hereupon they made the sovran grandchild's augustness to know in a great DREAM, and made him to know their names, saying: 'Our NAMES, who have prevented the things made by the great PEOPLE of the region under heaven from ripening, and have spoilt them, by visiting them with bad winds and rough waters, are Heaven's PILLAR'S[7] augustness and Country's PILLAR'S augustness.' And they made him to know, saying: 'If for OFFERINGS which shall be set-up in our presence there be furnished various sorts of OFFERINGS, as to CLOTHES, bright cloth glittering cloth, soft cloth and coarse cloth and the five kinds of things, a mantlet, a spear, a HORSE furnished with a SADDLE, if our HOUSE[8] be fixed at Wonu in Tachinu at Tatsuta, in a place where the morning sun is opposite and the evening sun is hidden, and praises be fulfilled in our presence, we will bless and ripen the things produced by the great PEOPLE of the region under heaven, firstly the five sorts of grain, down to the least leaf of the herbs.'

"Therefore hear, all ye Kaññushi and Hafuri, my declaring in the presence of the sovran gods that, having fixed the HOUSE pillars in the place which the sovran gods had taught by words and made known, in order to fufil praises in the presence of the sovran gods, the sovran GRANDCHILD'S augustness has caused his great OFFERINGS to be lifted and brought, and has fulfilled their praises, sending the princes and councillors as his messengers."

He says: "As to the great OFFERINGS set-up for the youth-god[9], I set-up various sorts of OFFERINGS, for CLOTHES, bright cloth, glittering cloth, soft cloth and coarse cloth, and the five kinds of things, a mantlet, a spear, a HORSE furnished with a SADDLE; for the maiden-god[10] I set-up various sorts of offerings, providing CLOTHES, a golden thread-box[11], a golden *tatari*[12], a golden skein-holder[13], bright cloth, glittering cloth, soft cloth and coarse cloth, and five kinds of things, a HORSE furnished with a SADDLE; as to LIQUOR[14], I raise high the beer-jars, fill and range-in-a-row the bellies of the beer-jars; soft grain and coarse grain; as to things which dwell in the hills—things soft of hair and things coarse of hair; as to things which grow in the great-field-plain—sweet herbs and bitter herbs; as to things which dwell in the blue-sea-plain—things broad of fin and things narrow of fin, down to the weeds of the offing and weeds of the shore. And if the sovran gods will take these great OFFERINGS which I set-up, piling them up like a range of hills, peacefully in their HEARTS, as peaceful OFFERINGS and satisfactory OFFERINGS, and the sovran gods, deigning not to visit the things produced by the great PEOPLE of the region under heaven with bad winds and rough waters, will ripen and bless them, I will at the autumn service set-up the first fruits, raising-high the beer-jars, filling and ranging-in-rows the bellies of the beer-jars, and drawing them hither in juice and in ear, in many hundred rice-plants and a thousand rice-plants. And for this purpose the princes and councillors and all the functionaries, the servants of the six FARMS of the country of Yamato, even unto the males and females of them, have all come and assembled in the fourth month of this year, and plunging down the root of the neck cormorant-wise in the presence of the sovran gods, fulfil their praises as the sun of to-day rises in glory."

"Hear, all of ye the mandate: Kaññushi and Hafuri, deign to receive the great OFFERINGS of the sovran GRANDCHILD'S augustness, and set them up without omission."

NOTES.

[1] The five sorts of grain of the Japanese are rice, millet (panicum Italicum),

barley and two sorts of beans, *adzuki* or Phaseolus radiatus, and *daidzu* or Glycine hispida. This differs from the Chinese enumeration, in which hemp is given instead of one of the sorts of bean. In the *Kozhiki* the five kinds of grain are said to have sprung from the dead body of the Goddess of Food, Ohogetsu-hime; rice from the eyes, millet from the ears, *adzuki* from the nose, barley from the private parts and *daidzu* from the fundament. Hirata in the *Koshi Seibuñ* gives a slightly different form of the myth. The expression 'five sorts of grain' is evidently an imitation of Chinese phraseology, and its occurrence here is an indication of the comparatively late date of this *norito*.

[2] 'Spread-out islands,' *Shiki-shima.* This is generally explained to mean the palace of Suuzhiñ Teñwau, which tradition says was in the department of Shiki in the province of Yamato, now divided into Shiki no kami and Shiki no shimo. Reasons for thinking this view erroneous, and for regarding Shikishima as a general epithet of Japan, and hence capable of being used with respect to any Mikado, have been given in the introduction to this ritual.

[3] *Oho ya shima guni,* the Country of Many Islands. *Ya* originally signified 'many', but was afterwards adopted as the numeral 'eight,' and hence in the myth of the birth of the Japanese archipelago eight islands are always mentioned, though not the same set of eight in each form of the myth. In the *Kozhiki* the gods Izanagi and Izanami beget in succession, 1st, Ahaji, or the island on the road to Aha; 2nd, Iyo, an island with one body and four faces, *i.e.* the island of Shikoku, divided into the four provinces of Aha, Tosa, Iyo and Sanuki, 3rd, the triplet of Oki, a group which lies north of the province of Idzumo; 4th, Tsukushi, an island with one body and four faces, *i.e.* the island of Kiushiu, or Kiukoku, originally divided into four regions, namely, Tsukushi, which now forms the modern Chikuzeñ and Chikugo, Toyo, the modern Buzeñ and Buñgo, Hi, consisting of the modern provinces of Hizeñ, Higo and a part of Hiuga, and Kumaso, the modern Satsuma, Ohosumi and southern half of Hiuga; 5th, Iki; 6th, Tsushima (which probably means 'port island,' as containing the port of call for boats going from Japan to Korea); 7th, Sado, formerly famous for its mines, and 8th, last of all, Oho-yamato-Akitsushima, *i.e.* the main island of Japan. It is worth while noting how many of these names have in the course of time to be extended in application. Tsukushi and Iyo were parts only of the islands which were afterwards called by their names; Kumaso was the modern department of So in Ohosumi, and Yamato, applied later to the whole of Japan, originally meant only the province which still bears that name. Yamato-kotoba is the old Japanese language (or rather the words of which it is composed), and not, as some persons still seem to imagine, the language spoken in that province. Six forms of the myth are given in the *Nihoñgi* with slight variations, such as the birth of Koshi (now divided into the five provinces of Wechizeñ, Kaga, Noto, Wetsuchiu and Wechigo) separately from the main island, the inclusion of Ohoshima, which is one of the departments of Suhau forming an island by itself, and Kibi no Kozhima, a part of Bizeñ, also formerly an island. (See 國號考, *Kozhiki Deñ*, vol. 5, p. 1, *et infra*; 日本記集註, vol. 1, p. 6 verso, et *infra*.)

[4] 'Great' (*oho*) is a mere honorific, like mi (rendered by 'august'), applied to the people because they belong to the Mikado. A little further on the same epithet is applied to the dream in which the wind gods make themselves known to the Mikado.

[5] The word *ura*, which in one of its secondary uses signifies divination, means primarily that which is behind, and hence is invisible, e.g. the mental feelings of a person, in which sense it is equivalent to *kokoro*, which may be employed to denote the mental part of man and most of its modes of operation, such as will, sentiment, intention, meaning. The art of finding out that which is hidden was called *ura-waza* or *ura-goto*, and then for shortness' sake simply *ura*. Thus from this use of *ura* to mean 'heart,' it was transferred to the means of discovering the intentions of another, especially the intentions of a god, *i.e.* divination, and the verb *ura-nafu*, to divine, was formed from it by adding *nafu*, to spin. (See note 20 to the Praying for Harvest.) Various modes of divination were in use among the ancient Japanese,

of various degrees of solemnity. One of these has already been described in the introductory remarks to the service of the gods of Kasuga. Another, to which allusion is made in the *Mañyefushifu*, consisted in stepping out into the road, and listening to the fragmentary talk of passers-by, from which omens might be interpreted. This was called *Tsuji-ura*, or divinings in the roads; the word has lost its primitive meaning in the present day, and is now applied to the 'mottoes' placed inside sweetmeats, with which we are familiar in Europe also. As this sort of divination was usually practised at night it was also called *yufuke tohi*, 'questioning the evening passers-by,' and *yufu ura* 'evening divination,' under which names it is frequently alluded to in the *Mañyefushifu*. In its earliest form the ceremony consisted in planting a stick upright in the ground to represent the gods of roads, who according to the ancient myth was the transformation of the staff of Izanagi, which he threw from him when returning from the lower regions, in order to prevent the demons from pursuing him any further. Offerings were then made to this god, and he was besought to give an answer to the question propounded. A passage alludes to the custom of carrying a stick when going out to perform the *yafuke tohi*,

Tsuwe tsuki mo	I go and question the evening oracle,
Tsukazu mo yukite	(unconscious) whether I carry a stick
Yufuke tohi	or not.

(vol. 3, pt. 2. f. 28, line 3), and the presentation of offerings is indicated in the following stanza from the same (vol. 11, pt. 2, f. 6, 1. 9).

Ahanaku ni	As I have not met her, my sleeves
Yufuke wo tofu to	which I deposited as offerings in order
Nusa ni oku ni,	to question the evening oracle will
Wa ga koromode ha	have to be used again.
Mata zo tsugubeki.	

The meaning of *tsugu* is not quite certain. One commentator thinks that the lover has ripped up his clothes and reduced them again to the state of mere cloth to offer to the god, and that *tsugubeki* means that he will sew the pieces together again after obtaining an answer. But the other view, with which the translation above given accords, namely, that as he is unable to meet his love, it will be necessary to continue the offering until he gets a favourable answer, is more plausible. Sometimes the answer was deceptive.

Yufuke ni mo	When may I expect you,
Ura ni mo noreru	who do not come,
Koyohi dani	even on the night which
Kimasanu kimi wo	was told by the evening
Itsu to ka matamu.	oracle and by the divination too.

The woman in this case has tried both ways of finding out when her lover will come, the 'evening oracle' and divination by scorching either a deer's shoulder-blade, or a tortoise-shell, and both have promised that she shall see him on a certain evening, but he disappoints her after all. The following extracts also illustrate this practice, which seems to have been very common in ancient times, ten or eleven centuries ago. The poet Yakamochi in reply to a lady writes:

Tsukuyo ni ha	On a moonlight night
Kado ni idetachi	I stood at the house-door,
Yufuke tohi	questioned the evening oracle
A ura wo zo seshi	and performed foot-divining
Yukamaku wo hori.	because I longed to go to you.

(M. Y. S. 4, pt. 2, f. 21 verso, 1. 1.) *A ura* is the same as *ashi ura*, which Bañ Nobutomo thinks may have consisted in walking up to a string stretched across

the road, and drawing omens from the position of the feet when the string stops
further progress, but this is simply a conjecture.

Kotodama no	I question the evening oracle
Yaso no chimata ni	in the many road-forkings
Yufuke tofu;	of the language-spirit;
Ura-masa ni nore	tell me truly
Imo ni ahamu yoshi.	how I shall meet my love.

(Bk. 11, pt. 1, f. 34, 1.6)

Ima sara ni	Does he now call me
Kimi ka wa wo yobu,	after all, or does
Tarachine no	my august mother
Haha no mikoto ka	who suckled me,
Momo tarazu	ask the evening oracle for me
Yaso no chimata ni	in the many road-forkings,
Yufuke ni mo,	or ask by divination,
Ura ni mo zo tofu	for me who must die.
Shinubeki wa ga yuwe.	

(M. Y. S, 16, f. 19, 1. 8.)   This is part of a lament by a lady whose husband
is far away. She pictures herself dying broken-hearted, and wonders whether he is
near her pillow to call her back, as the Japanese custom is, in her last moments,
and whether her mother, anxious about her welfare, is at this moment consulting
the oracle or inquiring of the diviner. In bk. 17, pt. 2, f. 8, 1. 5 we have the
following extract from a *naga-uta* written in *kana.*

Shita gohi ni	Feeling melancholy with
Omohi urabure	hidden longing,
Kado ni tachi	I stand at the house-door,
Yufuke tohitsutsu.	questioning the evening oracle.

(See also vol. 14, pt. 2, f. 5 verso, 1. 12).   Generally, however, this sort of divination was performed by going away from the house, as in the following *naga-uta.*

Ki no kuni no	When I went out
Hama ni yoru tofu	and stood in the road,
Ahabidama	and asked the evening oracle
Hirohamu to ihite,	when he would come back
Imo no yama	who went over the sweetheart's mount
Se no yama koyete,	and the lover's mount,
Yukishi kimi ha	saying that he would
Itsu ki masamu to	pick up the *ahabi* shells
Tamaboko no	which come ashore
Michi ni idetachi	in the "Region of woods,"
Yufu ura wo	the evening oracle said to me:
Wa ga tohishikaba,	"Sweetheart!
Yufu ura no	"he for whom you wait
Ware ni noraku;	"is searching for
Wagimoko ya	"the white shells which
Na ga matsu kimi ha	"come near on the waves
Oki tsu nami	"of the offing, the white shells
Ki yoru shira tama	"which the shore waves
He tsu nami no	"bring near.
Yosuru shira tama	"He does not come,
Motomu to zo.	"he picks them up.
Kimi ga ki masanu.	"He does not come.
Hirofu to zo.	

Kimi ha ki masanu.	"if he be long,
Hisa naraba,	"'twill be but seven days;
Ima nanuka bakari;	"If he be quick
Hayakaraba,	"'twill be two days.
Ima futsuka bakari	"He has heard you.
Aramu to zo.	"Do not yearn,
Kimi ha kikoshishi,	"my sweetheart."
Na kohi so wagimo.	(M. Y. S., bk. 13, pt. 2, f. 15.)

In the *Ohokagami* (vol. 5, f. 6 from the end) an instance of *yufuke tohi* is related as follows: "Her mother, impelled by some unknown motive, when she was yet quite young, went out into the Second Broad-street and performed the *yufuke tohi* (questioning the evening oracle), when a woman with dreadfully white hair who was passing by stopped, and said: 'What are you doing? If it is questioning the evening oracle that you are bent on, then may everything you can think of fall out as you wish, and may your fortunes be broader and higher even than this Broad-street;' and so saying she departed altogether."

The book from which this is taken dates from the beginning of the 11th century. In the *Shifu gai seu*, or Collection of Rubbish (拾芥抄) is preserved the following stanza used by women in addressing the god who gave the oracle:

Funadosahe	When we ask things
Yufuke no kami ni	of Funadosahe,
Mono toheba,	the god of the evening oracle,
Michi yuku hito yo	deliver the oracle truly,
Ura masa ni se yo.	ye who go along the way.

The women used to go out in threes to the nearest cross-road, and repeat this stanza thrice. They marked out a certain portion of the road, and scattered rice about it as a charm against demons. Then each turning towards a separate road drew her finger along the edge of a box-wood comb which she carried, and they inferred good or evil fortune from the words uttered by the first person who happened to pass that way. The use of the box-wood comb was a sort of pun, the word *tsuge* meaning both 'box-wood' and 'tell,' and drawing the finger along the teeth was a request to the god to speak out. Bañ's work on divination, the 正卜考, mentions several other ancient methods, such as *kama no wa no ura*, divining by the boiler-bed, *kome ura*, rice divination, *ashi-ura* and *ishi-ura*, foot and stone divination, of which little more is known than the mere names.

Shitodo dori was a method of divination in which a species of bird played a prominent part, but whether it resembled the Chinese method of divination by observing the direction in which certain birds fly and their number, is not known. Another method, *koto-ura*, was employed at the temple of the Sun-goddess in Ise, with the object of ascertaining whether the priests who are to take part in a religious service and the tables and vessels used in presenting the offerings are pure or not. At midnight on the night preceding the service a priest (called a *mi kamu no ko no uchiudo*, evidently a person of peculiar sanctity) sat with a harp outside a certain gateway of the temple. Turning towards the shrine he prayed that the goddess would enable him to discover by divination whether the above persons and things possessed the requisite purity. He then struck the harp thrice with a piece of yew wood in the form of a *shiyaku* (Chin. 笏 hwuh), a loud "Hush!" being uttered each time, and then uttered the following three verses, by which all the gods were besought to descend from heaven and give answer to the question put.

I.

Ahari ya	Ah! ah!
Asobi ha su to mausanu,	we do not merely amuse ourselves;

Asakura ni	on to your splendid seat
Ama tsu kami kuni tsu kami,	gods of heaven and gods of the country
Orimashimase.	descend.

II.

Ahari ya	Ah! ah!
Asobi ha su to mausanu	we do not merely amuse ourselves;
Asakura ni	on to your splendid seat
Naru Ikadzuchi mo	sounding Thunderbolt also
Orimashimase	descend.

III.

Ahari ya	Ah! ah!
Asobi ha su to mausanu	we do not merely amuse ourselves;
Asakura ni	on to your splendid seat
Uha tsu ohoye shita tsu ohoye	upper great elder brother and lower great elder brother (?)
Mawiri tamahe.	deign to come.

The names of all the priests were then called over one by one, and the question was asked, "Is he clean or unclean." The same priest as before repeated the words, and striking the harp again, tried to whistle by drawing in his breath. If the whistle was audible, the person whose name had been called was considered to be free from impurity, and vice versâ. The same proceeding was observed with respect to the persons who had prepared the offerings, and the boxes, pails, ladles, tables, pottery and food-offerings. Afterwards the priest struck the harp again three times, with a solemn "Hush!" and intoned similar verses, in which the gods who had been called down were asked to return to their abodes. This ceremony is first mentioned in the Calendar of the Sun-goddess' Temple drawn up about the end of the 8th century, but the minute details are taken from a Calendar of the end of the 12th century, and there is nothing surprising in the use of the Chinese *shiyaku* or courtier's tablet, which had been part of ceremonial dress for several hundred years. Everything else in the proceedings, and certainly the verses, seems purely Japanese.

The most important mode of divination practised by the primitive Japanese was that of scorching the shoulder-blade of a deer over a clear fire, and finding omens in the direction of the cracks produced by the heat. It is allude to in the following verses from the *Maōyefushifu.*

1.

Musahi no ni	On Musashi moor
Urahe kata yaki	I burnt the divining shoulder-blade,
Masade ni mo	And distinctly too
Noranu kimi ga na	Your name which they would not tell me
Ura ni ide ni keri.	Has appeared in the divination.

Urahe is explained to be a contraction of *ura ahase, hase* being naturally contracted into *he* and the two *a* coalescing; but it is simpler to regard *ahe-* as the transitive verb corresponding to the *i.v. ahi-* to meet. The meaning of the expression is that the seeker after divine guidance as to the right conduct to be followed, by means of the process called divination ascertains whether his own mind is in harmony or unison with that of the god or gods appealed to. The verse is supposed to have been the composition of a girl whose parents are about to give her in marriage, but refuse to disclose beforehand the name of her husband, and she has recourse therefore to divination by scorching the shoulder-blade of a deer. Being written entirely in *kana,* with the exception of the words *musashi no* and *na*, there is no dispute about the reading of this verse. It is to be found in bk. 14, pt. 1, folio 12 verso, Riyakuge edition.

2.

Oju shimoto	My love's name
Kono moto-yama no	which I tell not even to the grass (or, not grudgingly even)
Ma shiba ni mo	of this tree-mountain
Noranu imo ga na	where grow many trees
Kata ni idemu kamo	will appear in the shoulder-blade!

(Ib. folio 12 verso.)

There is a play on the words *shiba ni*, which mean 'to the grass' and 'frequently,' or they may perhaps be read *shiba ni*, grudgingly. The allusion to divination by means of the shoulder-blade of a deer is here not very distinct, but *kata* cannot be satisfactorily explained in any other way.

3.

Watatsumi no	When I had toiling come
Kashikoki michi wo	without enjoying ease
Yasukeku mo	along the awful road
Naku nayami kite,	of the sea-possessor,
Imada ni mo	and yet again was
Mo naku yukamu to,	about to go
Yuki no ama no	after burning the shoulder-blade
Hotsute no urahe wo	for the divining for a fair wind
Kata yakite	by the fishermen of Iki,
Yukamu to suru ni,	in order to go untroubled,
Ime no goto	thou didst depart from me,
Michi no soraji ni	in the sky of my road
Wakare suru kimi.	like a dream.

(Ib. vol. 15, f. 34.)

This seems to be a lament by a traveller to Korea, who on arriving at the island of Iki lost his companion by death while they were awaiting for a fair wind. *Hotsute* is explained by *ho*, sail, and *te*, as used in *haya-te*, a gust; hence the compound may mean a wind that suits the sails, a fair wind. Here the reference to scorching a shoulder-blade is distinct, but the animal from which it was taken is not mentioned. It is clear, however, from the following passage from the *Kozhiki* that the shoulder-blade of a deer was used: "He summoned Ame-no-koya-ne no mikoto and Futo-dama no mikoto, and caused them to pull out completely the shoulder of a stag of Ame-no-kagu yama, and taking *hahaka* [the name of a tree] of Ame-no-kagu yama, to perform divination." Nothing is here said about sorching the bone, which part of the process is known from the verses previously quoted and from a passage in a Chinese account of Japan which dates from the latter part of the third century, A. D. This account is to be found in the appendix to the *Wei che* (魏志), in the 三國志, *San kwo che*, or History of the Three States, but it is more conveniently referred to in a collection of passages from Chinese works bearing on Japan called 異稱日本傳 (*Wi shiyou Nihoñ deñ*), in the first volume of which book it is to be found, on the reverse side of folio 10. The Chinese author, in describing the custom of the Japanese, says: "They have the custom, when entering upon an undertaking or starting on a journey, or saying or doing anything of importance, of scorching a bone, and by divining, to discern good and evil. They first announce what is to be divined, and the language used is the same as in divination by the tortoise-shell. They discern the omens by observing the cracks produced by the fire." The last sentence but one is an allusion to the Chinese practice of muttering over the tortoise-shell the question which it is required to answer. It is interesting to notice that a similar method of divination was in vogue among the Kirghiz. In Pallas' Reise durch Verschiedene Provinzen des Russischen Reichs, vol. 1, p. 393, he says: "There is a sort of diviners called Jauuruntschi, who from the shoulder-blade of a sheep predict the future, and can answer all sorts of questions. It is said that the shoulder must be simply scraped with a knife, and not touched with the teeth, because it would thus become unfit for the purposes of magic. When a question has been proposed to the diviner, or he has proposed something mentally to himself, he lays the shoulder-blade on the fire, and waits until the flat side gets all kinds of cracks and splits, and by means of these lines he divines." The Chinese history of the Mongol dynasty called Yüan (元史) relates that Genghis Khan used to 'scorch the shoulder-blade of a sheep and compare the results thus obtained with those of the astrological diviners, whose advice he always sought before undertaking an expedition, so that the Kirghiz method was also formerly practised by the Mongols. Another Chinese work (the 皇宋事實類苑, which appears to have been reprinted in Japan about two centuries ago) says: "The western barbarians use divination by the sheep. * * They scorch the shoulder-blade of a sheep on a fire of worm-wood, and observe the cracks." These western barbarians (西戎) are explained in Dr. Williams' Dictionary to be 'the wild tribes in Turfan and west of China generally.' Lubbock (Origin of Civilization, p. 163) mentions that the Lapps have this method of divination by a shoulder-blade, and quotes Klemm to the effect that it also exists among the Mongols and Tunguses of Siberia and the Bedouins. In the Okugi seu (奥儀抄), written about the middle of the 12th century, a tradition is quoted to the effect that 'the savages of Mutsu practised divination by scorching the shoulder-bone of a deer (vol. 6, § 8), and the Shintau priests of Yahiko in Wechigo (near Nihigata) had a similar tradition concerning their own temple. The Ichi-no-miya Zhiyuñkei shi of Tachibana no Masayoshi (dated 1696) contains the following account of a similar practice then observed at the temple called Hatsumu no Zhiñ-zhiya, the chief Shintau temple of Kaudzuke, not far from the town of Takasaki. The shoulder-blade of a deer presented by the villagers of Akibata is taken out, carefully polished, and divided into slips about five inches in length. These are placed on a tray and touched with an owl heated in purified fire, and omens are discerned from the extent to which the point penetrates the bone, complete penetration being accounted a fortunate omen and vice versâ. This practice seems to be a survival from the ancient method of divining by the cracks in the scorched bone. It is interesting to note the existence of this sort of divination amongst so many different races of central and eastern Asia. The substitution in Japan of the tortoise-shell for the deer's bone seems to have taken place as early as the 8th century at least, for it is alluded to in a poem which was composed about 730 (M. Y. S. 16, f. 19), and in the Riyau no Gige there is a note explaining that divination was performed by 'scorching a tortoise (shell) and discerning good and evil omens from the lines across and up and down the scorched shell.' It is said that the tortoise-shell has been used for this purpose by the islanders of Hachi-jiyau from the earliest times, and it is evident that a maritime people would find the tortoise-shell more convenient than the deer's shoulder-blade, especially as the neighbouring sea abounds in turtle, and the island is inhabited by no species of wild quadrupeds except rats.

[6] What gods were in the earliest ages regarded as 'heavenly' and what as 'country' gods is unknown, but the Riyau no Gige makes an attempt to give a definition of the two Chinese terms Teñzhiñ (天神) and Jigi (地祇), which were in old Japanese translated by ama tsu yashiro and kuni tsu yashiro or kami (see Wa miyau Seu, bk. 2, f. 1). Among the former it ranks the Sun-goddess and the other goddess worshipped in Ise, the god of Kamo near Kiyauto in Yamashiro, those of Sumiyoshi or Suminoye between Ohosaka and Sakahi, and the god worshipped by the kuni no miyatsuko of Idzumo; and as representatives of the latter it names the gods of Oho-Miwa in Yamato, of Oho-yamato and of Katsuragi no Kamo in Yamato, and lastly Oho-namuchi no mikoto in Idzumo. That this division is wrong seems clear from the fact that the god of Kamo in Yamashiro is identical

with the god of Kamo in Yamato; Koto-shiro-nushi, who is worshipped at the latter place, being simply the 'intelligent spirit' (*nigi mi tama*) of Aji-suki-taka-hiko-ne, to whom the former temple is dedicated. It is of course impossible that the same god can have belonged to both classes at once. Of the two goddesses of Ise, the Sun-goddess must evidently be ranked in the first class, but Ukemochi no kami, the personification of the earth as 'the supporter,' can only belong to the second. The gods of Sumiyoshi were chiefly sea-gods, and therefore more earthly than heavenly in their nature, while the god worshipped by the hereditary chieftains of Idzumo was Susanowo, who was evidently a human being, though not a native of Japan. Among the deities classed by the *Gige* as 'earthly,' those of Oho-miwa, namely Oho-mono-nushi the 'intelligent spirit' of Oho-namuchi, and of Katsuragi no kamo are deified human beings, while the deity of Oho-yamato, called Oho-kuni-mitama, is probably the earth looked upon as the abundant giver of food. It is impossible to discover what principle of classification was here acted upon by the compilers of the *Gige*, and it is most natural to suppose that the original meaning of the terms *Ama tsu yashiro* and *Kuni tsu yashiro* was no longer remembered in their time. In fact, they were simply trying, by the aid of such lights as they possessed, to explain the two Chinese terms *teñzhiñ* and *jigi*, which they seem to have misunderstood. According to the orthodox Chinese view, these two expressions simply signify the two spirits of Heaven and Earth, and if *Ama tsu yashiro* and *Kuni tsu yashiro*, which the *Wamiyau Seu* gives as their equivalents in Japanese, really correspond to them, then the Japanese terms can only mean the Sun as the Celestial deity and the Earth as Terrestrial deity. A second interpretation is that *ama tsu yashiro* denotes all gods of supernatural origin, while *kuni tsu yashiro* should only be applied to deified human beings. A third view is that which looks on the latter class as the gods of the race which Zhiñwau Teñwau found in possession of the land, and *Ama tsu kami* (or *yashiro*) as those whose worship was brought from beyond the sea by his ancestor, the ancient idea concerning foreigners having been that they descended from heaven. But on the whole, the safer conclusion is that the two expressions at first meant only Amaterasu-oho-mi-kami and Uke-mochi no kami, the Sun and the Earth, and that when their original signification was afterward forgotten, various erroneous interpretations were put upon them.

[7] See Introductory remarks.

[8] *Mi ya*, HOUSE, has now various meanings, palace, temple, prince of the imperial family by special patent. Anciently it was also applied to a tomb, which suggests how a chieftain who had once inhabited a palace, passed at death into a tomb which was at the same time a temple. In the *Mañyefu*, *toko mi ya*, eternal HOUSE, is several times applied to tomb.

[9] The youth-god, that is Shinatsu-hiko no mikoto, the 'long-breathed youth', which is the other name of the god of wind.

[10] The maiden-god, that is Shinatobe no mikoto, 'the long-breathed maiden'. These are the pair of wind-gods spoken of in the preceding part of the Ritual as Heaven's PILLAR and Country's PILLAR; see also introductory remarks.

[11] *Wo-ke* 麻筍, a thread-box. *Wo* is 'thread', but as hemp-fibre in ancient times was the chief material used for that purpose (as it continues in modern times to be considerably employed) the character 麻, which properly means 'hemp', was used to denote thread in general. *Wo* in *tama-no-wo*, bead-string, and perhaps *wo*, tail, are identical with it. *Ke* is usually a wooden vessel made by forming a thin board or a stout shaving into a circle and applying a flat bottom, to which the nearest European approach in form is a shallow band-box; *ke* is found in *woke*, pail (which is probably the same word), and in *kushi-ge*, casket (literally, comb-box). *Wogoke* is the modern term in use for the ancient *woke*, and the article known by this name is applied to the same purpose, namely, that of holding hempen thread used for coarse needle-work.

[12] *Tatari*, supposed to have been formed of a flat stand 3.6 Japanese inches square, with an upright piece of wood in the centre, 1 ft. 1.6 inches high, Japanese measure.

[12] *Kasehi.* *Kase* is 'skein', and *hi* is commonly translated 'shuttle', but it probably had originally the wider meaning of something to wind a skein on. In the *Daizhiñ guu shiki* (大神宮式) amongst the treasures of the goddess two *kasehi* are mentioned, one of gold, the other of copper, '9.6 inches long, the length of the handles 5.8 inches'. In the *Mañyefu,* vol. 6, p. 56 verso. line 3, we have

Wotome ra ga,	The mountain of the skein
Umi wo kaku tofu	[holder] on which the
Kase no yama.	maidens hang the twisted thread.

There is a play here on the first half of *kasehi* and the name of a mountain. The *kasehi* kept at the sun-goddess' temples in Ise is simply a sort of reel in the shape of a letter **H**, the upright strokes being curved to hold the thread which was wound round it, and the horizontal stroke representing the *te* or handle.

[14] From this point the offerings are common to both deities.

ANCIENT JAPANESE RITUALS.—PART III.*

(Nos. 5, 6, 7, 8 & 9.)

BY ERNEST SATOW.

[Read before the Asiatic Society of Japan on May 10th, 1881.]

No. 5—HIRANU NO MATSURI, OR SERVICE OF THE TEMPLE OF IMAKI.

The temple of Hiranu, now called Hirano, is situated in the village of Kogitayama on the N. E. of Kiyau-to, and according to the usually accepted account, derived from the Ku-zhi Koñ-geñ, the gods worshipped at the four shrines which it contains are the following:

At the Imaki shrine, Yamato-dake-no-mikoto; at the Kudo shrine, Chiu-ai Teñ-wau; at the Furuaki shrine, Niñ-toku Teñ-wau, and at that of the *hime-gami* (goddess), Amaterasu-oho-mi-kami (the Sun-goddess). These four deities are regarded as the ancestral gods (*Uji-gami*) of the Minamoto, Tahira, Takashina and Ohoye families respectively.

Mabuchi supposes the first of these four deities, to whom the present ritual is addressed, to have been brought from a place called Imaki in Yamato by Kuwañ-mu Teñ-wau, when he founded the present city of Kiyau-to. He adds that a temple called Kudo no Zhiñ-zhiya, situated near the temple of the Gods of Wind at Tatsuta (see Yamato Mei-shiyo Dzu-we vol. 3, f. 50), is mentioned in the "Catalogue of Temples," but that where the god of Furuaki came from is unknown. Another point which Mabuchi was unable to explain was that besides the four families above mentioned, the Yamato family was also represented among the persons who took an official part in the ceremony. In fact, all

*Reprinted from the Transactions of the Asiatic Society of Japan, First Series, Vol. IX, Pt. II, pp. 183-211

that he is able to tell us about the service amounts to very little, nor does Motowori throw any additional light upon the matter.

The following solution of the difficulty has lately been proposed by a native scholar of independent views. He reads 今木 Ima-ge, instead of Imaki or Imagi, and explains *Ima-ge no Kami* to be 'the god of New Food,' whose name was Waka-toshi no Kami (god of the new harvest).* The spot where a certain temple of this god stood came to be called Ima-ge after the god. But it was, in fact, the ancient custom in every household to make offerings to the God of New Food, in the palace of the Mikado as in the dwellings of the common people. Besides this God of New Food, the Japanese worshipped the god of the cauldron in which water and rice are boiled and the goddess of the saucepan in which food is cooked, under the names of *Oki-tsu hiko* and *Oki-tsu hime*,** names derived from the construction of the fire-place, which is built up with clay, and always contains

---

Ima-ge did not always mean 'this year's crop of rice,' but seems to have been also used in a slightly different sense. It was the custom in the very earliest times to perform every month at the Mikado's palace a rite called *Kamu Ima-ge no Matsuri* (神今食祭), the "Service of the Divine New Food," which evidently could not have been, on every occasion, the lately harvested crop of rice. It was probably freshly hulled rice that was offered to the gods at these celebrations, and afterwards partaken of by the Mikado. In later times this *Matsuri* was held only twice a year, on the 11th day of the 6th and 12th months, immediately after the *Tsuki-nami no Matsuri* or so-called "Monthly Service." Detailed directions are given in the *Gi-shiki* (bk. 1, f. 26 v.), which show the nature of the ceremonies observed in the 9th century. Towards evening the Mikado proceeded to a special building called the Naka no Win, which stood west of the Palace, where he immediately took a bath, and then the service called the *Oho-tono Hogahi* or "Luck-wishing of the Great Palace," was performed, after which mats were brought in and his bed was made. This was supposed to be symbolic of the rejoicings on the occasion of the completion of the first palace of the first Mikado, and of his taking possession of it as his residence, sleeping in a house being regarded as the sign of ownership. (For this reason a pillow is often placed in the shrine of a Shiñ-tau temple, as a symbol of the god's presence.) The Chief Cook, who bore the ancient title of *Kashihade no tomo no miyatsuko*, kindled fire by means of the fire-drill and began to cook the rice, while the *Adzumi no sukune* (originally called *Watadzumi no murazhi*, a superintendent of fishers) blew up the fire. Other persons prepared various dishes to be eaten along with the rice. Towards eleven o'clock the procession was formed, headed by the Chief Cook bearing a torch, and followed by other functionaries carrying the utensils, dishes, soups, water and *sake*, part to be offered to the gods, part for the Mikado. About midnight the meat was cleared away. The Mikado and his suite passed the night in the building, and about half-past three next morning his breakfast was served in the same style. About five o'clock he changed his clothes, and returned to his own apartments, where the *Oho-tono Hogahi* was again performed.

**See Ko-zhi-ki Deñ, bk. 12, f. 29. Hirata suggests that *Oki-tsu* is a contraction of *Oki-tsuchi*, earth put or piled up, which seems a probable derivation. (古史傳, bk. 16. f. 5).

two compartments, one for the *kama*, or boiler, the other for the *nabe*, or saucepan. Other names for the same things are *kudo* and *kobe*, after which the pair of deities Kudo no kami and Kobe no kami were called.† The first of these is one of the gods to whom the next ritual is addressed, and the second is what, through a slip of the pen, has come to be called Furuaki. Originally written 古閇 , in which the characters are used merely as phonetic symbols, by some mischance or other it appeared as 古開 in the MSS. from which the printed copies are descended; and the ordinary reading Furuaki rests entirely on a conjecture of Mabuchi, who himself confesses that he does not know whether the characters should be read as *on* or as *kun*, by the Chinese sound or the Japanese translation. Another household deity was Toyo-uke-bime, the earth conceived of as the goddess of Abundant Food. The rites in honour of these gods were at first performed by the head of the household (*to-nushi*, contracted into *tozhi*), but in after times the duty came to be delegated to the women of the family, whence the word *tozhi* to denote women. In the same way the word *miyazhi* (*miya-nushi*), from meaning the 'lord of the palace,' came to be the title of the priest who discharged the function of worshipping the gods of the kitchen. After Kuwañ-mu Teñ-wau founded this temple of Hirano about the end of the 8th century, it became the custom for all the branches of the monarchical family to be represented at the two annual celebrations. His own mother belonged to the Yamato family, and his grandmother to the Hazhi family, from whom were descended the Ohoye. The Tahira were sprung from an illegitimate son of Kuwañ-mu himself, the Minamoto from his successor Saga Teñ-wau, and the latter had a secondary wife who belonged to the Takashina family. In this way all these five families came to share in the worship of the Mikados's household gods, being either connected with him by ties of agnatic relationship, or, what was not recognized in earlier times, through females. It was Kitabatake Chikafusa (1293-1359) who first invented the popular account of the gods worshipped at Hirano, and knowing that they were in some manner family deities, proceeded to allot as ancestors to the Tahira, Minamoto,

† *Kudo* is still commonly used in the province of Ise for 'fire-place,' the usual term for which in other parts of the country is *hetsui*.

Ohoye and Takashina families, ancient members of the royal line taken here and there at random, beginning with the Sun-goddess and coming down to the prehistoric Niñtoku Teñ-wau.

In the middle of the 9th century the service was performed twice a year, in the 4th and 11th months, on the first day of the ape, and nearly the same *norito*, with slight variations, was read before each of the first three shrines. Whether any, or what, ritual was read before the fourth is unknown. The ceremonies are laid down with great minuteness in the Gi-shiki (bk. 1, f. 15). From the fact that the Heir-Apparent and several Princes of the Blood, together with Ministers and Councillors of State, were obliged to take part in it, it is evident that the service was one of great importance in ancient times. As already observed, members of the Minamoto, Tahira, Takashina and Ohoye families were expected to be present, on account of their relationship to the Mikado. In some points the ceremonial observed resembled that of the Kasuga service, which has already been described. Horses were led in solemn procession round the temples, pieces of music were executed on wind and stringed instruments, and a long succession of grave dances were performed by officials of high rank, such as lords-in-waiting and vice-ministers of the Department for the Worship of the Gods (神祇官), as well as by the women who prepared the rice-offerings and the soldiers who took the part of peasants (*yama-bito*). The principal point of difference is that at the beginning of the service these fictitious peasants, twenty in number, entered the courtyard of the temple carrying branches of the sacred tree, *sakaki* (Cleyera japonica), and recited in turn the praise of the four gods (*kami no yogoto*), the words of which have unfortunately been lost. This incident harmonizes completely with the opinion that the deities here worshipped were originally such as would be all-important in the eyes of a peasant, namely, those who provide him with his food and the means of cooking it.

RITUAL.

[TRANSLATION.]

He says: The sovran *who is called* "According to his great

WORD"[1] deigns to say in the wide presence of the sovran great
GOD who has been brought[2] from Imaki:

The divine treasures which *he* offers up after having, in accordance with the request which the sovran great GOD has deigned
to make, widely planted the HOUSE-pillars on the bottom-most
rocks and exalted the cross-beams to the plain of high heaven,
and having fixed on it as his SHADE from the heavens and SHADE
from the sun, and having fixed on [surname, name, office, rank]
of the Office of the Gods as Kañ-nushi, *are* a BOW, a SWORD, a
MIRROR, a bell, and a silk baldaquin, and a HORSE is led and
ranged *with them;* for CLOTHING, providing bright cloth, glittering cloth, fine cloth and coarse cloth, and having taken and ranged
with them the first parcels of tribute set-up by the regions of
the four quarters; as to LIQUOR, raising high the beer-jars, filling-
and-ranging-in-rows the bellies of the beer-jars; as to things of
the mountains and wilds,—sweet herbs and bitter herbs; as to
the things of the blue-sea-plain,—things wide of fin and things
narrow of fin, even unto the weeds of the offing and weeds of
the shore,—piling-up high the various kinds of things like a
range of hills, he fulfils praises saying: Peacefully accept the
great OFFERINGS thus set-up, and glorify the AGE of the sovran
eternally and unchangingly, and blessing it as a luxuriant AGE,
cause *him* greatly to be for a myriad ages.

Again *he* says: *I* fulfil praises, *saying:* Cause the CHILDREN,
the princes, the councillors and all the functionaries to deign to
guard with nightly guarding and daily guarding, and flourishing
like the perpetual growth of luxuriant trees ever higher and ever
wider in the count of the sovran, humbly to serve *him.*

NOTES.

[1] See Note 1 to the Kasuga Ritual.

[2] The expression here rendered "brought" is *tsukahe matsuri kitaru,* lit., "came
serving." See notes 1 and 4 to the Kasuga Ritual.

There is some doubt as to whether *"he* says" in this ritual means that the
Mikado says, or that the reader of the Norito says, a doubt which arises in connection with nearly all the rituals, and different views have been taken by different commentators, as observed in Note 1 to the praying for Harvest.

[3] Toy swords and mirrors are still used very commonly as ex-voto offerings to
both Buddhist and Shiñ-tau gods, the former by men, the latter by women, being
symbolical of what is most valued by each sex respectively.

No. 6.—KUDO AND FURU-AKI.

As has been observed in the introduction to the 5th Ritual, *Furu-aki* ought probably to be read *Kobe*.

The text of the *norito* is almost identical with the last, with the exception of the substitution of the words "being the two House of Kudo and Furu-aki' for "from Imaki" and the omission of the words "Office of the Gods," further down. It is therefore unnecessary to translate it.

No. 7.—MINADZUKI NO TSUKINAMI NO MATSURI.

This service was celebrated in honour of the 304 shrines, distinguished as Great Shrines, the offerings to which were arranged upon tables or altars. These shrines formed a portion of the much larger number at which the "Praying for Harvest" was celebrated, distributed as follows, according to the Catalogue in the Yeñ-gi Shiki:

Kiyau-to	34
Yamashiro	53
Yamato	128
Kahachi	23
Izumi	1
Tsu	26
Ise	14
Idzu	1
Musashi	1
Aha	1
Shimo-fusa	1
Hitachi	1
Afumi	5
Wakasa	1
Tañ-go	1
Harima	3
Aki	1
Kii	8
Aha	2
Total	305

There is evidently a mistake of a unit here.

According to one view the object of this service was to render monthly thanks to the gods for the protective care they bestowed on the country in response to the petitions offered up at the Praying for Harvest. It was, however, probably more ancient than the Praying for Harvest (see Vol. VII, p. 108). The ritual is identical with that of the Praying for Harvest, with the exception of the latter part of the second paragraph, which runs as follows: "As to the monthly OFFERINGS for the sixth month of this year (in the twelfth month say monthly OFFERINGS for the twelfth month of this year), providing bright cloth, glittering cloth, fine cloth, coarse cloth, I fulfil praises *by setting-up* the great OFFERINGS of the sovran GRANDCHILD'S augustness, as the morning sun rises in glory," and by the omission of the third paragraph containing the petition to the gods of the harvest.

A list of the offerings made at the 304 or 305 shrines is given in the "Ceremonies of the Services of the Four Seasons" (四 時 祭 式), Deha-boñ edit., vol. 1, f. 28 v. For an account of the history of this service see the "Materials for a History of Shiñ-tau" (神 祇 志 料) of Kurita Hiroshi, vol. 5, f. 19.

No. 8.—OHOTONO HOGAHI, OR LUCK-WISHING OF THE GREAT PALACE.

This was one of the Occasional Services, and in later times was always celebrated before and after the *Kamu Ima-ge no Matsuri* (see above note on p. 184) and the *Ohonihe* or *Ohoñbe* (Coronation Festival.) It dates, however, from the very earliest ages, namely, from the establishment of the capital at Kashihara in Yamato by Zhiñ-mu Teñwau. In language closely resembling that of the ritual, the author of the *Ko-go Zhifu-wi* (古語拾遺) describes how on that occasion the timber was cut in the forests with a sacred axe, and the foundations of the great hall or palace dug with a sacred spade. The pillars of the house were firmly planted on the rocks beneath the surface, and the ends of the rafters, crossed over the ridge-pole, were raised high towards the sky. Offerings, or 'divine treasures,' as they are called,

namely, a mirror, beads, spear, mantlet, paper-mulberry bark
and hemp were prepared by the *imibe,* who then, under the
guidance of the head of their tribe, deposited in the great hall
the sword and mirror, which constituted the sacred symbols of
sovereignty, hung the building with strings of red beads, laid
out the offerings in due order, and read the ritual. The service
of the Palace Gates (Ritual No. 9) was performed immediately
afterwards.

Another indication of the extreme antiquity of the composition is the comparatively large number of archaic words
which it contains. For some of these no precisely corresponding
expression could be found in the Chinese language, and though
equivalents were assigned to others, it was still judged necessary to mark by a note in *kana* the exact way in which the
Chinese characters were to be read. These *kana* were not the
derivative signs usually denoted by that term, but whole Chinese
characters used as phonetic symbols, such as are found in all
the early remains of Japanese literature before the 10th century.

The object of the service was chiefly to propitiate two deities
who are described as the Spirits of Timber and Rice, and to
obtain their protection for the sovereign's abode, so that it
should be preserved from decay, and its occupier from snake-
bite, pollution through birds flying in at the smoke-hole in the
roof and from night-alarms. From the language in which these
petitions were offered up, we learn incidentally that at the period
when this service was first instituted, the palace of the Japanese
sovereign was a wooden hut, with its pillars planted in the
ground, instead of being erected upon broad flat stones as in
modern buildings. The whole frame-work, consisting of posts,
beams, rafters, door-posts and window-frames, was tied together
with cords made by twisting the long fibrous stems of climbing
plants, such as Pueraria Thunbergiana (*kuzu*) and Wistaria
Sinensis (*fuji*). The floor must have been low down, so that
the occupants of the building, as they squatted or lay on their
mats, were exposed to the stealthy attacks of venomous snakes,
which were probably far more numerous in the earliest ages
when the country was for the most part uncultivated, than at
the present day. In the Ritual of the General Purification, snake-
bite is counted as an 'offence' or cause of pollution, which has

to be expiated by the sacrifice of a certain quantity of valuable property, and it was in accordance with a very natural impulse that the protective deities were besought to avert such a misfortune. There seems some reason to think that the *yuka*, here translated floor, was originally nothing but a couch which ran round the sides of the hut, the rest of the space being simply a mud-floor, and that the size of the couch was gradually increased until it occupied the whole interior. The rafters projected upward beyond the ridge-pole, crossing each other as is seen in the roof of modern Shiñ-tau temples, whether their architecture be in conformity with early traditions (in which case all the rafters are so crossed) or modified in accordance with more advanced principles of construction, and the crossed rafters retained only as ornaments at the two ends of the ridge. The roof was thatched, and perhaps had a gable at each end, with a hole to allow the smoke of the wood-fire to escape, so that it was possible for birds flying in and perching on the beams overhead, to defile the food, or the fire with which it was cooked. This is also one of the causes of pollution mentioned in the General Purification as requiring expiation. Such a description of the residence of the sovereign also seems to point to a very early origin for the main part of the ritual, though the separation of the members of the sovereign's family into two classes, CHILDREN (*miko*), who correspond to the modern Princes of the Blood and princes (*kimi*), as the grand-children and other agnates who are not themselves sons and daughters of a Mikado are called, is an arrangement which dates from the historical period (reign of Teñ-mu Teñ-wau), and the ending of the ritual where these terms occur must therefore be regarded as more modern.

The following account of the ceremony is taken from the *Gi-shiki* (middle of the 9th century). The Office of the Gods (神祇官) took four boxes containing precious stones, cut paper-mulberry bark, rice and *sake* in bottles, and placed them on two eight-legged tables, which were then borne by four attendants (*kan-domo*), preceded by functionaries belonging to the Nakatomi and Imibe tribes, the priests (*miya-zhi*), archivists and other attendants, all wearing wreaths and scarfs of paper-mulberry bark, walking in double line, the rear being brought up by virgin priestesses. On the procession arriving in front of the palace gate, the tables were deposited under the arcade which ran along the outside of the wall. A servant (*oho-doneri*) called out for admittance, and the porter having announced the procession by saying that an officer of the Imperial Household had asked for admission in order to pronounce the Luck-wishing of the Great Palace, the order "Let him pronounce it" was transmitted back from the Mikado. The porter thereupon called out. "Let him declare his name and surname," in reply to which the officer advanced to a spot previously marked out by a wooden ticket with his name on it, and said: "It is so-and-so (giving his name) of the Office of the Gods who wish to perform the Luck-wishing of the Great Palace." To this the Mikado's answer was: "Call them." The officer of the Household replied "O" (the old word for "Yes"), and retiring, called the functionaries of the Office of the Gods, who in their turn replied "O." The Nakatomi and Imibe then put on their wreaths of paper-mulberry, to which the latter added sashes (*tasuki*) of the same material, and advanced ahead of the tables up to the "Hall of Benevolence and Long-life" (one of the principal buildings of the palace). The virgin priestesses had meanwhile entered by another gate, and were waiting in the Palace enclosure. They now followed the tables, and came up to the verandah on the east side of the building, where they took charge of the boxes of offerings. The procession thereupon entered the building. One Virgin Priestess went to the Hall of Audience (*shi-shin-den*) and scattered rice about it, while another proceeded to the gate on its south side and performed the same ceremony there. The Imibe took out the precious stones and hung them at the four corners of the Hall, and the priestesses withdrew, after sprinkling *sake* and scattering rice and cut paper-mulberry fibre at the four corners of the interior. The Nakatomi stood on the south side of the building while the Imibe turned to the south-east, and in a low voice read the ritual. The whole company next went to the Mikado's bath-room and hung precious stones at its four angles, and the same at his privy, while the priestesses scattered rice and sprinkled *sake* as before. After this they retired through a gate on the west of the palace, with the exception of the priests and attendants, who proceeded to the palace kitchen to hang up paper-mulberry fibre and scatter rice and sprinkle *sake*. When all was over gifts were distributed to all those who had taken part in the ceremony.

RITUAL.

[TRANSLATION.]

He felicitates and brings to rest with the heavenly mysterious congratulatory words,[1] thee Yabune[2] no Mikoto, *who art* the fresh ABODE which has been made for the sovran GRANDCHILD'S augustness' SHADE from the heavens and SHADE from the sun, by setting up the sacred[3] pillars with the sacred spade, *after* cutting down with the sacred axe of the Imibe the trees which grew in the great gorges and small gorges of the remoter hills, and offering the two ends to the god of the mountains, and bringing forth the central parts—the ABODE *namely* of the sovran GRANDCHILD'S augustness, who in succession to heaven's sun rules over the region-under-heaven, the dominion to which he deigned to descend *after that* the sovran's dear progenitor and progenitrix, who divinely remain in the plain of high heaven, had caused the sovran *grandchild's* augustness by their WORD to sit on the heavenly high SEAT, and deigning to lift and bring the mirror and sword[4] which are the heavenly symbols, had pronounced the words of luck-wishing, and appointed him, *saying;* "Let our sovran great CHILD, the sovran GRANDCHILD'S augustness, sitting on this heavenly high seat here,[5] tranquilly rule the succession of heaven's sun,[6] the Great Many-islands, the Luxuriant Reed-plain Region of Many Spikes[7] for long autumns, a myriad thousand autumns, as a peaceful country," and by the heavenly COUNSEL-TAKING[8] the rocks, trees and the least leaf of the herbs likewise that had spoken, had been silenced.

He says; *I* repeat the NAMES of the gods who tranquilly and peacefully watch[9] so that the great HOUSE where he sits ruling, *as far as* the limit of the bottom-most rocks, may not have the calamity of crawling worms *among* the lower cords *which tie it together, as far as the* limit of the blue clouds of the plain of high-heaven, may not have the calamity of birds flying in at the smoke-hole[10] in the roof; the meeting[11] of the firmly planted[12] pillars, cross-beams, rafters, doors and windows have no movement or noise, have no loosing of the tied rope-knots or unevenness of the thatch with which it is roofed, and no harmful rustling in the joints of the FLOOR or alarms at night.   And having humbly praised their names as Yabune Kukunochi[13] no Mikoto and Yabune Toyo Ukebime no Mikoto, *I say:* "In consequence of your humbly praising the AGE of the sovran GRAND-CHILD'S augustness, eternally and unchangeably, and humbly blessing it as a luxuriant AGE, sufficient AGE and long AGE, let the Divine Corrector's augustness and the Great Corrector's augustness[14] tranquilly and peacefully govern *the proceedings,* correcting any omissions which they may have seen or heard in the luck-wishing and bringing-to-rest *uttered* by the Imibe no Sukune So-and-so, who hangs a thick sash on his weak shoulders, and adds bright fine cloth and glittering fine cloth to the fresh ever-bright red-stones, the innumerable strings of beads of luck-wishing, which the sacred bead-makers have made with due-care-to-avoid-pollution and attention-to-cleanness."

Parting the words, *he* says: As to declaring *her* NAME as Woman-of-the-great-HOUSE'S augustness, *I* fulfil *her* praises by *declaring her* NAME as Woman-of-the-great-HOUSE'S augustness, because blocking up the way within the same great HOUSE as the sovran GRANDCHILD'S augustness, *she* chooses and knows the persons who come in and go out, by *her* word corrects and softens the grumbling and wildness of the gods, prevents the scarf-wearing attendants and the sash-wearing attendants[15] who present the morning FOOD and evening FOOD of the sovran GRANDCHILD'S augustness from erring with hand or foot, and prevents the CHILDREN, princes or counsellors and all the functionaries from indulging their own separate inclinations, causes them to attend in the HOUSE and serve in the HOUSE without bad hearts or foul hearts, and correcting whatsoever faults and errors she may see or hear, causes them to serve tranquilly and peacefully.

NOTES.

[1] *Ama tsu kusushi ihahi-goto.*   Here we have first, the Chinese characters which were thought to correspond most closely to the Japanese words of the original, and second, in a note, those very words repeated in *mañ-yefu-gana*, so that there is no doubt whatever about the reading.   Perhaps 'miraculous' would be as good a

rendering as 'mysterious' for *kusushi,* which seems to contain an allusion to the magical effect of the words which follow, and which act as a charm to ward off every kind of calamity from the building.   Hence the word *ihahi,* rendered 'congratulatory,' is written with 護 'to protect.'   The words in the translation here referred to begin with: *"He* says: I repeat the NAMES of the gods who tranquilly and peacefully watch," etc.   In all the editions of the Yeñ-gi-shiki and in the Norito kau the reading is *ihahi-goto mochite koto-hogi shidzume mawosaku,* but Motowori proposes *ihahi* instead of *shidzume.*   Hirata has restored the earlier reading, which there seems to be no adequate reason for altering.

² *Mi araka imashi Yabune no mikoto,* Yabune no mikoto *who art* the abode. *Ya* is simply 'house,' as the Chinese character indicates, and *fune* is a general term for all wooden things that contain, such as brewers' vats, bathing-tubs, as well as 'boat' or 'ship,' which is its most common use.   Mabuchi, indeed derives the word *ya-fu-ne* from *iya ofu ne,* 'ever-growing root, and considers it to be an epithet of trees and the rice plant; but this seems rather far-fetched.   'Abode' is the closest attainable rendering of the ancient *araka* (modern form *arika*), which is here given in a note as the proper reading of 殿.   These notes embedded in the text of the Norito are of the highest value, because they preserve to us archaic words which would otherwise have been utterly lost.   The first syllable of *kado,* 'house-door,' is perhaps identical with the *ka* of *araka.** Observe that *mi araka, imashi, and Yabuñe no mikoto* are all in apposition, thus justifying the insertion of 'who art,' to help out the meaning.

³ The foundation and construction of sacred buildings was always attended with these formalities. In the ceremonial rules for the Coronation of the Mikado (*Gi-shiki,* bk. 2, f. 15), we read that a special granary was built for storing the rice used on that occasion. Young virgins first cleared and levelled the ground with a sacred spade, and then dug the holes to receive the four corner-posts. After this a large party proceeded to the mountain where the timber was to be cut, and after rites had been performed to propitiate the forest god, the virgins took the sacred axe and made the first cut. Labourers were afterwards sent to cut down the timber and bring it in. On all similar occasions the virgins are represented as taking a sacred spade to dig the holes for the uprights. In the "Yamato-hime no Sei-ki" the foundation of the Sun-goddess' temple in Ise is thus described: "On the *ki-no-ye ne* day of the winter, tenth month of the 26th year, *hi-no-to mi,* they removed the From-heaven-shining-great-deity to the bank of the I-suzu-gaha in Watarai. This year Yamato-hime no Mikoto commanded Oho-hata-nushi no Mikoto and all the men of the eighty companies of the *mono-no-fu* to cut away the rough herbage and trees on the plain of I-suzu, to level the big stones and the little stones, to cut the timber standing in the big ravines and little ravines of the distant hills and near hills with the sacred axe of the Imibe, and bring it away, to offer the end to Yamatsumi and bringing out the central part to set up the sacred pillars with the sacred spade, to raise-up the cross-beams to the plain of high heaven, and widely plant the great HOUSE-pillars."   It was important to propitiate the forest god beforehand.   In the province of Tohotafumi, says Mabuchi, the woodmen, after cutting down a tree, break off a branch and stick it upright in the stump.   Elsewhere the woodman lops off a branch, and setting it up in front of the tree, together with his axe, clasps his hands and bows down, in order to obtain permission to cut it down from the spirit which is supposed to inhabit it.   Some such practice as this is alluded to in the text where the 'ends' are said to be offered to the god of the mountains.

⁴ The Mirror and Sword are two out of the three precious objects regarded as the regalia of the Japanese sovereigns, the possession of which was the evidence of their title to reign. The third is a stone (or perhaps a necklace of stones), of what kind is not precisely known. Its existence was denied by the Imibe, and hence

---

*This word occurs also in *inaka* (rice dwellings), the country districts; "sumika," dwelling-place; "kakureba," hiding place; and *yamaga,* mountain village.

the omission of it in this Norito, which had to be read by a member of their tribe. These treasures, commonly called the 'Three Kinds of Divine Treasures' (*San shiyu no Zhin-pau*, 三種之神寶) or 'Utensils' (*ki* 器) are mentioned in the Kozhi-ki on the occasion of Ninigi no Mikoto's descent, where they are called the *Yagaka no Maga-tama, the Kagami* and the *Kusa-nagi no Tsurugi*, the 'Ever-bright Curved-jewel,' the 'Mirror,' and the 'Herb-quelling Sabre.' In the Ni-hoñ-gi the names of the first two differ slightly, being *Yasaka-ni no Maga-tama, Ya-ta no kagami*.   The Stone and Mirror are supposed to be identical with those which play such an important part in the episode of the Sun-goddess' retirement into the cave, when they were hung on the sacred *sakaki* bush, together with other offerings, as inducements to her to come forth again and shed the light of her countenance of the earth.   In the latter passage of the Ko-zhi-ki the Mirror is called *Yata kagami*, the 'Many-angled Mirror.''   *Ya-ta* is a contraction of *Ya-ata, ya*, which eventually came to mean eight, having originally been used to denote any large number, while *ata* may either be the root of *atama*, head, or *hata*, fin, from the resemblance in shape and position to the fin of the fish, looked on as a mere appendage to the body.   A mirror, called *Yatama kagami*, which is figured in the Guñ-shiyo Ruwi-zhiyuu, vol. 28, f. 23, is circular, with a raised design not unlike the conventional form of the sacred lotus of the Buddhists.

The material of the sacred Mirror is said to have been iron.   Although the traditional reading is simply *kane*, which might mean any kind of metal whatever, the Chinese character in the text is 鐵, iron, and by the Chinese character we must be guided when there is any doubt as to the meaning.   In the Ko-go Zhifu-wi the mirror is said to have been made of copper or bronze (銅), but this book is exactly a century later than the Ko-zhi-ki, and a hundred years after the discovery in Japan of copper.   The use of that metal having by that time become well-known, the author of the Ko-go Zhifu-wi would naturally be inclined to suppose that it must have been the metal employed in making this mirror.   The word handed down by tradition was simply *kane*, which the compilers of the earlier work understood was "iron," while the later author by the light of additional knowledge, interpreted it to mean "copper."   In the Ni-hoñ-gi the mirror is called by the same name (*ya-ta kagami*), but nothing is said with respect to the metal of which it was formed.   It would be curious if the Japanese should be proved to have possessed the knowledge of iron earlier than that of copper.   According to one version of the legend in the Ni-hoñ-gi, it was suggested by Omohigane no kami that a likeness of the goddess should be made, and it is added that the image then made (i.e. a mirror) is now the deity of Hi-no-mahe in the province of Ki-shiu.   The Ko-go Zhifu-wi also says that the mirror was made in the sun's likeness: "The first made was not quite perfect, but the second was beautiful.   The former is the god of Hi-no-mahe, in the province of Kii; the latter is the great deity of Ise."

The full name of the Jewel is *Ya-saka no Maga-tama no iho-tsu mi sumaru no tama*.   Motowori acknowledges that he cannot explain *ya-saka*.   Numerous etymologies have been suggested, as, for instance, that *ya=iya*, and *saka* the root of *sakayeru*, hence the meaning 'ever-flourishing.'   Again, that *maga-tama*, being taken to signify 'bent stone,' *yasaka* may be interpreted, according to the Chinese characters with which it is written, 'eight feet' or 'many feet' (reverting to the original meaning of *ya*), that being the length of the stone if it could be straightened.   This seems rather far-fetched.   Other conjectures are that *yasaka* was the name of the place whence the stone was procured, as well as that the *tama* being beads, *yasaka* (eight or many feet) denotes the length of the string upon which they were threaded.   Hirata's derivation of *saka* from *sa-aka*, 'very bright, seems the best, and I have accordingly adopted it rendering *yasaka* by 'ever-bright.   Motowori takes ==maga-tama to be 'curved jewel,' such as are from time to time dug out of the ground and are shaped like a tiger's claw.==   They are formed of "nephrite, crystal, serpentine, agate or more rarely topaz, amethyst or jasper; soapstone and even clay has occasionally been used."—(*Henry von Siebold*.)   Hirata, however explains *maga* to be a contraction of *ma kaga*, 'very sparkling,' *kaga* being the radical of *kaga-yaku*, 'to

ANCIENT JAPANESE RITUALS—PART III

glitter, sparkle,' and identical with *kage*, 'brightness' as in *tsuki-kage*, 'moonshine.'
The former etymology is supported by the evidence of the Chinese characters used,
though there is nothing to prove that the modern so-called *maga-tama* are identical
with those spoken of in ancient writings, while the latter is convenient, because it
allows us to include amongst *maga-tama* precious stones of other forms, especially
the cylindrical beads popularly known as *kuda-tama*, as well as globular beads that
have been found in tumuli. *Iho-tsu*, literally 'five hundred,' is merely used to
express a great number. *Mi* is the honorific prefix, and *sumaru* is the equivalent of
the Chinese 統 t'ung, to bring together, being in fact the same word as *sumeru* and
suberu (see note 4 to the "Praying of Harvest"). The whole, therefore, signifies' the
'ever-bright curved (or glittering) jewels, the many assembled jewels,' and the
natural conclusion is that this member of the regalia ought to be a long string
of, perhaps claw-shaped, stone beads.

The *Kusa-nagi* was originally called *Ame no Murakumo no Tsurugi*, the
'Sabre of the Assembled-clouds of Heaven.' In the Ko-zhi-ki there is a very
curious account of its discovery. As a punishment for the misconduct which had
been the cause of the Sun-goddess' retirement, a large fine was imposed upon
Susa-no-wo no Mikoto, and he was banished from heaven. "So, being driven
away, he descended on Tori-kami by the source of the river of Hi, in the province
of Idzumo. Then there came a chop-stick floating down the river. So Susa-no-
wo no Mikoto thought that people must dwell up that river, and went up it in
search of them. There he found an old man and an old woman, two of them,
who had placed a young girl between them, and were weeping. Then he asked,
'Who are you'? Whereupon the old man replied, saying: 'I am a god of the
earth, the child of Oho-yama-tsu-mi no Kami (the god of mountains). My name
is called Foot-stroker (Ashi-na-dzu-chi) and my wife's name is called Hand-strok-
er (Te-na-dzu-chi), and my daughter's name is called Miraculous-rice-field-sun-
maiden (Kushi-inada-hime).' Again he asked, 'What is the reason of your
weeping?' He (the old man) answered and said: 'My daughters were originally
eight young girls, but the Eight-forked Serpent of Koshi came every year and
devoured them, and I weep because it is now the time for him to come.' Then
he (the god) asked, 'What is his form like?' He answered and said, 'His eyes
are red-glistering, his body is one, with eight heads and eight tails, and on his body
grow moss, *hi* and *sugi* (Chamaecyparis and Cryptomeria). His belly extends
over eight valleys and eight hills, and if one looks at his belly, it is all constantly
bloody and inflamed.' Then Haya-Susa-no-wo no Mikoto said to the old man,
'If this is your daughter, will you offer her to me?' He replied, saying, 'With
respect, but I do not know your august name.' Then he replied, and said, 'I am
the dear elder brother of the From heaven-shining-great-deity, and have just
descended from heaven.' Hereupon Ashi-na-dzu-chi-no kami and Te-na-dzu-chi
no kami said, 'If that be so, with respect (i. e., we obey), we will offer [her to
you].' So Haya-Susa-no-wo no Mikoto transformed the young girl into a many-
and-close-toothed comb, which he stuck in his hair, and then said to them, 'Brew
some eight-fold filtered beer. And make a fence round about, and in that fence
make eight gates, and at each gate tie togeher a bench, and on each bench place
a beer-vat, and in each vat pour beer, and wait.' And when they had thus
prepared [every thing] in accordance with his bidding, the Eight-forked serpent
came truly as [the old man] had said. Then it dipped a head into each vat and
drank the beer. And thereupon it became drunk with drinking, and all [the
heads] lay down and slept. Then Haya-Susa-no-wo no Mikoto, drawing the sword
of ten hand-breadths [length] which he wore, cut the serpent in pieces, and
the Hi river turned into blood and flowed on. Now, when he cut the middle
tail, the edge of his sword broke. Thinking it strange, he took the point of his
sword, thrust, split and looked, and there was a keen-cutting blade [within]. So
he took this sword, and thinking it a strange thing, sent it up with a message to
the From-heaven-shining-great-deity. This is the 'herb-quelling sword' (*Kusanagi no
tachi*). Thereupon Haya-Susa-no-wo no Mikoto sought for a place in Idzumo where
he might build a HOUSE. So he came to the place called Suga, and said this:

Grosscutter?

'Having come to this place my heart is pure,' and there he built a HOUSE. Wherefore that place is yet called Suga. When this great god first built the HOUSE of Suga, clouds rose up from the place. So he made a SONG, and that SONG was:

Many clouds arise.
The manifold fence of the forth-issuing clouds
Makes a manifold fence
For the spouses to be within.
Oh! that manifold fence.

"Then he called that Ashi-na-dzu-chi no kami, and said to him, 'Thee do I appoint chief of my HOUSE', and also he gave him a name, calling him Inada no miya-nushi Suga no yatsu-mimi no kami."—(Ko-zhi-ki.)

In the Ni-hoñ-gi version of the myth the locality is placed in the province of Aki, and the parents of the maiden are called Ashi-nadzu-te-nadzu and Inada no miya-nushi. They besought Susa-no-wo no Mikoto to protect their new-born babe from the serpent, and by his orders made eight jars of wine from the fruits of trees, which he poured into the mouths of the serpent, and the monster became an easy victim. The sword used by him in slaying the serpent was called "Worochi no Aramasa," the Rough-perfect-one of the Serpent, and is said to be worshipped as a god at the ancient temple of Furu in Yamato. In another account this sword is called "Worochi no Kara-sabi," the Foreign-spade of the Serpent. A third version given in the Ni-hoñ-gi differs considerably, but is worth translating chiefly on account of its connecting Susa-no-wo with Korea, and showing that tradition affords ground for conjecturing that the original civilisers of Japan crossed over to Idzumo from that country. This version is as follows:

"Susa-no-wo no Mikoto's conduct was indecent, wherefore all the gods imposed upon him a penalty of a thousand tables [of offerings], and finally banished him. Then Susa-no-wo no Mikoto, taking with him his child Iso-takeru no Kami, descended into the country called Shiraki, and dwelt at a place called Soshimori. Then he commenced to speak, and said: 'This is a place in which I do not desire to dwell,' and consequently making a boat of clay, he embarked in it, and going across eastwards, arrived at Mount Tori-kami, which is at the source of the river Hi, in the province of Idzumo. At that time there was a serpent which swallowed human beings. So Susa-no-wo no Mikoto cut the serpent with the sword Ama-no-hawe-giri (the "Heavenly fly-cutter"), and cutting the serpent's tail, its edge broke. So he split up [the tail] and looked, and within the tail there was a strange sword. Susa-no-wo no Mikoto said, 'I must not make this my private property,' and sent his descendant in the fifth generation, Ama-no-fuki-ne no Kami, and offered it to Heaven. This is now called the Kusa-nagi no Tsurugi. When first Iso-takeru no Kami descended from heaven, he brought down a quantity of seeds of trees, but instead of planting them in Kara kuni (韓地) he brought them all back, and eventually sowed them all over the Great Many Island Country, beginning from Tsukushi, and made the mountains green. Wherefore Iso-takeru no Mikoto was called Isawoshi no Kami, 'The God of Merit,' and he is the great god who dwells in the province of Kii."—(Ni-hoñ-gi.)

The Sword, Mirror and Jewel (or Jewels) were brought to Japan by the ancestor of the Mikados, the mythical grandson of the Sun-goddess, Ninigi no Mikoto. In delivering the Three Sacred Treasures to him, the Sun-goddess said: "Look upon this mirror as my SPIRIT, and worship it as if you were worshipping my actual presence."—(Ko-zhi-ki.) One version of the myth which is given in the Ni-hoñ-gi makes the Sun-goddess deliver the precious mirror of her son Oshi-ho-mimi, with almost the same words, adding an injunction to keep the mirror always in the same house and on the same raised floor (toko) with himself. And this was actually done by the Mikados down to the reign of Su-zhiñ Teñ-wau, when, as he Ni-hoñ-gi says: "In the 6th year some of the people abandoned their homes, others rebelled, and the state of things was such that it was not to be remedied by the virtue [of the Mikado]. Wherefore he rose early in the morning and in the evening was solicitous, and besought punishment from the gods. Before this the two gods Ama-terasu Oho-kami and Oho-kuni-mi-tama, of Yamato, had both been worshipped within the RESIDENCE of the sovereign. But now fearing the might of these deities, he felt uneasy at living with them, wherefore he committed Ama-terasu Oho-kami to the charge of Toyo-suki-iri-hime no Mikoto, to worship at Kasa-nuhi no Sato (the Village of the Hat-makers) in Yamato, and there he built a stone-walled brushwood hut (*shiki himorogi*), and he entrusted Oho-kuni-mi-tama of Yamato to Nu-na-ki-iri-bime no Mikoto to worship, but Nu-na-ki-iri-bime no Mikoto's hair fell off and her body wasted, so that she could not worship."—(*Ni-hon-gi.*)

The Ko-go Zhifu-wi says: "In the reign of Shiki no Midzugaki (i.e., Su-zhiñ Teñ-wau), fearing at last the power of the god, and not feeling at ease in the same palace, the Mikado ordered the Imibe tribe to bring the two families descended from Ishi-kori-dome no kami and Ama-ma-hitotsu no kami, to cast a new mirror and make a new sword, to be the EMBLEMS to guard his person, and these are the mirror and sword which are offered to the Mikado at his accession as the divine symbols. At the same time he built a stone-walled brushwood hut at the Village of the Hat-makers in Yamato, and removing thither the From-heaven-shining-great-deity and the Herb-quelling sword, ordered the princess Toyo-suki-iri hime no Mikoto to worship them. On the evening of the removal the people of the palace all came and feasted throughout the night, singing:

> *Miya-bito no*
> *Oho-yo sugara ni*
> *iza tohoshi*
> *Yuki no yoroshi mo*
> *oho yo sugara ni.*"

The Yamato hime no Mikoto no Sei-ki (倭姫命世記) is the history of the Mirror and Sword from the time they left the Mikado's Palace until they were finally established on the banks of the Isuzu-gaha in Ise, at the present Nai-kuu Temple. After the first priest-princess had been in charge of the sacred symbols for some fifty-three years, in the course of which she had frequently removed them from one site to another, finding herself getting old and feeble, she delivered them into the care of her niece, Yamato-hime, a sister of Kei-kau Teñ-wau, who wandered about with her trust until the 26th year of Suwi-niñ Teñ-wau (B. C. 4 according to the popular chronology), when she settled down in Ise at a spot indicated by a revelation from the Sun-goddess.

This princess appears to have lived to a great age, for she is still found as the high priestess of the Sun-goddess' temple in the 28th year of Kei-kau Teñ-wau. Here she was visited by Yamato-dake no Mikoto, when on his way to subdue the barbarians of the east. She lent him the sacred sword for use against the enemy, and it was an incident of his campaign that gave to the weapon the name of "Herb-quelling Sabre." On his return he left the sword at Atsuta in Wohari, where a temple was built for it, which still exists, and is well-known to travellers. The story is recounted in the Ko-zhi-ki as follows: "Now when the sovereign again commanded Yamato-dake no Mikoto, saying, 'Subdue and pacify the violent gods and disobedient men of the twelve eastern roads,' and sent him, attaching to him the the ancestor of the Omi of Kibi, whose name was Mi-suki-tomo-mimi-take hiko, he gave him a many-fathom-long spear of *hihira-gi* (Olea aquifolio). So when he departed having received the command, he came into the HOUSE of the great DEITY of Ise, and worshipping the court of the deity, said to his aunt Yamato-hime, 'The sovran's augustness apparently desires that I should die [as] quickly [as possible], for after he had sent me to take the unsubmissive men of the west, as soon as I came up back, before any interval has elapsed, without bestowing on me any fighting men, he now sends me to subdue the unsubmissive men of the twelve circuits of the east. Consequently, I think he certainly desires me to die [as] quickly [as possible].' When he went away, having spoken thus with grief and weeping,

Yamato-hime no Mikoto bestowed on him the 'Herbquelling blade,' and also bestowed
on him a BAG, and bade him open the mouth of the bag on an emergency. So, coming
to the province of Wohari, he entered into the house of Miyasu hime, ancestress of
the 'Miyatsuko of Wohari, and thereupon thought to marry her, but thought again
that he would marry her when he came back again, and having entered into a promise,
went forth to the eastern provinces and subdued and softened all the turbulent gods
and unsubmissive men of the mountains and rivers. And when he came to the province
of Sagamu, the Miyatsuko of that province lied to him, saiyng, 'There is a lake in
this province, and the god who lives in that lake is a very turbulent god.' So, when
he entered into the prairie in order to visit that god, the Miyatsuko of the province
set the prairie on fire. So knowing that he had been deceived, he opened the mouth
of the bag which his aunt Yamato-hime no Mikoto had given him, and looked [into
it,] and there was a steel in it. So he first mowed away the herbage with his
SWORD, and with the steel he struck fire, and kindling a counter-fire, set it [the
herbage] on fire and drove-back [the other fire], and returning forth killed and
destroyed all the Miyatsuko of that province. He then set them on fire and burnt
them. Wherefore [that place] is now called Yaki-dzu."—(*Ko-zhi-ki.*)

In the Nihoñ-gi version, the prince, after first suggesting that the charge of
subduing the rebels should be entrusted to his feebler brother Oho-usu no Mikoto,
finally offers to undertake the task himself. The Mikado appointed him to command the expedition, and describes to his son the savage enemies which he would
have to encounter, and says: "I have heard that the Eastern barbarians have a rough
and violent disposition, and make violence their chief pursuit. Their villages have
no chief and their hamlets no heads, but every one encroaches on his neighbour's
boundary, and they all rob one another. In the mountains, too, there are evil gods,
and in the open country wicked demons who obstruct the roads and block up the
paths, causing great annoyance to others. Amongst the eastern barbarians the Yemishi
(Prawn barbarians) are the strongest. Male and female dwell together promiscuous-
ly, and there is no distinction between parent and child. In the winter they lodge
in caves and in the summer dwell in huts. They wear skins and drink blood.
Brothers are suspicious of each other. Their ascending the hills is like the flight of
birds, and their walking though the herbage is like the running of quadrupeds. If
they receive a favour they forget it, but if they suffer an injury are certain to
requite it. For this reason they conceal arrows in their hair and swords underneath
their clothes. Sometimes they assemble in bands and harry the frontier, or spy the
peasants at their work and carry them off. If attacked, they hide in the herbage;
and if pursued, enter the hills. For this reason, from ancient times till now they
have not been affected by the monarch's teachings." [It would appear from this that
these Yemishi, the modern Yezo or Ainos, were only one tribe out of many, but in
nearly all passages of the ancient chronicles, where savages are mentioned, the
term Yemishi is used. This name is said to have been given to them on account
of the resemblance in appearance between their hairy faces and the prawn's head.]
The Mikado then proceeds to extol the qualities which seem specially to fit his
son for the undertaking, and he sets forth with two companions and a cook
called Seven-span-shin (Nana-tsuka-hagi). On his way he calls upon his aunt in
Ise, and upon his saying that he is going to fight the savages, she gives him the
sword, bidding him to be diligent in the performance of his duty. When he reaches
the province of Suruga, the local rebels pretend to submit, and tell him a story
about a prairie full of deer, who are so numerous that their breath resembles a mist,
and their legs a plantation of young trees. He falls into the trap, and goes off to
hunt the deer on the prairie, whereupon the rebels set fire to the herbage with the
intention of destroying him. He pulls out a flint and steel, kindles a counter fire,
and so escapes. Another account is that the sword, Murakumo, which he wore, of
itself left the scabbard and cut down the herbage all round, thus enabling him to
escape, whence it was re-named Kusa-nagi, Herbqueller.—(*Ni-hoñ-gi.*)

On returning victorious from his expedition, the prince turned aside to the
dwelling of Miyasu-hime in Wohari, and married her. After a month's stay, he
departed, leaving the sword with her as a pledge that he would send for her as soon

as he reached his home at the capital, telling her to keep it as a precious treasure, but met with his death when engaged in an adventure with the god of Ibuki yama and she never saw him again. Miyasu-hime fulfilled his injunctions, and laid the sword in the couch which the prince had occupied, but the weapon soon manifested its divine character by working miracles in favour of those who prayed to it, and she finally resolved to build a temple for its safe keeping. To this 'the name of Atsuta "Hot-field," was given, from the circumstance of a tree which stood there having burst into flame, and so fallen prone into the swampy soil of a rice-field, where it continued to burn and so heated the ground.—(*Ni-hoñ-gi*).

This concludes the supernatural part of the history of the regalia.

⁵ The reader of the *Norito* thus makes the gods refer to the throne in the Hall of Audience.

⁶ *Hi-tsugi*, written 日嗣 , by following closely the meaning of the Chinese characters, may be interpreted either 'sun's succession' or 'sun's successor,' in the latter of which senses it is usually understood by modern writers. In that case the phrase *Ama-tsu hi-tsugi* is in apposition to *Oho-ya-shima Toyo-ashi-hara no midzu-ho no Kuni*. It has been, however, suggested that disregarding the strict meaning of the Chinese characters, *hi-tsugi* may be taken as if it were written 日 次 , 'succession of days,' i.e., continuation of existence, governed by *yorodzu chi aki naga aki ni* (where in modern Japanese we should have *ni shite* instead of simply *ni*), 'making the celestial continuation of days a myriad thousand autumns of long autumns,' i.e., live forever. Another way of writing this word is 日繼 , as in Ko-zhi-ki Deñ, vol. 14, f. 36. Motowori here proposes to explain *tsugi* by 給 'to give,' and to interpret *Ama-tsu hi-tsugi shiroshimesamu* as equivalent to *Oho mi kami no tsugi-yosashi-tamafu ine wo mochite kashiku mi ke wo shiroshimesamu*, literally, 'shall enjoy the food prepared from the rice-plant bestowed upon him by the great goddess,' or more shortly, 'enjoy the gift of heaven's sun.' But against such a theory there is the fact that *ama-tsu hi-tsugi* is the traditional reading of such Chinese expressions as 天業 , and 膺極.

⁷ *Oho ya shima Toyo ashi-hara no midzu-ho no kuni*. The first part of this honorific and descriptive title of the Japanese realm, Oho ya shima, is explained in a note on p. 61, above. *Toyo* is an honorific which may be variously rendered by 'flourishing,' 'luxuriant,' 'abundant,' 'powerful,' according to the context *Ashi* is perhaps Phragmites Roxburghii, and *hara*, rendered 'prairie' or 'moor,' means any wild uncultivated ground. When the name of a plant or tree is prefixed to it, it then means a tract of ground chiefly covered with that species, as for instance *matsu-bara*, a pine wood. *Ashi-hara* is therefore ground covered with the reed known as *ashi* (also called *yoshi*). Japan is sometimes called *Ashi-harano naka-tsu kuni*, the country in the middle of reed-covered wilds, which perhaps may have been a good description of the country as it appeared to the eyes of its first settlers when unreclaimed swamps covered the flat ground now cultivated as rice-fields. Some writers suggest that *naka-tsu kuni* should be understood as meaning 'Central region,' and that it was adopted in imitation of the Chinese 中國, central region or "Middle Kingdom." In the compound here used it must not be supposed that *Toyo* refers to the luxuriance of the reeds but it is rather to be taken as an epithet of the country. *Midzu* is found in the modern colloquial in the word *midzu midzu-shii*, applied to anything that is both young, fresh-looking and beautiful, the essence of the idea conveyed by it being youthful freshnesss. It would not be applied to anything old, however beautiful the thing might be. *Ho* is the ear of the rice-plant, and the most general signification that can be given to it is 'spike.' Hence we get as the equivalent of the whole, 'Great Many islands, the luxuriant reed-plain region of fresh-young spikes.'

⁸ This means the deliberations amongst the gods, assembled in Council by the Sun-goddess and Taka-mi-musubi no Mikoto, to consider what measures should be adopted for the conquest of Japan, which was then inhabited by the descendants of Susa-no-wo no Mikoto. In Note 4 the myth of his settlement in Idzumo has

already been related, and also his marriage with Kushi-inada-hime, who is probably a personification of agriculture. The seventh in descent from the pair, counting both extremes, was Oho-kuni-nushi, also called Oho-na-muji. "He had a large number of brothers, but all left the country to him, the reason of which was as follows: All of them wanted to marry Yakami hime of Inaba, and going to Inaba in company, they took him with them as a servant to carry their bag. When they came to Cape Keta (in Inaba) they found a perfectly bald hare lying on the ground, and addressed it, saying: 'You are to bathe in the brine, and lie upon the spur of a high mountain breasting the breeze,' and the hare did as they bid him. As the brine dried upon him, the skin was split all over his body by the wind, and he lay there weeping with pain. Oho-na-muji, who came by last of all, seeing the hare in this plight, asked him why he lay there weeping. The hare replied: 'I was in the Island of the Offing and wished to cross over to this land, but having no means of doing so, cheated the sea sharks (*wani*), saying: I should like to enter into a rivalry with you as to which of us has the largest tribe. If you will bring all your tribe with you, and let them lie in a row from this island to Cape Keta, I will tread on them, and count them as I run across, thus learning which of our tribes is the largest. When I said .this to them, they were deceived, and lay down in a row, and I treading on them, counted them as I came across. Just as I was about to land, I said: You have been cheated by me, and as soon as I had finished speaking, the very last of the sharks seized me and stripped off my clothing. As I was lamenting and weeping thereat, the many gods who preceded thee commanded me to bathe in the brine, and to lie exposed to the wind. And when I did as they had told me, the whole of my body was hurt.' Thereupon Oho-na-muji no Kami bade the hare go quickly to the mouth of the river, and after washing his body with the fresh water, to collect the pollen of the sedges which grew in the stream, and spreading it on the ground, to roll upon it, so that his body would be restored. And [the hare] having done as he was bid, his body became as before. This was the 'White hare of Inaba,' and even now they call it the 'Hare god.' The hare then said to Oho-na-muji: "These many gods shall certainly not get Yakami hime, but thou shalt, though thou bearest the bag."

The scene then changes to the abode of the damsel, who rejects the suit of the brothers, and declares her preference for Oho-na-muji. The disappointed suitors determined to take the life of their fortunate rival, which they did by rolling a huge red-hot stone down hill to Oho-na-muji, who supposed it to be the wild boar for which they had told him to be on the look-out. The ruse succeeded, and he was burnt to death. His mother appealed to the celestial gods, who sent down Kisa-gahi hime and Umugi hime (the shells called *aka-gahi* and *hama-guri*). The first calcined her shell, while the second brought water in hers, and they made a paste with which they besmeared the burnt corpse. By this process he was restored to life again, and made much more beautiful than before. Next his brothers beguiled him into the forest, where they made him pass through the split trunk of a tree, in which they had inserted a wedge, but as soon as he was in the middle of the tree they suddenly withdrew the wedge, so that he was caught as in a trap. His mother rescued him, and to save him from their machinations, sent him to the care of Ohoyabiko, who lived in the province of Kii, and was probably related to the ruling family of Idzumo. After that he visits Susa-no-wo in the infernal regions, and after many adventures there, finally returns with a famous sword, bow and arrows, which have the power of conferring long life on their possessor. With their aid he slays his brothers, and becomes ruler of the whole country. While in the infernal regions he had married Suseri-hime, the daughter of Susa-no-wo, and now he takes as a second wife his previous love Yakami hime, who is afraid of the legitimate spouse, and takes to flight, leaving the child she had borne to him in the fork of a tree. By other women he begot a large number of children, amongst whom the most famous are Aji-shiki-taka-hiko-ne (the god of Kamo ni Yamato), Shitateru hime and Koto-shiro-nushi, and in conjunction with Sukuna-hikona he brings the country under cultivation.

Suddenly the Sun-goddess resolves to make a grant of the Luxuriant Reed-plain region of Fresh-young Spikes to her adopted child Masaka-a-katsu-kachi-haya-bi-ame-no-oshi-ho-mimi no Mikoto, and despatches him on the journey downwards. Taking his stand on the Floating Bridge of Heaven (which formed the means of communication between heaven and earth in those days) he observed that the earth was violently disturbed, and straightway returned to heaven. Upon this Take-mi-musubi no kami and Ama-terasu-oho-mi-kami "assembled all the many hundreds of myriads of gods by the bed of the Peaceful River of heaven, and spoke thus to Omohi-gane no kami: 'This region in the midst of the reed plains has been granted by us to our child to rule over. We see that the country contains countless gods of great energy who behave turbulently, and ask you what god shall we send down to subdue them.' Then Omohi-gane no kami and all the many myriads of gods took counsel, and advised that Ame-no-hohi no kami should be sent. So Ame-no-hiko no kami was sent, but he sought to curry favour with Oho-kuni-nushi, and three years passed without his returning to make a report."—(Ko-zhi-ki). In the Nihon-gi, the god with the long name, which is usually shortened to Ama-no-oshi-ho-mimi, marries a daughter of Taka-mi-musubi, and begets Ninigi no Mikoto. Taka-mi-musubi was very fond of his grandson, and resolved to make him prince of Ashi-hara no Naka-tsu kuni. "But in that region were gods who glittered like the fire-fly's light, and bad gods who buzzed like bees, besides whom there were plants and trees which could speak. Taka-mi-musubi no Kami therefore assembled the gods (八 諸神), and said to them: 'I want to subdue the gods of Ashi-hara no Naka-tsu kuni. Whom would it be best to send? Let none of you conceal his opinion.' All replied: 'Send Ama-no hobi no Mikoto, for he is a valiant god, and it would be well to try him.' So Taka-mi-musubi no Mikoto deferred to their advice, and sent down Ama-no-hohi no Mikoto to conquer the country. This god, however, flattered and cajoled Oho-na-muji no kami, and three years passed without his making any report."

The Ko-zhi-ki says that under these circumstances Taka-mi-musubi no kami and Ama-terasu-oho-mi-kami again asked the gods whom they should send, seeing that the former messenger had not returned. Omohi-gane no kami suggested the name of Ame-waka hiko who was accepted. Armed with a deer-bow and winged arrows, the gift of the gods, he descended on to the earth, where he married Shita-teru hiru hime, one of Oho-kuni-nushi's children, hoping to inherit the kingdom, and eight years passed without anything being heard from him. A council of the gods was again held to determine who should be sent to inquire the reason of the delay, and the result was the despatch of a pheasant, whom the Supreme Pair commanded to go and ask Ame-waka hiko for an explanation. "So the pheasant descending to the earth, perched upon the umbrageous katsura outside the gate of Ame-waka-hiko's house, and repeated to him what the heavenly gods had bid him say. Thereupon Ame no Sagume (an evil spirit) and to him: 'The voice of that bird is very ugly; shoot it.' So he took the bow and arrow given to him by the heavenly gods, and shot the pheasant, and the arrow passing through its bosom, flew back to heaven and came where Ama-terasu Oho-mi-kami and Takagi no kami were sitting in the bed of the Peaceful River. Takagi no kami is another name for Taka-mi-musubi. Taking up the arrow and looking at it, he saw blood on its feather, and said: 'This was the arrow given to Ame-waka hiko.' Then showing it to all the gods, he said: 'If this arrow came hither after Ame-waka hiko, faithful to the command laid upon him, had shot the wicked gods, let it not strike him, but if he has an evil heart, let Ame-waka hiko die.' With these words he took the arrow, and thrusting it downwards through the hole by which it had entered, sent it back. It struck Ame-waka hiko on the top of his breast, as he was sleeping on his couch, and killed him.

"Then Ama-terasu Oho-mi-kami said: 'What god shall we now send?' Whereupon Omohi-gane no kami and the other gods said: 'Send Itsu no Wo-habari no kami, who dwells in the heavenly rock-built house near the source of the Peaceful River of Heaven. Or if not then send Take-mika-dzuchi-no-wo no kami, the son of that god. But as Ame-no-Wohabari no kami has turned aside the waters of that river and blocked up the road, no other god can get to him. Send, therefore, Ame-no-kaku no kami.' So she sent Ame-no-kaku no kami to ask Ame-no-Wohabari no Kami, who said: 'I obey. But you should send my son Take-mika-dzuchi no kami,' and he gave [his son]. So Ama-terasu Oho-mi-kami attached Ame-no-tori-fune no kami to Take-mika-dzuchi no kami, and despatched them down to the earth."

The two gods descended to the province of Idzumo, and obtained the submission of Koto-shiro-nushi, and the original proceeds to say: "So they asked Oho-kuni-nushi: 'Your son Koto shiro-nushi no kami has thus spoken; have you any other son who wishes to speak?' He replied: 'There is my is my son Take-mi-na-gata, but none other,' and as he thus spoke, Take-mi-na-gata came up, bearing on the tips of his fingers a rock such as a thousand ordinary men would be required to move, and saying: 'Who is it that thus comes to our country and secretly talks? Come, I will have a trial of strength with you. To begin with, let me take your hand.' So Take-mika-dzuchi no kami let him take it, whereupon it changed into an erect icicle, and then into the edge of a sword, which frightened him so that he drew back. After that Take-mika-dzuchi asked permission to take Take-mi-na-gata's hand, which he grasped and crushed like a young reed, and flung roughly from him. Take-mi-na-gata fled, and the other pursuing him to the lake of Suwa, in the province, Shinano, was about to kill him, when Take-mi-na-gata said to the god: 'I submit. Do not kill me. I will never leave this spot, rebel against the commands of my father Oho-kuni-nushi no kami, nor violate the promise given by Yahe-koto-shiro-nushi no kami, but will surrender this land in accordance with the commands of the CHILD of the heavenly gods.'

"So they returned, and asked Oho-kuni-nushi no kami, saying: 'Your son Koto-shiro-nushi no kami and Take-mi-na-gata no kami have declared that they will not violate the commands of the CHILD of the heavenly gods. What are your feelings?' He replied, saying: 'Just as my two sons have said, I too will not violate them. In accordance with the (heavenly) command, I will give up this reed-plain central region. But as to my place of residence, if you will make stout the HOUSE pillars on the bottom-most rocks, and make high the cross-beams to the plain of high heaven, like the rich and sufficing NEST where the CHILD of the heavenly gods enjoys the succession of heaven's sun, and will order matters well, I will hide in the many road-windings (i.e., the abode of the dead) and serve him. And if my children, the numberless gods, serve under the guidance of Yahe-koto-shiro-nushi no kami, there will be no disobedient gods.' And having said this he disappeared."—(Ko-zhi-ki.)

In the Nihoñ-gi version, Take-mika-dzuchi is accompanied by Futsu-nushi instead of Ame-no-tori-fune. They learn from Oho-kuni-nushi (who in this chronicle is called Oho-na-muji) that it is necessary to obtain the consent of his son Koto-shiro-nushi, and despatch a messenger to the latter, who at once gives in his submission and disappears. Upon the messenger's return with this information, Oho-na-muji announces his own determination to depart, in order to prevent the gods of the country from offering resistance, and having delivered to them the spear with which he had originally acquired his donations, he disappears.

"So they built a heavenly residence at Tagishi no Obama, in the province of Idzumo, and Kushi-ya-tama no kami, the grandson of Minate no kami, was appointed cook, and offered up heavenly cookery. Then, after prayers had been offered, Kushi-ya-tama no kami ('god of miraculous and numerous offerings') changed into a cormorant, and entering the bottom of the sea, took clay from the bottom in its mouth and made many heavenly dishes, and cutting a seaweed stalk made a fire-mortar, and made a pestle out of Komo (a kind of seaweed), and drilling out fire therewith said: 'The fire which I have drilled will I burn until the soot of the rich and sufficing heavenly new nest of the PARENT Kami-musubi in heaven hangs down many hand-breadths long, and the earth below will I bake down to its bottom-most rocks, and stretching a thousand fathoms of paper-mulberry rope, will draw together and bring ashore the fisherman's large-mouthed small-finned suzuki, [and] will offer up the heavenly fish-food on bending split bamboos.'

"Then Take-mika-dzuchi went back up (to heaven), and reported how he had subdued and pacified the reed-plain central region."—(*Ko-zhi-ki.*) Everything was therefore ready for the descent of Ninigi no Mikoto.

[9] Hirata reads *ihahi* ('felicitate,' apparently on the ground that it is the reading of 護 no f. 23, col. 5. prescribed in the note of the original transcriber. It has no justification here.

[10] For *chidari* and *tobu tori* consult Ko-zhi-ki Deñ, XIV., f. 39, and Oho-barahi Go-shiyaku, I, ff, 59 and 60.

[11] *Kikahi.* Mabuchi supposes this to be a corruption of *yuki-ahi*, meetings.

[12] Lit., dug, i.e., the holes for the pillars.

In the Japanese text the following gloss is here inserted: "This is the Spirit of Wood," and after the name of the second deity here addressed, is another: "This is the Spirit of the Rice-plant, commonly called Uga no Mi-tama. Just as, at the present day, in the hut of a woman in child-birth, pieces of split wood and bundles of the rice-plant are placed near the door, and then rice is scattered about the interior of the hut." These glosses are perhaps as old as the beginning of the 10th century, when the present collection of *norito* was made, or may be even earlier. The reference to the practice of removing a parturient woman to a hut built for the purpose, where the worship of the spirits of timber and the rice-plant was performed, and rice scattered about as a charm against evil spirits, shows that the ceremony was at one time observed universally upon the erection of a new house, no matter what the station in life of its owner, and not exclusively at the inauguration of a palace belonging to the sovereign. *Yabune* has already been explained. *Kukuchi* is the old reading, for which Mabuchi, and others following him, have substituted *kukunochi*, without any good reason, as far as I can see. *Kukuchi* is probably the same word as *hukide*, 'to sprout forth.' Toyo-uke-bime is the Goddess of Food, to whom Ritual No. 3 is addressed. It has been suggested that this deity is primarily the Earth-goddess, *uke*, and *uke-mochi* in one of her other names, being taken in the sense of 'supporter.' If this be so, her worship here as the supporter of the foundation of the palace would be perfectly logical.

[14] In the Ko-zhi-ki's account of Izanagi's lustration by bathing in the sea, after his return from visiting his dead spouse Izanami in the nether world, we read that "the name of the first god who was produced when he dived into the central current was Yaso-maga-tsu-bi no kami and next Oho-maga-tsu-bi no kami. These two gods were generated from the pollution contracted by him when he went to the dirty and ugly region (i.e., of the dead). And the names of the gods who were next generated to correct the evil were Kamu-naho-bi no kami and next Oho-naho-bi no kami, and next Idzu-no-me no kami." *Naho* is 'straight' (*Latin*, *rectus*) and *nahosu*, *nahoru* are the transitive verb and intransitive verb 'to straighten,' 'to correct.' *Bi* is evidently the same as in *maga-tsu-bi*, and perhaps in *musu-bi*, which forms part of the names of the Creators. (According to the Yamato-hime Sei-ki, Kamu-naho-bi and Oho-naho-bi are two names of one god, Ibukido-nushi, who is the 'Rough Spirit' of Toyo-uke-bime.) These were the gods to whom was assigned the task of counteracting all the evil of whatever kind, whether moral, physical, ceremonial or natural, that might arise in the world.

[15] These are general expressions for female and male attendants. The *hire* rendered 'scarf,' was worn by the women, called *uneme*, who waited on the Mikado, the *tasuki* was a cord or sash passed over the shoulders, round the back of the neck, and attached to the wrists, to strengthen the hands for the support of weights, whence the name, which means 'hand-helper.' It was thus different both in form and use from the modern *tasuki*, a cord with its two ends joined which is worn behind the neck, under the arms and round the back, to keep the modern loose sleeves out of the way when household duties are being performed.

No. 9.—MIKADO MATSURI OR SERVICE OF THE GATES OF THE PALACE.

This service was held twice annually, but nothing is known of the ceremonies by which it was accompanied, beyond the fact that certain Virgin Priestesses of the Gates officiated in chief. Some remarks upon the names of the two gods Kushi-iha-ma-do no Mikoto and Toyo-iha-ma-do no Mikoto, will be found in Note 31 to the "Praying for Harvest," to which nothing need be added here. Motowori suggests that some such introductory sentence as "He declares in the presence of the sovran gods of GATES" has been omitted by a copyist's error from the MS. of the Yeñ-gi Shiki, which seems very probable.

RITUAL.

[TRANSLATION.]

He says, with reference to declaring the NAMES Wonderful-rock-Gate's *Augustness* and Powerful-rock-Gate's Augustness, *I* fulfil the praises of the NAMES Powerful-rock-Gate's Augustness and Wonderful-rock-Gate's Augustness, because *you* deign to obstruct like innumerable piles of rock in the inner and outer GATES of the four quarters, prevent *the servants of His Majesty* from being poisoned and seduced by the wickedness which may be uttered by the god called Ame no Magatsuhi, who may come unfriendly and turbulent from the four quarters and the four corners, and *because you* guard when they come[1] from the top, and guard the bottom when they come from the bottom, and waiting repel, sweep and send *them* away, and refute *them:* in the morning open the gates, inquire and learn the names of the persons who come in and of those that go out, see and correct, hear and correct with divine-correcting and great-correcting[2] the faults and errors that may be committed *by them*, and cause *them* to serve peacefully and tranquilly.

NOTES

[1] More literally 'go' (*yukaba*). From this it appears that the service was held at a temple situated just outside the Palace gates.

[2] I.e., in the same way as the gods called Divine-corrector and Great-corrector.

ANCIENT JAPANESE RITUALS.—PART IV.*

By Dr. Karl Florenz.

In volumes VII and IX of the Transactions of the Asiatic Society of Japan *Sir Ernest Satow* has published an English translation, with commentary, of the Norito, or Ancient Japanese Rituals. His three papers on this subject constitute one of the monumental works of Japanese philology. Unfortunately the learned author has not seen his way to give us more than the smaller moiety of the Rituals (nine out of twenty eight) which is the more regrettable as no abler hand could have undertaken the task. It is difficult for anybody, and rather bold, to continue a work begun by a Satow, for the inferiority of the continuation will be only too palpable. As the Norito belong, however, to the most important, interesting and beautiful products of Japanese literature, a reliable translation of all of them is an urgent necessity, and the present writer has therefore ventured to come forward and supply the omission. His original intention was to publish the result of his studies in German, his native tongue; having now undertaken to produce it in English, he believes himself entitled to a certain degree of indulgence on the part of the reader, because he labours under no small disadvantage in doing a work of this kind in a foreign language. The writer has endeavoured to use as much as possible Satow's phraseology, in order to preserve in the English rendering the same uniformity of style which exists in the Japanese text. For quotations from the Kojiki and Nihongi the admirable translations by *Chamberlain* and *Aston* have been placed under frequent contribution, though the present writer has in all cases consulted the originals themselves, and, with regard to the Nihongi, also his own German translation and commentary. For students of the original text a full glossary will be added.

*Reprinted from the Transactions of the Asiatic Society of Japan, First Series, Vol. XXVII, Pt. I, pp. 1-112.

No. 10.—*Minadzuki Tsugomori no Oho-harahe*, OR
GREAT PURIFICATION CELEBRATED ON THE
LAST DAY OF THE SIXTH MONTH
(AND ALSO IN THE *Shihasu* OR
TWELFTH MONTH.)

LITERATURE USED: Besides the older commentaries of Mabuchi, Motowori Norinaga and Fujiwi, mentioned by Satow, vol. VII pag. 101, I have made use of *the Noritoshiki-kōgi* (祝 詞 式 講 義) by Haruyama Tanomu, the *Norito-bemmō* (祝 詞 辨 蒙) by Shikida Toshiharu (5 vols.) the *Norito-shiki-kōgi* by Ōkubo (2 vols), the *Norito-ryakkai* (祝詞略解) by Kudo (6 vols), and notes of lectures delivered by Motowori Toyokahi in the Imperial University of Tōkyō. The big commentary *Noritokōgi* written by the late Suzuki Shigetane in 34 vols. is unfortunately, like his huge commentary on the Nihongi, not yet accessible to the general public. The Government would render an invaluable service to all students of Japanese archaeology by printing these two works of one of the greatest scholars Japan ever possessed. I have also had the advantage of consulting a very interesting paper on the Oho-harahe by *Dr. H. Weipert* (Trans. of the German As. Soc., Heft 58, page 365-375), in which special attention has been paid to the ritual as being a monument of the most ancient judicial ideas of the Japanese, and the learned essay "The Mythology and Religious Worship of the Ancient Japanese" by Satow, published in the Westminster Review, July 1898, p. 27-57. Unfortunately this latter paper became known to me, through the kindness of its author, only after the present essay was finished, so that the valuable information given by it could only be made use of in the form of additional notes.

INTRODUCTION.

§ 1. DEFINITION.

The *Oho-harahe* or Great Purification is one of the most important and most solemn ceremonies of the Shintō religion; by it the population of the whole country, from the Princes and Ministers down to the common people, is purified and freed from sins, pollutions and calamities. In the earliest times, i. e. until the beginning of the 8th century A. D., the service seems not to have been celebrated at fixed regular intervals, but only when special reasons offered (see § 3) ; since then it has been celebrated twice a year, on the 30th day of the 6th and 12th months. The chief ceremony was performed in the capital, near the South Gate or *Shūjaku-mon* (Gate of the Scarlet Bird) of the Imperial palace, and might be styled the purification of the court, because it was to purify all the higher and lower officials of the Imperial court. In a similar way the ceremony was celebrated also, at all the more important (public) shrines of the whole country, and therefore the Shintoists speak of an Oho-harahe of the provinces, in contradistinction to the Oho-harahe of the court. Beside the regular celebration on the 30th day of the 6th and 12th months we find, however, the ceremony not infrequently performed at other times, e. g. on the occasion of the *Dai-jō-we* (festival after the ascension to the throne of a new Emperor), or when the *Itsuki hime-miko* (an Imperial princes, chosen as Vestal) was sent to the temple of the Sun-goddess in Ise.

There are four ways of spelling and pronouncing the name 大祓 , viz. *Oho-harahe, Oho-harahi, Oho-barahe, Oho-barahi.* The first deserves to be preferred. It is derived from *oho* "great" (stem of the adjective *ohoki*) and the verb *harafu* "to clear away," "to sweep." *Mi-na-dzuki* (水無月   water-less month) is an old name of the 6th month O. S. (approximately our July), *shihasu* of the 12th month O. S.; *Tsugomori* means "last day" of a month. The 6th month is often called *nagoshi-no-tsuki* "month of leave-taking from summer" (the summer comprised the 4th, 5th and 6th months), and so we find for the summer purification also the popular name *nagoshi no harahe* 夏越ノ祓 .

The regular celebrations in the 6th and 12th months are designated as *Kōrei Oho-harahe* (恒例大祓) usual or regular O. H., the extraordinary ones as *Rinji Oho-harahe* (臨時大祓) occasional O. H. When a year had an intercalary 6th or 12th month, the last day of the intercalary month was chosen. Since the introduction of the Gregorian calendar (1st January, 1873), the regular ceremony has taken place on the 30th of June and 31st of December.

The Oho-harahe consists of certain ceremonial actions, chiefly the offering and throwing away into the water of the so-called *harahe-tsu mono* (祓物) "purification-offerings (lit things)," and the reading of a Ritual.

§ 2. OHO HARAHE, HARAHE, MISOGI.

The *Oho-harahe* must be distinguished.

A) from the simple *Harahe*, i. e. the purification of an *individual person from the pollution contracted by some offence,* in which case the guilty person himself had to provide certain offerings to the Gods. This was originally a mere religions ceremony, the offerings provided by the offender being, in the beginning, probably only such things of his personal property, as were considered to have been polluted. They were thrown away into the water. But out of this developed, in the course of time, the idea of a penalty. Now it is highly interesting to observe, for what reasons, in what way, and to what extent penalties were exacted from offenders. The archaic Japanese society possessed neither law-codes, nor clear descriptive rights at all, so that the punishment of offences was left entirely to the discretion of the injured individual or community. The Kojiki and Nihongi report numerous instances, in which an Emperor, or a chieftain, or some other individual metes out punishment to an offender, the punishment varying usually between the penalty of death, making the criminal a slave, banishment, and wholesale or partial confiscation of property. The punishment of transgressions being thus, until about the end of the 7th century, purely arbitrary, it is no wonder that frequent abuses occurred, and that there arose a regular system of squeezing under the hypocritic disguise of a legitimate *Harahe* (purgation). The Emperor Kōtoku, the great admirer of Chinese institutions, is reported by the Nihongi to have issued, on the 22nd day of the third month of the second year of his reign (12th April, 646), a decree in order to abolish existing bad customs, from which I extract the following interesting paragraphs:

Sometimes a wife who has lost her husband, marries another man after the lapse of ten or twenty years and becomes his spouse, or an unmarried girl is married for the first time. Upon this, people, out of envy of the married pair, have made them perform *purgation*.

Again, there have been cases of men employed on forced labour in border lands who, when the work was over and they were returning to their village, have fallen suddenly ill and lain down to die by the roadside. Upon this the [inmates of the] houses by the roadside say:—'Why should people be allowed to die on our road?' And they have accordingly detained the companions of the deceased and compelled them to do *purgation* [i. e. their valuables were taken away from them under the pretext that these had to serve as purification-offerings in the ceremony necessary to purify the road from the pollution]. For this reason it often happens that even if an elder brother lies down and dies on the road, his younger brother will refuse to take up his body [for burial].

Again, there are cases of peasants being drowned in a river. The bystanders say:—'Why should we be made to have anything to do with drowned men?' They accordingly detain the drowned man's companions and compel them to do *purgation*. For this reason it often happens that even when an elder brother is drowned in a river, his younger brother will not render assistance.

Again, there are cases of people who, when employed on forced labour, cook their rice by the roadside. Upon this the [inmates of the] house by the roadside say:—'Why should people cook rice at their own pleasure on our road?' and have compelled them to do *purgation*.

Again, there are cases when people have applied to others for the loan of pots in which to boil their rice, and the pots have knocked against something and have been upset. Upon this the owner of the pot compels *purgation* to be made.

All such practices are habitual among the unenlightened vulgar. Let them now be discontinued without exception, and not permitted again.

It goes without saying that this primitive kind of judicial procedure did not long survive the introduction of the Chinese system of administration, at least to no great extent. Also in a purely religious sense the *Harahe* of single individuals from pollutions contracted through crimes seems to have disappeared.

B) A second kind of *Harahe,* generally called *Misogi* (禊)
"ablution," practised in ancient times, has been preserved to
the present day, viz. the purification of a single individual or a
place *from pollutions through coming into contact with something
ceremonially impure,* like dead bodies, etc. Comp. notes 37 and
35 to the translation of the ritual.

C) As a third species of *Harahe* we may mention the purification preceding every greater festival (*matsuri*) of a Shintō
shrine, through which the *priests and others taking part in the
Matsuri are purified.*   This ceremony takes place in a hall or
open place specially prepared for the purpose, called *harae-dokoro*
"purification-place."   It consists in the *Kami-oroshi* "bringing
down the spirits of the purifying deities" (see note 74, 76, 79
and 81) into the *himorogi* (a Sakaki branch with cut paper
hangings) which stands on an eight-legged table in the middle
of the Harahe-dokoro, the recitation of the purification-prayer,
various subsequent symbolic ceremonies, and the *Kami-age* or
"sending back the gods" (to their abodes).   Thereupon the
priests are considered to be pure, and the Matsuri proper can
begin.   A detailed description of this ceremony I shall give on
another occasion.   Only the wording of the prayer addressed to
the gods may be mentioned here:

"In reverence and awe:

"The great gods of the purification place who came into
existence when the great god Izanagi deigned to wash and purify
himself on the plain of Ahagi [east] of Tachibana [near] the
river Wotō in Himuka in Tsukushi, shall deign to purify and
deign to cleanse whatever there may be of sins and pollutions
committed inadvertently or deliberately by the officials serving
[here] to-day.   Listen ye to these my words.   Thus I say
reverentially."

D) Fujiwi mentions in his *Gogoshaku* a sort of *private
Harahe* which, like the Oho-harahe, was performed on the last
day of the sixth month.   People fastened *yufu-shide,* strips of
mulberry-tree fibres, to hemp leaves, and taking these to the
bank of a river performed the purification.

These statements about *Harahe* and *Misogi* do not at all
exhaust the subject, but will perhaps convey a sufficiently clear
idea of it.

§ 3. AGE OF THE CEREMONY.

The earliest historic reference to the ceremony of general purification we find made on the occasion of the death of the Emperor Chiūai, said to have taken place in the year 200 A. D. This date is, of course, entirely untrustworthy, like all the dates before the fifth century; but this much at least can be inferred from it, that the existence of the ceremony is ascribed to a very early time. The Emperor had died a sudden death which was attributed to the curse of some offended god, and the Empress Jingō therefore "commanded her Ministers and functionaries to *purge offences* (i. e. celebrate the Oho-harahe) and to rectify transgressions, eac." (NIHONGI). The corresponding passage of the KOJIKI enumerates a great number of the crimes with which we shall become acquainted in the text of our ritual. It says: "Then, astonished and alarmed, they set [the dead Emperor] in a mortuary place, and again taking the great offerings of the provinces, seeking out all sorts of crimes, such as flaying alive and flaying backwards, breaking down the divisions of rice-fields, filling up ditches, etc., etc., evacuating excrements and urine, marriages with cattle, marriages with fowls, and marriages with dogs, and having made a *Great Purification of the land,* the Noble Take-uchi again stood in the pure court and requested the Deities' commands." (Chamb. page 230). Then there is complete silence for a long time, until the reign of Emperor Temmu in the second half of the seventh century. On the 16th day, 8th month, 5th year of this Emperor (i. e. 28th September, 676) an Imperial edict commanded (this and the following quotations are from the NIHONGI):

"Let a Great Purification be held in all quarters! As for the articles needed for this purpose, there are to be forwarded as *harahe-tsu-mono** (purification offerings) by the Kuni no Miyatsuko (Country-Rulers) of each province: one horse and one piece *(Kida=13* feet) of cloth; moreover, by each district governor: one sword, one deerskin, one mattock, one smaller sword, one sickle, one set (i. e. ten pieces) of arrows, and one

---

*Aston's version "to be forwarded to the shrines of purification" is based on the text of the Nihongi-shūge; the editor of this text has, however, arbitrarily changed one Chinese character (祓柱 into 祓社), and I have gone back to the original reading.

sheaf of rice in the ear; moreover, by each house: one bundle of hemp.

This Great Purification was obviously celebrated in order to avoid the evil influence of a comet that had appeared in the seventh month, seven or eight feet in length, and disappeared from the sky in ninth month.

The third reference is made in the spring of the seventh year of Temmu (678): "This spring, as the preparation for worshipping the Gods of Heaven and Earth, a *Purification* was held *throughout the Empire.* An *imi-no-miya* (Purification-palace or Abstinence Palace, for the Emperor) was erected on the bank of the Kurahashi river (in the Tōchi district of Yamato).

The fourth reference, on the 30th day, 7th month, 10th year (19th August, 681) runs: "Orders were given to the whole Empire to hold a great *Purification ceremony.* At this time each Kuni no Miyatsuko supplied as purification-offering one slave, and thus the purification was done."

The fifth, on the 3rd day, 7th month, 1st year Shuchō (28th July, 686): "The Emperor commanded all the provinces to perform the ceremony of the *Great Purification.*" The reason for the celebration of the last mentioned ceremonies (fourth and fifth) is not apparent from the context. The last book of the Nihongi, treating of the reign of the Empress Jitō, Temmu's successor, has not a single reference to the ceremony. It is next mentioned again in the 11th month of the 2nd year of the Emperor Mommu (698), as an occasional performance. With the first year of the period Taihō, 701, we come at length to the time when the Great Purification was ordered to be performed at regular intervals, viz. twice a year, on the last day of the sixth and twelfth months. After this date the regular ceremony on the fixed days is no more specially mentioned by the annals, being considered as a matter of course, whilst its performance on other extraordinary occasions is frequently referred to. Under the influence of the increasing power of Buddhism and Chinese philosophy during the middle ages and the Tokugawa period, the Shintō religion, as a whole, lost much of its hold on the people, and naturally the general observation of its rites suffered in consequence. The Central Government certainly did nothing for their encouragement or preservation. But while a number of ancient Shintō customs fell thus into complete oblivion, the Oho-harahe has always been practised to a certain extent. The restoration of the Imperial power in the present Meiji era was shortly followed by a thorough, and almost extravagant, rehabilitation of Shintō in its so-called "pure" form, and the newly established Council for Spiritual Affairs (*Kyōbushō*) issued, first on the 25th June, 1871, and subsequently on the 18th June, 1872, decrees by which all public Shintō shrines of the country were directed to celebrate the Great Purification on the last day of each June and December as an official ceremony, in the presence of the local officials. The latter decree to which I shall refer again in § 6, gave also detailed instructions in regard to the ceremonial, and a new abridged version of the ritual. Another decree, dated the 3rd September of the same year, fixes the official contribution to the expenses for the Oho-harahe ceremony in each Kwankoku-Hei-sha (i. e. Shintō shrines whose fêtes are observed under the direct supervision of the Central Government, or under the supervision of the governor of the province respectively) as one yen fifty sen.

§4. AGE OF THE RITUAL.

The Ritual read at the ceremony of the Great Purification is usually called *Oho-harahe no Kotoba* "words of the Great Purification." It is also called *Nakatomi* (or *Misogi*) *no Kotoba* "purification words of Nakatomi" (see § 5) which is a very old name, occurring already in the KOGOSHUI (compiled 807 A. D.). Other designations are *Nakatomi-(harahe) no saimon* (祭 文 written Shintō prayer), or simply *Nakatomi-harahe*.

Mabuchi ascribes the Oho-harahe no Kotoba to the end of the reign of Emperor Tenji (662-671) or the reign of Emperor Temmu (673-686); the congratulatory address of the chieftains of Idzumo (Norito No. 28) to the reign of Emperor Jomei (629-641); the service for the removal and dismissal of avenging deities (No. 25) and the Luck-wishing of the Great Palace (No. 8) to the reign of the Empress Jitō (687-697); the Praying for Harvest (No. 1), the service of Hirose oho-imi (No. 3) and the service of the gods of wind (No. 4) to the beginning of the reign of the Emperor Kōnin (770-782). All the others are, according to the same authority, later and inferior, the latest being the worst. His grounds for assuming these dates do not, however, bear any deep critical investigation, and we must side with Motowori who rejects his hypothesis as untenable. To be quite sincere, we must confess that we have not sufficient means for determining the age of the Norito. Motowori remarks justly: In the most ancient times the Norito cannot have existed in a definite form, but must have been composed anew on each occasion, according to circumstances. But what was repeated every year at a fixed time, became by and by crystallized into a definite form. We cannot now make out when the Norito were first committed to writing, and at what time of the year they were originally used. Most of the old Norito have been handed down to us in their original wording, though, of course, some minor changes have been unavoidable. Something has probably been omitted, something probably been added, and interpolations from other texts may have crept in. The collection of the Norito, as we possess it embodied in the Engi-shiki (promulgated 927) was probably made in the Taihō period, or even a little earlier, during the reign of the Emperors Tenji or Temmu. Among the Norito there are some which were composed for festivals of later origin, or were put in the place of older lost rituals. Such rituals are inferior in style to the earlier ones, but have been composed in imitation of them, the old words and phrases being used. It is, therefore, not at all easy to determine the time of their composition; at least, not as easy as with the later Mono-gatari (novels) and Jobun (prefaces). In the present Oho-harahe ritual some passages seem to date from time immemorial (Motowori says fantastically from the time of the descent of the Heavenly Grandchild) while others seem to have been added in the periods of the Mikados, Tenji, Temmu and Jiō. It is useless and wrong to draw any inferences with regard to the age of the Oho-harahe ritual from the sporadic occurrence of several later expressions in its text.

§ 5. RECITATION OF THE RITUAL.

The ritual was recited at the public ceremony of the Oho-harahe as well as on the occasion of private purifications (*wata-*

kushi no harae). In consequence of its use for the latter purpose, frequent changes took place in the wording in order to adapt it to special circumstances, and this accounts for the existence of so many corrupted texts.

The Oho-harahe no Kotoba was recited only *once* at each ceremony of purification, and this is perfectly natural. But later on the influence of Buddhism began to tell upon it. It is a peculiar custom of the Buddhists to read their Sutras again and again, to indulge in an endless and really stultifying repetition of the same text (as the Roman Catholics do with the Ave Maria in the prayer of the rosary), and unfortunately the Shintōists also were, for a long time, influenced in the same direction and read the ritual several times in succession. Now they have returned to the original method of reading it only once.

Though the ritual is originally and properly only a part of the ceremony of purification, it not infrequently happens that it is recited without performing the ceremony.

The *reader* of the ritual was, in ancient times, always a member of the *Nakatomi* family, a family of priestly character (comp. note 51) which derives its origin from the god Ama no Koyane no Mikoto (meaning Heavenly-Beckoning-Ancestor-Lord according to Motowori; but the etymology is obscure. See Satow, above, p. 42). This god played a conspicuous part in the arrangements made for enticing the Sun-goddess out of the Heavenly Rock-cave into which she had retired in consequence of Susanowo's misconduct: he was made to *recite a grand liturgy.* Since that time he and his earthly descendants, the Nakatomi, are said to have filled the hereditary office of reciters of the Oho-harahe no Kotoba and other rituals. Towards the end of the ritual the *Urabe* or diviners are mentioned. Their function at the Oho-harahe ceremony was originally only to throw the purification-offerings away into the river; but in the middle-ages it became the practice for them to recite the ritual itself, in stead of the Nakatomi. At the present time, the office of the Nakatomi as reciters of the Norito is no longer in existence; the ritual is now read by a priest of the temple concerned.

§ 6. THE PRESENT OHO-HARAHE CEREMONY, ACCORDING TO THE DECREE OF THE 18TH JUNE, 1872.

On the last day of June and December, i. e. twice a year, the ceremony of the purification shall be performed in all public Shintō shrines (官 社 以 下　all shrines both those supported by the Government and those maintained by the people of a particular locality.)　The officials of the Fu and Ken as well as the common people shall then visit the shrine and partake in the purification.

In the court yard in front of the shrine, to the right and left, coarse matting is spread, and small round, or square mats (*Enza* or *ko-hanjō*) are laid down to serve as seats for the local officials and priests during the purification.　The officials sit on the left, the priests on the right hand side viewed from the temple.　In the middle between them stand tables (ta-katsuwe) on which are deposited the purification-offerings (harahe-tsumono), consisting of two feet of bleached cloth made of paper-mulberry bark (木 綿) and two feet of bleached linen (布). Before these, i.e. between the tables and the shrine, is the seat for the [reciter of the] purification ritual.

At 2 o'clock p.m. the local officials and priests occupy their seats.

Then the chief priest (*gūji*, or, if there is no *gūji*, the next highest priest) proceeds to the Main shrine (*shinden*), mounts up [the stairs] and opens the door.

Then he recites the following prayer, bowing twice:

"In reverence and awe: In the honorable front of the.... Shrine, I, the chief priest, of such and such a rank and such and such a name, say in awe, in awe:　As for the various sorts of sins that may have been committed either inadvertently or deliberately by the officials of this.....Fu (or Ken), and the divine officials (i.e. priests) serving the great god [of this shrine], and moreover by the common people of all the Sato under his sway, the sins which we purify and cleanse at the setting of the evening-sun of the last day of the sixth (or twelfth) month of this year, depositing in abundance various sorts of purification-offerings on the tables,—

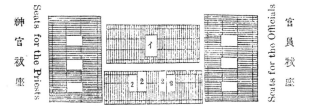

```
┌─────────────────────────────┐
│         Main Shrine         │
│      本 (Honsha) 社         │
└─────────────────────────────┘

┌─────────────────────────────────┐
│            ORATORY              │
│         拜 (Haiden) 殿          │
└─────────────────────────────────┘
```

神官祓座   Seats for the Priests   Seats for the Officials   官員祓座

COMMON PEOPLE.

1. Seat for the [reader of the] Purification Ritual.
2. Tables with the purification-offerings (harahe-tsumono).

Give first the description of the modern ceremony, because it is easier to understand than the rather fragmentary report on the old one, and throws also some light upon it.

"I humbly pray to the gods of the place of purification: Deign to consult in divine consultation, and deign to purify and deign to cleanse the evils, sins and pollutions of all people. Hear this my prayer [pricking your] ears higher and higher like the swift-running horse! This I say reverentially."*

Then the chief priest descends from the shrine and occupies again his seat at the place of purification.

Hereupon a priest (神官) takes the seat in the middle (the above mentioned for the ritual) and turning his face towards the people (with his back towards the shrine), he recites the ritual of purification.

(Some changes in the wording of the ancient ritual were necessitated by the different conditions of the time; but apart from this it has also been abbreviated in such a manner, that all the poetic charm of the original text, which may be justly called one of the most impressive productions of Japanese poetry, has entirely vanished. I cannot help calling the new official text a barbarous mutilation. It runs as follows:) †

"I say:" Hear all of you! The various sorts of sins that may have been committed as heavenly sins, or earthly sins, either inadvertently or deliberately by the officials of this.... Fu (or Ken), and the divine officials (priests) who serve in this....Shinto shrine, and moreover by the common people of all the places (Sato) under the sway of the great god of this shrine; the sins which we purify and cleanse in the great Purification, at the setting of the evening-sun on the last day of the sixth (or twelfth) month of this year, depositing on the tables the purification-offerings,

"will be carried out under mutual consent by the goddess Se-ori-tsu-Hime, the goddess Haya-aki-tsu-Hime, the god Ifuki-do-nushi and the goddess Haya-sasura-Hime into the river and sea, and breathed away and made to disappear without trace in the Root-country, the Bottom-country.

* In order to understand all details in this prayer and the following abbreviated version of the ritual of purification, the reader is requested to look up the corresponding passages in the ancient ritual, to which explanatory notes are appended.

† My translation is based on the text given in the official *Jinja-saishiki* (神社祭式), published in August 1875. It differs slightly in the choice of some expressions from the text in the above mentioned decree (See *Horei-zensho* 法令全書, Meiji 5th year.)

"After they have thus made them disappear, it is to be expected that, what one calls sin (tsumi) and what one calls transgression (toga) will from to-day no longer exist with the officials of this Fu (or Ken), the priests, and moreover the men and women of all the houses in all places, and in this expectation I recite [this Norito] and perform the purification."

Hereupon the local officials and priests grasp the *Kiri-nusa* and execute with it the purification.

The *Kiri-nusa* 切 麻 is a wand with hemp-fibres hanging from its upper end (on the whole identical with the *Gohei*). After the officials and priests have taken their seats on the place of purification, the *Kiri-nusa* are distributed, and one is placed before each of the officials and priests. As for the common people taking part in the ceremony, they also manipulate the *Kiri-nusa* in the same way, or simply bow down, if they cannot procure any for themselves.

Then the chief priest mounts up again to the main shrine, closes the door and having finished doing this, descends from the shrine and returns to his seat.

Hereupon the priests retire and go out.

The purification-offerings are now cut into small pieces, and thrown away into the river or the sea. The same applies to the *Kiri-nusa*. (If neither river nor sea is close by, a tub of water is used instead).

§ The Ancient Ceremony, According to the
Ceremonial Regulation of the
Jōgwan-period (859-876).

"As for the great purification in the sixth and twelfth months, the officials, of the Department of the Shintō Religion (Jingi-kwan), the Imperial Household Dapartment (Kunai), the Bureau of Sewing and Embroidery at the Imperial Court (Nuhidono), etc. shall present themselves in the fourth division of the hour of the horse (i.e. between 1½ and 2 o'clock p.m.) outside of the En-sei-mon (a gate on the east side of the Dairi or Inner Palace). All the officials assemble at the spot chosen for the ceremony of purification (Harahe no tokoro). Before

this, the officials of the Department of the Shintō Religion
spread out the purification-offerings south of the way before the
Shūjakumon (Gate of the Scarlet Bird, the Middle South gate
of the outer enclosure of the Palace)—distributed at six places:
the horse stands South, with its head facing the North. The
officials arrange the seats at the Shūjakumon and at the eastern
and western Jōsha (伕舍 , watch houses in front of the gates
of the Palace).

All persons from Ministers down to officials holding the fifth
rank have their seats at the eastern side of the platform, facing
the West and being drawn up in double line according to their
rank, from North to South. The first space east of the southern
staircase is the stair for persons of the fourth rank downwards,
and the second space is the staircase for the State-Counsellors
(Sangi) and officials of higher rank. The female officials are
also on the western side of the same platform, separated by a curtain. The Fubito of the Geki-kwan (i.e. the scribes and under-
secretaries of the Council of State) and the officials of the Central Department (Naka-tsukasa), Board of Civil Office (Shikibu)
and Board of War (Hyōbu) have their seats at the eastern Jōsha,
facing the West and being drawn up in lines according to their
rank from North to South. The members of the Board of
Police (Danjō) are at the western Jōsha, facing the East and
being drawn up in lines according to their rank from North to
South. The seat for the Norito (i.e. for the reader of the ritual
of purification) is at the south-western side of the way, and
before the seat is spread a cloth as Hizatsuki (small square mat
to squat upon). In the first division of the hour of the sheep
(i.e. 2-2½ o'clock p.m.) the secretaries (Geki) take each their
seats; the [officials of the] other offices stand at the eastern end
of the eastern Jōsha, etc. The Geki and their inferiors rise from
their seats, go down to the southern end of the eastern building
(sha) and post themselves there. The secretaries (Matsurigoto
bito) and Clerks (Sakwan) of the Board of Civil Office and
Board of War take their place at the head of the civil and military officials, and stand in lines, facing the West, and being
drawn up according to their rank from North to South. The
Secretaries and Clerks of the Board of Police go down to the
southern end of the western building (sha) and post themselves

there, facing the East, and being drawn up according to their rank from North to South. After they have thus posted themselves, the officials of the Department of the Shintō Religion distribute the *Kiri-nusa* (cut *nusa*) i.e. white wands with hemp-fibres hanging from the upper ends, the symbol of the primitive offerings of greater value)—among the Sangi and superiors, these are distributed by Clerks; among the officials of the fourth rank upwards (but lower than the Sangi) by scribes; among the

IMPERIAL CASTLE (宮 城 *Kyūjō*).

Ōkura   Ōkura

Offices

Dairi
Inner
Palace-ground

Ensei-mon

Offices

Kōka-mon   *Shujak-mon*   Bifukumon

North

West   East

South

PALACE GROUND.

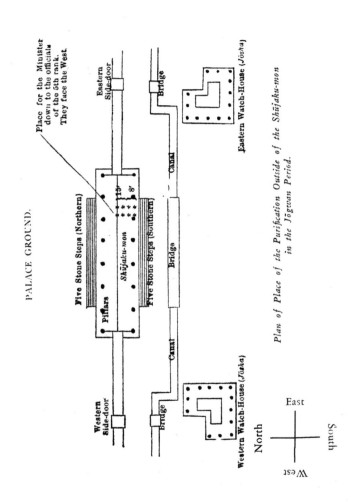

Plan of Place of the Purification Outside of the Shūjaku-mon
in the Jōgwan Period.

ladies and other officials by Kamu-Tomo-nowo.* Thereupon Nakatomi takes his seat and recites the ritual. When he says *kikoshimese* "hear!", all the officials exclaim *wo!* After the purification is finished, the [ceremony with the] *Oho-nusa*† is performed. Hereupon the *Kiri-nusa* of the persons from the fifth rank upwards are taken back. Shortly afterwards all go away.

§ 8.   DETAILS ON VARIOUS PRACTICES.   CEREMONY AT THE SUMIYOSHI SHRINE IN TOKYO.

During the middle ages—it is impossible to fix the time even only approximately—various popular practices have sprung up in connection with the purification ceremony and have partly been preserved to the present day. I shall proceed to mention some of the more important ones of them, in the course of a minute account which I am going to give, with illustrations, of the ceremony performed at the *Sumiyoshi-jinja*, situated on the small island Tsukuda-shima in the mouth of the river Sumidagawa, at Tokyo. This Shinto shrine, which is a branch shrine of the famous Sumiyoshi-jinja of Osaka, is one of the few shrines in the country, where, at least in June (the December ceremony is an abridged one), the ceremony is performed exactly in the same way as in the middle-ages. The information which I have been able to gather thereabout I owe mostly to the kindness of the priest of the temple, Mr. Hiraoka Yoshibumi （平岡好文）.

Towards the 25th or 26th of June (or December) the parishioners and other believers who wish to be purified go to the shrine and get from its official a so-called *kata-shiro* （ 形 代 ） i.e. a white paper cut in the shape of a human garment. On this the person to be purified, writes the year and month of his birth, and his sex; then he rubs the paper over his whole body, and breathes his breath on it, by which procedure his sins are transferred to it, and takes it back to the shrine before the beginning of the ceremony. It is therefore also called *nade-mono* （ 撫 物 ） "stroke-thing." (The article in *Fuzoku-gahō*, No. 6

---

* Attendants in the Department of the Shintō Religion, also called *Kamibe* There were thirty of them in the Department.

† A wand (*kushi*) with cut paper (*shide*). The *Oho-nusa* is taken and rubbed over the body, by which process the sins of the performer are believed to be transferred to it.

reports that in the Tokugawa time the people wrote on the *kata-shiro* such phrases as *kanaianzen* （ 家 内 安 全) "peace for my house," or similar ones). All the *kata-shiro* brought back are packed into two *ashi-dzutsu* （葦筒） "reed-sheath" which are placed on a table of black wood (*kuroki no tsukuwe*), and are called *harahe tsu-mono* "purification-offering" (see above).

head

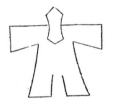 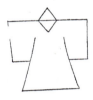

Length about 3″;   KATA-SHIRO.
Width about 2″.

KUROKI-NO-TSUKUWE
"Black-wood-table," made of Haji branches, bound with rattan vine.
Length 2′; width 1′2″; height 1′.

The *Tori-wi* in front of the shrine is decorated in the following way: On the left and right is placed a large bamboo, called *imi-dake* (齋竹) "sacred bamboo"; a *shime-nawa* is stretched across, and the inner space of the Tori-wi is filled out with a huge *chi no wa* (茅の輪) "reed ring," from the upper part of which hang down *shide* (paper cuttings) and *kata-shiro*. In June the ring is made of reed, in winter of rice straw. Its circumference is about 8 *ken* (=48 *shaku*).

長さ凡ソ四尺餘

ASHI-DZUTSU
Length about 4' or more;
Circumference about 2'
or more. (2 pieces).

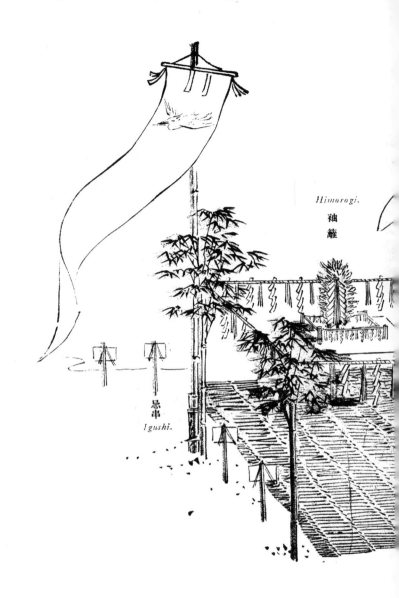

Himorogi.

袖籬

忌串

Igushi.

White flag with emblem
of a heron (*sagi*).

祓
白　式
幟　塲

Imi-dake.

Ara-komo.

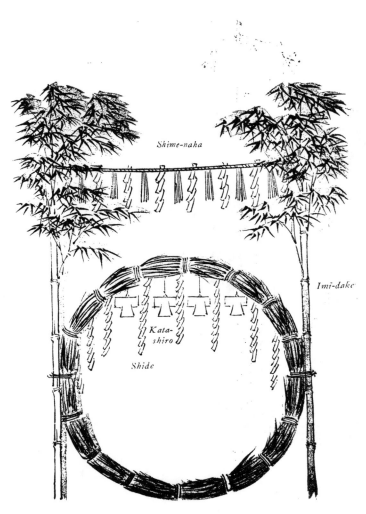

CHI NO WA (Reed-ring) with IMI-DAKE.

The place for the purification-ceremony proper (the *Harahe do*) is chosen in front of the shrine, in the immediate neighbourhood of the border of the river; it covers a space of about three *ken* (18 feet) square. After the place has been made ceremonially pure, *imi-dake* are erected at its four corners, *shimenawa* are stretched between them, and the whole space is covered with *ara-komo* "fresh rush mats." An eight-legged table (*yotsu-ashi no tsukuwe*) is put there, and thereon the *Himorogi* (into which the gods are called down by prayer) is placed. Round about the purification place so-called *i-gushi*, "sacred

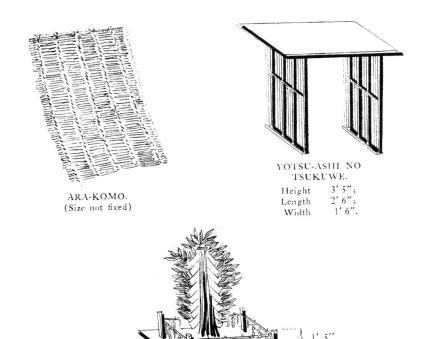

ARA-KOMO.
(Size not fixed)

YOTSU-ASHI NO
TSUKUWE.
Height   3′ 5″;
Length   2′ 6″;
Width   1′ 6″.

HIMOROGI.
The middle part, the Himorogi proper, consists of a *Sakaki* or *Kashi* (oak) branch, with eight-fold white paper *shide*, and hemp fibres hanging down in the middle. Round about is a kind of fence.

1′ 5″

1′ 4″

stakes", are planted in the ground, and on the side where the river flows, two "flags of the gods" (神 旗 *shin-ki*) are erected.

I-GUSHI.

8 pieces (2 on each side).

A green bamboo, of about 4′ length. The paper insected above is six-fold, the material being *hōsho* paper (a kind of fine paper, so called from its having been used in writing the *hōsho*, a letter of instruction issued through the secretary of the Kamakura Shogunate by order of the latter. Brinkley's Dict.). Hemp slips bound in a peculiar way are hanging down from the top of the stake on the left and right hand side.

STAFF OF PRIESTS TAKING PART IN THE CEREMONY:

1) One *Ihahi-nushi* (齋 主) master of rites. The chief priest of the shrine functionates as such. He opens and closes the door of the main shrine (shinden) at the beginning and end of the service, and recites the prayer. On the purification place he performs the *kami-oroshi* (calling down the purification gods into the *Himorogi*) and *kami-age* (sending back the gods), and recites the prayer.

2) One *Kotoshiribito* (典 禮) connoisseur, director of the ceremony.

3) One *Norito-shi* (祝 詞 師). He announces to the assembled people, on the place of purification, the intention of

the performance of the Oho-harahe, and afterwards recites the Oho-harahe no kotoba.

4)   One *Mike no Osa* (神饌長) chief of the divine food. He places the food-offerings to the gods on the sacrificial table in the main shrine, and afterwards takes them again away (after the essence of the food has been consumed by the gods).

5)   One *Shiho-yu-gyoji* (鹽湯行事).   He purifies the Himorogi with salt-water.   The salt-water is in a white earthen vessel, this on a *Sambō* (wooden stand used in offering sacrifices to the kami) which the priest holds with the left hand, whilst

Eight-legged sacrificial table (*yatsu-ashi no shinsen-an*).   Length 8'; width 1'5"; height 2' 5".

Earthen vessel with salt dissolved in warm water.

Sakaki branch.

Sambō.

he sprinkles the water with a small *Sakaki* branch held in the right hand.

6)   One *Oho-nusa-gyoji* （ 大麻行事 ）.   He purifies the assembled people with *Oho-nusa* (holding it with both hands and brandishing it over the assembly, first in the direction of his left, then his right, then again his left shoulder: the so-called *sa-yu-sa* "left-right-left").

A kind of helmet, made of paper, and called *ebōshi-kami*, i-e. paper in the form of an *ebōshi* cap.

Shide (cut paper), in eight layers.

Hemp (*asa*).

Two stakes (*kushi*), one of plum-tree wood, the other of bamboo, on which the paper and hemp are fastened.

Octangular stand (*dai*) for the Oho-nusa.

OHO-NUSA, 大麻 (lit. big hemp), about 4' high from the top to the bottom.

7) Two *Shidori* (後取), companions and assistants of the *Ihahi-nushi*.

8) *Te-na ga* (手長), "long-armed," assistants in the offering of the food to the gods. The various articles of food for the gods, placed on a number of *Sambō*, are kept ready in the *Shinsen-ya* "divine food-hall" outside the shrine. In offering, one *Sambō* after the other is brought from the *Shinsenya* and placed on the sacrificial tables. This is done in the following way: The sacrificer proper, the *Mike no Osa*, posts himself directly before the sacrificial tables, and from him to the *Shinsenya*, at a distance of one Ken from each other, stand a number of *Te-naga*, but not in straight line:

The Sambō are passed from one Tenaga to the other (who have covered their mouth with a white paper fillet, *fukumen*, in order not to pollute the food by their breath) with arms outstretched at the height of their eyes; the receiver claps his hands once before taking the Sambō, in token of his readiness, for it would be a high offence to the gods to let anything drop. Finally the *Mike no Osa* receives the Sambō and places it on the table. In the same way, the offerings are taken away again: what has been brought last, is taken away first, and so on. There are fixed regulations for the number of Sambō and the kinds of food to be offered on each occasion. The first Sambō is placed in the middle, the following ones are alternatively placed to the right and left of it. (Seen by the public).

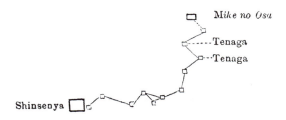

Mike no Osa
Tenaga
Tenaga
Shinsenya

9) One *Kamu-koto-shi* （ 神琴師 ） player on the divine Koto. He plays the so-called *Suga-gaki* (melody on the Yamato-koto, without accompaniment of ringing) on the *Yamato koto* (sinico-jap. *Wagon*), a six-stringed harp, during the opening and closing of the door of the Main Shrine and during the *kami-oroshi* and *kami-age*.

10) Two *Yosohi-shi* （ 裝飾師 ） decorators. They bring and take the tables and other things used in the ceremony.

11) *Reijin* （ 伶人 ） musicians; their number is not fixed.

It may be observed that, though the above list of officiating priests is fixed by the regulations, in reality several functions are mostly performed by one man, because it is rarely the case that so many priests are at disposition.

The whole service may be divided into two phases:

A)   the preliminary service in the *Shinden;*

B)   the purification service proper on the *Harahe-do*.

A)   IN THE SHINDEN:

When, at about 3 o'clock in the afternoon, all preparations have been finished, the divine officials take their seats before the *Shinden* at a sign of the drum (*dai-ik-ko*, first drum).

First, the *Ihahi nushi* mounts up to the *Shinden*, accompanied by the *Shidori* who roll up the *misu* (a blind made of fine bamboo strips, hung before the door of the *Shinden*).

Then the *Ihahi-nushi* steps forward and opens the door with a key. Whilst he does so, the two *Shidori*, squatting behind him, bow down and make the *keihitsu*, i.e. utter three times a long-sustained cry ō!, by which they warn the people to be respectful, at the same time, playing on the *koto*.

Then the *Ihahi-nushi* bows twice and claps his hands without causing a sound （ 短手 *Shinobi-te*）.

4″5″.   四寸五分

Length 4′2″.
YAMATO-KOTO

Then the *Ihahi-nushi* and *Shidori* go back to their seats.
Then the divine food (*shinsen*) is offered to the gods in the
way described under No. 8 (*Tenaga*).   First the tables are
placed before the sanctuarium, and then the Sambō with the
food are brought one after the other.   In this instance nine
Sambō are offered, on which are the following articles.

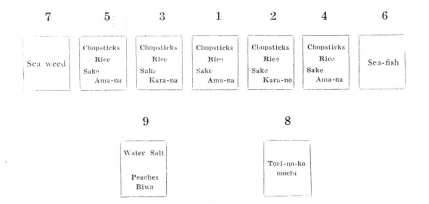

7	5	3	1	2	4	6
Sea weed	Chopsticks Rice Sake Ama-na	Chopsticks Rice Sake Kara-na	Chopsticks Rice Sake Ama-na	Chopsticks Rice Sake Kara-no	Chopsticks Rice Sake Ama-na	Sea-fish

9	8
Water Salt Peaches Biwa	Tori-no-ko mochi

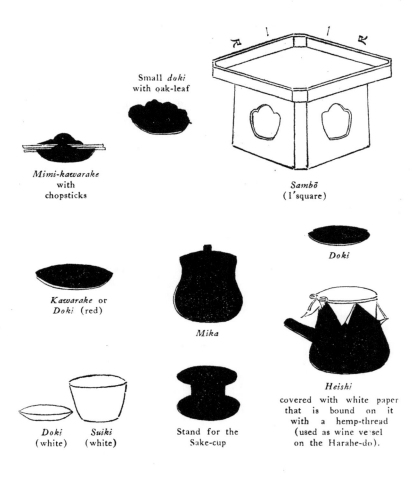

Small *doki*
with oak-leaf

Mimi-kawarake
with
chopsticks

Sambō
(1'square)

Doki

Kawarake or
Doki (red)

Mika

Heishi
covered with white paper
that is bound on it
with a hemp-thread
(used as wine vessel
on the Harahe-do).

Doki   *Suiki*
(white)   (white)

Stand for the
Sake-cup

The *chopsticks* are made of willow-tree and placed on a
a *mimi-kawarake*, i.e. an unglazed earthen vessel with handles
in the shape of an ear.

The *rice* is put on a small *doki* (=*kawarake* unglazed
earthen vessel), an oak-leaf being first spread on the *doki*.

The *sake* is kept in 2 bottles (*mika*).

The *kara-na* "sharp-tasting greens" (such as *wasabi*, horse-
radish, *shōga*, ginger, *negi*, onion, etc.) and *ama-na*, "sweet
greens" (such as *seri* Oenathe stolonifera, *nasubi*, egg-plant,
yama-imo, mountain-potato, *ninjin*, carrot, etc.) are placed on a

doki with an oak-leaf under them. The same is the case with the sea-fish, sea-weed, peaches, *biwa* etc.

The *torinoko-mochi,* "egg-shaped *mochi*" (i.e. cakes made of pounded glutinous rice) are placed on paper.

The *salt* is put on a *doki,* and the water in a *suiki* (water-vessel).

During the offering music.

Then the *Ihahi-nushi* recites a prayer (*norito*). He invokes the three gods of Suminoye (Soko-dzutsu no Wo, Naka-dzutsu no Wo and Uha-dzutsu no Wo) produced when Izanagi washed himself to clean away the pollution contracted in Hades, and the two deities Oki-nagatarashihime no Mikoto and Adzuma-mi-oya no Mikoto, and asks them to consult with the great gods of the purification-place, in order to remove to Hades all evils, sins and pollutions from the people of Tsukuda-no-shima, the merchants who come to the shrine, and the families and relations of the officiating priests, and to bestow upon them peace, protection and bliss.

Then twice double bows (i.e. bowing 4 times: *ryōdan saihai*).

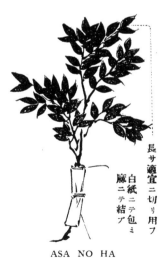

長サ適宜ニ切リ用フ

白紙ニテ包ミ

麻ニテ結ブ

ASA NO HA
(wrapped in white paper which is bound with a hemp string).

Then the *Ihahi-nushi* and all others return to their seats.

Then, on the second signal of the drum, all leave the temple hall, the *Ihahi-nushi* with an *Asa-no-ha* (hemp leaves) in his hand. They go one after the other through and round the *Chi-no-wa*, singing a song, under the leadership of the *koto-shiri-bito*, and proceed to the purification-place. The going-round the *Chi-no-wa* (chi-no-wa wo meguru) is done in the following way: one steps into the ring, turns to the left and goes three times round the left pillar in the *sa-yu-sa* fashion (i.e. once to the left then to the right and then again to the left); then he turns three times round the right pillar in the same fashion, and goes on to the Harahe-do. The two songs sung when making the round of the Chi-no-wa, are:

> Minadzuki no.
> Nagoshi no harahe
> Suru hito ha
> Chitose no inochi
> Nobu to ifu nari.

"The people who perform the Nagoshi no harahe (see above §1) of the watery moon, are said to prolong their lives to a thousand years."

> Omofu koto
> Mina tsukine tote
> Asa no ha wo
> Kiri ni kirite zo
> Harahe tsuru kana.

"What [we] think, shall all be annihilated. With this intention, cutting hemp-leaves with cuts, [we] have performed purification."

B. ON THE HARAHE-DO.

The *Harahe-tsu-mono* are brought, laid, as stated above, on a table of black wood which is placed on a convenient spot of the purification-place.

First salt-water (*shiho no yu*) is sprinkled.

Then the Ihahi-nushi and Shidori proceed before the *Himorogi* and squat down.

Then the Ihahi-nuchi recites the words by which the gods of purification are called down (*kami-oroshi*) into the Himorogi.

Meanwhile the *Suga-gaki* is played by the koto-player, and the shidori make the *keihitsu*.

Then the Ihahi-nushi bows twice and makes the *shinobi-te* (soundless clapping of the hands).

Then the Ihahi-nushi and Shidori return to their seats.

Then the *Oho-nusa* is brought out (from the shrine.)

Then the *Norito shi* announces to the people his intention of performing the *Harahe*. The people utter their consent (lit. say "yes," which means that they are ready). The *Norito-shi* says: Kore no yu-niha ni ugonohareru hito mina ga ayamachi-okashikemu kusagusa no tsumi-goto wo harahe-do no oho-kami-tachi umi-kaha ni mochi-idete Ne no kuni Soko no kuni ni ibuki-hanachi sasurahi ushinahitemu. Kaku ushinaihiteba kefu yori hajimete tsumi to ifu tsumi wa araji to harahi-tamahi kiyome tamafu koto no yoshi wo moro-moro kikoshimese to noru. I.e. "The great gods of the purification-place will take out into the river and sea all sorts of offences, that may have been committed either inadvertently or deliberately, by the people assembled in this pure court-yard, and blow them away and completely banish them and get rid of them into Hades. Hear you all the circumstance (*yoshi*) of the purification [which is performed with the intention] that from to-day there will be no longer any offence which is called offence, after they have thus got rid of them."

Then offering of divine food. Meanwhile music. [This time only *seven* Sambō are offered, viz.

6	4	2	1	3	5	7

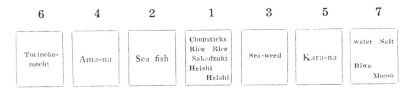

| Toi inoko-mochi | Ama-na | Sea fish | Chopsticks
Rice Rice
Sakadzuki
Heishi
Heishi | Sea-weed | Kara-na | water Salt
Biwa
Momo |

Then the Ihahi-nushi recites the prayer (*norito*) and at the same time all proceed forward before the Himorogi and squat down. The prayer is directed to the four gods of the purification-place, and asks them to bless the people by their lofty spirit, to take away their offences without leaving any trace, and to enjoy the food and wine presented.

Then *ryō-dan saihai* (bowing 4 times). All do the same.

Then the *Norito-shi* recites the *Oho-harahe no kotoba* (our present ritual).

Then the Norito-shi bows twice, with *shinobi-te*.

Then the manipulation with the *Oho-nusa*.

Then the divine food is again removed (in the reverse order to that in which it has been brought from the Shinsen-ya). Meanwhile music.

Then the Ihahi-nushi and Shidori proceed before the Himorogi and squat down.

Then the double bow and *shinobi-te* of the Ihahi-nushi.

Then the Ihahi-nushi recites the words of the *Kamiage* (sending back the gods). *Suga-gaki* and *keihitsu*, as in the *kami-oroshi*.

Then the Ihahi-nushi and Shidori return to their seats.

Then the *Himorogi* is removed.

Then *ushiro-de* (退手) hand clapping to mark the act of retiring.

Then the *Harahe-tsu-mono* are packed into a boat which is rowed out into the sea in order to throw them away there. In the mean-time, after the *ushiro-de*, the Ihahi-nushi and those priests who have not gone into the boat, return to the shrine and again take their seats there.

Now the Ihahi-nushi ascends to the Main shrine: double bows and *shinobi-te*.

Then the divine food offered in the Main shrine is removed. Meanwhile music.

Then double bows and *shinobi-te* of the Ihahi-nushi.

Then the Ihahi-nushi goes and shuts up the door of the Main shrine. Meanwhile *Suga-gaki*, and *keihitsu* by the Shidori.

Then the curtain (*misu*) is let down again.

Then *ushiro-de*.

Then the *Ihahi-nushi* and *shi-dori* go back to their seats.

Finis.

§ 9. THE PRESENT CEREMONY IN THE IMPERIAL PALACE.

The Kwanpō (Official Gazette) publishes twice a year, towards the end of June and December, regulations with regard to two special ceremonies which take place in the Imperial Palace for the sake of the purification of the Emperor and the officials of the various ministerial departments.

A) The *yo ori* "breaking [bamboo-] joints" ceremony for the Emperor. At 12 o'clock (noon) the decoration of the so-caller *Hō-ō no ma* "Phoenix Hall," a room of the palace in which the ceremony takes place, is undertaken. At 1 p.m. the officials of the Kunaishō enter, and the Shōten-chō (Grand Master of the Ceremonies) goes and asks the Emperor to be present. He and all his subordinates wait for His Majesty under the eaves (*hisashi ni;* at present they wait in the corridor). After the Emperor has made his appearance, the Shōtenchō steps forward and inquires after His Majesty's health. Then a Chamberlain (*jijū*) hands to the Emperor an *arayo* cloth[1]. The Emperor takes it, gives it back to the Chamberlain, and this one hands it over to the Shōtenchō. Next, a Shōten (Master of the Cere-monies) takes bamboo canes, called *ara-yo no take*[2], and hands them to a Chamberlain. The Chamberlain takes with this bam-boo five times the measure of the body of the Emperor[3], and, this done, he gives the bamboo back to the Shōten. Hereupon a Shōten takes an *ara-yo no tsubo* "rough-joint jar" and hands it to a Chamberlain. The Chamberlain hands it to the Emperor, and after his Majesty has done with it, the jar is given back to the Chamberlain and then to the Shōten. The whole ceremony is then gone through a second time, only *nigo-yo* cloth, bamboo, and jar being used instead of the *ara-yo* objects. Then the Emperor retires. After he has gone, the Shōten betakes himself to the Oho-kawa (great river, in order to throw away all the objects used; the Sumida-gawa is here understood), and a Shōten-ho Vice Master of Ceremonies goes with the *mi-nusa* (御 麻) to the purification-place (harahe-do). Thereupon all retire.

NOTES.

[1] Ara "rough," in contradistinction to *nigo* "soft," used in the same way as in the Shinto expressions *ara-mitama* "rough or enraged august spirit" (of a god or deceased person) and *nigi-mitama* "soft or propitious spirit;" *yo* "bamboo joint." The *arayo* cloth is made of *nuno*, which probably is here equivalent to *asa* "hemp" (I was not able to make it out positively), whilst the *nigo-yo* cloth, mentioned farther down, is made of silk. Wherein the material distinction between *ara-yo no take* and *ara-yo no tsubo* on the one side, and *nigo-yo no take* and *nigo-yo no tsubo* on the other side, lies, I am not prepared to say.

[2] The number of the bamboo canes is *nine*.

³ In taking the measure of His Majesty's body, one cane after the other is used, each cane being used only once. First of all the entire length of the body is measured, and the exceeding piece of the cane is broken off, wherefrom the name of the whole ceremony: *yo-ori* "the breaking off of the [superfluous] joints [of the bamboo]." Then the measure is taken, in the same manner, from both shoulders to the feet, then from the middle of the breast to the finger-tips of both hands, then from both loins (*koshi*) down to the feet, then from both knees down to the feet. The whole action is of course a symbolic one.
⁴ He breathes his breadth into it.

B). The *Oho-harahe for the officials*, in the court-yard of the place.

At 1½ p.m. arrangements are made in the yard (*teijō*) for the preparation of a *harahe-do*, and the *harahe-tsumono* are deposited there. At 2 p.m. the Shōtenchō and others take their seats, together with one official of Chokunin rank, one of Sōnin rank, and one of Hannin rank, of each ministerial department respectively. The two Shōten-ho put rice into the *mi-nusa* which is laid on a table standing in the yard. Then the Shōten-chō calls a Shōten and commands him to perform the purification. The Shōten proceeds to the front of the table and reads the *Oho-harahe no Kotoba*. Then a Shōten steps forward, takes the *Oho-nusa* from the table, steps back, turns his face to all the people sitting in the yard and purifies them standing (he purifies them by flourishing the *Oho-nusa* over them, as described above). Having done, he delivers the *Oho-nusa* to a Shōten-ho. During this procedure the sitting persons stand up. Then the Shōten, turning in the direction of the great river, calls out: "*Harahe-sare!*" (purify away!). Then the Shōten-ho takes the *harahe-tsu-mono* and goes with them to the great river (to throw them away into the water). Thereupon all retire.

§ 10. LEGENDARY ORIGIN OF THE PURIFICATION CEREMONY,
AND CHARACTER OF THE HARAHE-TSU-MONO.

The origin of the ceremony of purification is ascribed by Japanese scholars, to two mythical occurrences related in chapters 10 and 17 of the Kojiki, and the corresponding passages of the Nihongi. It is hardly necessary to remind the critical student that, in point of fact, the two mythical occurrences are not the origin of the ceremony, but on the contrary the framing of the myths, presupposes the existence of the ceremony. The truth is that the two myths, represent only the most ancient Japanese tradition with regard to this peculiar religious custom, and as such they are of the highest value.

The first occurrence is the *ablution of the god Izanagi* after his visit to the lower regions, the land of Yomi (*Yomo*) or Hades, whence he had tried to fetch back his deceased wife Izanami (parallel to the Greek legend of Orpheus and Eurydice!). After his return from the unsuccessful task which had severely tried his nerves, he was seized with regret, and said (Nihongi version): "Having gone to—Nay! a hideous and filthy place, it is meet that I should cleanse my body from its pollutions." He accordingly went to the plain of Ahagi [east] of Tachibana [near] the river Woto in [the province of] Himuka in Tsukushi, and purified himself. When at length he was about to wash away the impurities of his body, he lifted up his voice and said: "The upper stream is too rapid and the lower stream is too sluggish, I will wash in the middle stream." By his plunging down and washing, a number of Deities were produced, some of whom play a leading part, later on, in the religious ceremony of purification and are mentioned in our ritual.

Izanagi's ablution is the prototype of the ceremonial lustration required after contact with death, birth and other things impure. Lustrations are a widespread practice, as may be seen from Tylor's Primitive Culture, vol. II, pag. 430 seqq. For comparison's sake I will quote two especially striking passages from this work:[1] Cremonial lustration to expiate a guilt was used in ancient Peru; after having confessed his sins, the Inca took a bath in a neighbouring river and spoke the following formula: "O river, receive the sins which I have confessed to-day before the Sun, carry them down into the sea and make that they never appear again."

The means most frequently used for removing impurities of the body or soul was the water, the divine waters to which the Hindoo prays: "Take away, ye waters, everything that is bad in me, what I have done by violence, or in swearing or with untruth."[2]

---

[1] Possessing only the German edition of Tylor's book, I am not able to reproduce the author's exact words.

[2] This is verse 22 of hymn 23, first Mandala of the Rig-veda. In the original: Idam apah pravahata yat kim ca duritam mayi, Yad va ham abhidudroha yad va cepa utanritam.

The second mythical occurrence alluded to is the *punishment of the god Susa-no-Wo*. After the Gods had succeeded in enticing the Sun-goddess out of the Heavenly Rock-cave into which she had retired, enraged on account of the misconduct of her brother Susanowo, the chief text of the Nihongi[3] reports: After this all the Gods put the blame on Susanowo no Mikoto, and imposed on him a fine of one thousand tables [of offerings], and so at length chastised him. They also had his hair plucked out, and made him therewith expiate his guilt. It is also reported that they made him expiate it by plucking out the nails of his hands and feet. In the second variant it says: After this Susanowo no Mikoto was convicted, and fined in the articles required for the ceremony of purification (*harahe*). [They took] the ends of his hands as good things to be thrown away (*yoshi-kirahi-mono*), and the ends of his feet as bad things to be thrown away (*ashi-kirahi-mono*), again, of his spittle they made white soft offerings, and of his nose-mucus they made green soft offerings, with which the purification was accomplished. Finally they banished him according to the law of Divine Banishment. The parallel passage in the third variant shows that by the "ends of the hands and feet" are meant the nails of his hands and feet.

The *yoshi-kirahi-mono* (*yoshi* good *kirafu* to abhor and throw away) are according to Suzuki Shigetane's Nihongiden, the signs and symbols of the purification, as it is performed before every divine service (comp. § 2 under C) and we might style them ritual or sacred offerings. The *ashi-kirahi-mono* (*ashi* bad) are penitential offerings provided by the offender in expiation of his offence. For in every process of purification two sides must be distinguished: a good side which aims at procuring luck, and a bad side which aims at doing away with calamity. Motowori is of the same opinion: under *yoshi-kirahi-mono* he understands the sacred utensils used for the rite (the *nusa*), and under *ashi-kirahi-mono* the objects which the offender has possessed and used, and which, therefore, must be thrown away as impure. He says that in the case of Susanowo the

---

[3] I prefer to quote the Nihongi, because, at least in this instance, it furnishes richer material than the Kojiki.

offence was so grave, that the usual purification-offerings were
not sufficient; the nails of his hands and feet had therefore to
be added.

The Rui-jū-san-dai-kyaku enumerates four categories of
harahe-tsu-mono, viz.:

a) 大 祓 米 物 Dai	no harahe-tsu-mono	(great)	28 sorts,
b) 上 „ „ „ Kami „	„	(upper)	26 „
c) 中 „ „ „ Naka „	„	(middle)	22 „
d) 下 „ „ „ Shimo „	„	(lower)	22 „

What kind of objects these were in the most ancient time,
is shown by the two passages quoted in § 3 from the Nihongi:
As Harahe-tsu-mono are to be forwarded by the Kuni no Miyatsuko of each province: one horse and one piece of cloth; moreover by each district-governor: one sword, one deerskin, one
mattock, one smaller sword, one sickle, one set of arrows, and
one sheaf of rice in the ear; moreover by each house: one bundle
of hemp. And: Each Kuni no Miyatsuko supplied as purification-
offering one slave, and thus the purification was done. These
things may fairly be considered as representing the entire property of the primitive household. As for the Harahe of a single
person, evidently his whole movable property was thrown away
in grave cases;[4] but with the purification of the whole people
such a sweeping procedure was, of course, impossible: certain
things were chosen as its symbols. In the course of time the
spirit of economy asserted itself more and more with regard to
the Harahe-tsu-mono, until they were reduced to the comparatively insignificant amount mentioned in § 6.

From what I have said above, the reader will already have
understood that the lustration of Izanagi and the punishment of
Susanowo are not two different kinds of Harahe, but only two
integral elements of one and the same process. Offence and
pollution are inseparable ideas with the ancient Japanese:[5] they

---

[4] In connection with this point the fact should be noticed that in his flight
from Hades Izanagi throws away all his personal wearing: his black head-dress,
many-toothed comb, staff, girdle, upper garment, trowsers and shoes (Nihongi, Aston
pag. 25 and 26).
[5] And not with them alone! Comp. E. g. Wurm, Geschichte der indischen
Religion, pag. 96: The offences against the law through which a man is liable to
bring down upon himself punishment in a future life, are pre-eminently regarded as
pollutions. The danger always in this conception of sin, is, with regard to the

are in fact identical. He who has committed a crime must be purified, as well as he who has come into contact with something impure; the purification extends to persons and things. The person is purified by lustration, the impure thing is trown away, or, where that is not possible or advisable (as e.g. when a temple compound has been polluted), it is made pure again by prayer and ceremony. The intimate connection between lustration and expiatory fine, is especially well shown by an incident reported by the Nihongi in the Annals of Emperor Richiū as having occurred on the 11th day, 10th month 404 A. D. (Aston, I 308). An Imperial concubine had died, and some one told the Emperor that her death was to be attributed to the impious action of a certain Kurumamochi no Kimi (i.e. Kimi or master of the Cart-keepers) who had gone to the land of Tsukushi, where he held a review of all the Cart-keepers' Be, and had taken along with them the men allotted to the service of the Deities (Kamube no tami). The Emperor straightway summoned to him the Kimi of the Cart-keepers and questioned him. The facts having been ascertained, the Emperor enumerated his offences, saying:— "Thou, although only Kimi of the Cart-keepers, hast arbitrarily appropriated the subjects of the Mikado. This is one offence. Thou didst wrongfully take them, comprising them in the Cart-keepers' Be after they had been allotted to the service of the Gods of Heaven and Earth. This is a second offence." So he *imposed on him the bad expiatory fine (ashi-harahe) and the good expiatory fine (yoshi-harahe)*, and sent him away to Cape Nagasu,[a] there to *purify and wash (harahe-misogashimu)*. After he had done so, the Emperor commanded him, saying:— "Henceforward thou mayest not have charge of the Cart-keepers' Be of Tsukushi." So he confiscated them all, and allotted them anew, giving them to the three Deities."

Another noteworthy case is told in the Annals of Emperor Yūriaku, 13th year (469 A.D.), 3rd month: "Hatane no Mikoto,

Hindoos, expressed by Wurm in the following words (same page): The effect of this propensity for external ceremonies has been that the Hindoo, in spite of his deeper conception of evil in the Indian doctrine of the Weltübel, has entirely lost the proper moral idea of sin and guilt, so that to-day by sin he understands nothing else but such external pollutions, and is nearly incapable of comprehending sin as having its seat in the human heart.

[a] In the province of Settsu. Nagasa (Aston) is a misprint.

great-great-grandson of Saho-hiko [who was again a grandson of Emperor Kogen), secretly seduced (*okaseri*, the same term which occurs so often in our ritual) the courtlady Yamanobe no Ko-shima-Ko. When this came to the Emperor's ears, he gave Hatane no Mikoto in charge to Mononobe no Me no Oho-muraji, and made him call him to account for it. Hatane no Mikoto *purged his offence* (祓除罪過 *tsumi wo harafu*) by the payment of eight horses and eight swords."

§11. THE RITUAL OF PURIFICATION
VIEWED FROM THE STANDPOINT OF JURISPRUDENCE.

Dr. Weipert puts, on page 371, the question whether the offences enumerated in the ritual, constitute the categories of the criminal law of the primitive Japanese, (die strafrechtlichen Kategorieen der japanischen Vorzeit), and whether their treatment in the process of purification can be called a penal resentment (strafrechtliche Ahndung)? He answers the question in the affirmative, without overlooking the fact that the treatment by purification was not the only method of reaction against crimes. There are in the Kojiki, and Nihongi, numerous instances of arbitrary punishment, inflicted by rulers, chieftains etc. or of private revenge (Dr. Weipert quotes some of them from the Kojiki), but nothing shows the existence of fixed punitive laws or conventions. The quiet national development of the Japanese criminal law, has been obstructed by the introduction of the Chinese criminal code of the Thang Dynasty, called Taiho-Ritsu (because promulgated in the first year of the period Taihō, i.e. 701 A.D.), and though, of course, nobody can say in what direction Japanese law would have developed if left alone, it is evident that arbitrary punishment and private revenge would have been checked considerably in the course of time. May I be permitted to conclude this chapter by quoting largely from Dr. Weipert's own words (on page 372 seq. of his essay), as it would be impossible to render a more lucid and concise account of this matter? Dr. Weipert says:

"If we confine ourselves to the prehistoric times of Japan, we find in them no other traces of conceptions of a binding law, than those handed down to us in the rituals dedicated to the gods. It was indeed the power of the ruler which held the community together, but the idea of the society being subject to lawful restraint was to be found only in the religious sentiments of the people. To the extent of these sentiments alone, can it be said that a lawfully regulated community and a consciousness of such existed in those days. Now, since we take Criminal Law to be the publicly regulated reaction of a community, against all acts of its members which are detrimental to the common interest, we can scarcely hesitate to describe the Oharai (Ohoharahe) as the first source of Japanese Criminal Law."

This statement by no means implies that the acts of purification imposed by the rite, are to be considered as punishments in the present acceptance of the word. On the contrary Motowori is perfectly right in emphatically objecting to an interpretation, which would imply that the tearing off of Susanowo's nails was a sort of corporal punishment, or which would make acts of restitution out of the offerings imposed. In either case the principal and original idea, was to symbolize purification, whilst the evils which resulted therefrom in the individual concerned were merely an effect. The same has to be said with regard to the banishment, which is finally pronounced against Susanowo. This measure was merely aimed, at the expulsion of the polluted from the community of the pure, it was a mere consequence of the purification, and not intended as a punishment in itself.

It will therefore be safe to state that in the case of an individual Harahe, a punishment was indeed inflicted on the wrongdoer; but it was inflicted for the sake of the whole procedure of purification, not for the sake of the punishment of banishment as such. This procedure bore an entirely religious character, and had no other aim than to settle the account with the gods. We may therefore conclude that the Criminal Law of ancient Japan belonged to the category of the so-called, sacred Criminal Laws ("Sacrales Strafrecht").

Respecting the prosecution of crime, one may perhaps be permitted to emphasize the fact, that frequently repeated purifications of the whole people were considered necessary; which enables us to arrive at the conclusion that the application of an individual Harahe was rarely resorted to, and perhaps only in cases of an exceptional character, so that private revenge had ample opportunity to assert itself.

RITUAL

[I.] He says[1]:

"Hear all of you, assembled princes of the blood, princes,[2] high dignitaries and men of the hundred offices."

[II.] He says:

"Hear all of you, that in the Great Purification of the [present] last day of the sixth month of the current year, [the sovran][3] deigns to purify, and deigns to cleanse the various offences which may have been committed either inadvertently, or deliberately,[4] especially by the [persons] serving at the Imperial court, [viz.] the scarf-wearing attendants, the sash-wearing attendants [of the kitchen],[5] the attendants who carry quivers on the back,[6] the attendants who gird on swords,[7] the eighty attendants of the attendants,[8] and moreover[9] by the people serving in all offices.[10]"

[III.] He says: Hear all of you:

Then sovran's dear progenitor and progenitrix,[11] who divinely remain in the Plain of High Heaven; deigned to assemble by their command[12] in a divine assembly, the eight hundred myriads of gods, and deigned to consult in divine consultation[13], and respectfully[14] gave the mandate with the word; "Our sovran Grandchild's[15] augustness shall tranquilly rule the Luxuriant Reed-plain Region of Fresh-young Spikes[16] as a peaceful country."

[The divine progenitor and progenitrix] deigned to arraign with divine arraignment the savage Deities[17] in the country thus given in charge; and deigned to expel them with divine expulsion; and silenced the rocks, and trunks of trees, and isolated leaves[18] of the herbs that [formerly] had spoken; and letting him go from the Heavenly Rock-Seat,[19] and dividing a road through the eightfold heavenly clouds with a mighty road-dividing,[20] they respectfully sent him down from Heaven, and respectfully gave [the land] in charge to him.

As the centre of the countries of the four quarters thus given in charge, was respectfully destined the country Great

Yamato, where the sun is seen on high[21], as a peaceful country; ....and making stout the House[22]-pillars on the nethermost rock-bottom, and making high the cross beams[23] to the Plain of High Heaven, [the builders] respectfully constructed the fresh Abode[24] of the sovran Grandchild's augustness, in order that He might hide [therein] as a shade from the heavens and as a shade from the sun,[25] and tranquilly rule the country as a peaceful country.

As for the various sorts of offences which may have been committed either inadvertently, or deliberately by the heaven's increasing population,[26] that shall come into being in the country, a number of offences are expressly distinguished[27] as heavenly offences;[28] [viz.] breaking down the divisions of the rice-fields,[29] filling up the irrigating channels,[30] opening the floodgate of sluices,[31] sowing seed over again,[32] setting up pointed rods[33] [in the rice-fields], flaying alive and flaying backwards,[34] evacuating excrements [at improper places].[35] [These are distinguished] as heavenly offences.[17] As for earthly offences,[36] there will be forthcoming a number of offences [viz.] cutting the living skin,[37] cutting the dead skin,[38] albinoes,[39] being effected with excrescences,[40] the offence of [a son's] cohabitation with his own mother,[41] the offence of [a father's] cohabitation with his own child,[42] the offence of [the father's] cohabitation with his step-daughter,[43] the offence of [a man's] cohabitation with his mother-in-law,[44] the offence of cohabitation with animals,[45] calamity through crawling worm,[46] calamity through the gods on high,[47] calamity through birds on high,[48] killing the animals [of other people],[49] the offence of using incantations.[50]

If such [offences] are forthcoming, the Great Nakatomi[51] in accordance with the ceremonies in the Heavenly Palace,[52]) cutting the bases, and cutting off the ends of the heavenly young little trees[53] shall [makes them] into thousand tables[54] and deposit [upon them] in abundance [the purification-offerings]; shall mow and cut off the bases, and mow and cut the ends of heavenly fine strips of rush,[55] and split them thinner and thinner with the needle[56]; and shall recite the powerful ritual-words of the heavenly ritual.[57]

If he thus recites [the heavenly ritual], the heavenly god,[58] pushing open the heavenly Rock-door,[59] and dividing a road through the eight-fold heavenly clouds, with a mighty road-dividing, will hear [the ritual-words]; [and] the earthly gods[58] ascending to the tops of the high mountains, and to the tops of the low mountains,[60] and tearing asunder the smoke[61] of the high mountains, and the smoke of the low mountains, will hear [the ritual-words].[62]

If they thus hear [the ritual words], it is to be expected that[63] any offence which is called offence[64] will disappear, especially in the court of the sovran Grandchild's augustness,[65] and [also] in the countries of the four quarters of the region under heaven;..........and it is to be expected that no offences will remain, like as the wind of [the wind-deity] Shinato[66] blows asunder the eight-fold heavenly clouds;..........as the morning-wind and the evening-wind blow away the dense morning-mist[67] and the dense evening-mist;..........as one unties at the prow and unties at the stern the large ships lying in the large harbour[68] and pushes them out into the Great Sea-plain[69];..........as one clears away the shrubs of the dense bushes yonder[70] with the sharp sickle of a tempered sickle[71].

The offences[72] which [the sovran][73] in this expectation deigns to purify and deigns to cleanse,..........will be carried out into the great Sea-plain by the goddess called Maiden-of-Descent-into-the-Current[74], who resides in the current of the rapid stream that in falling comes boiling down the ravines,[75] from the tops of the high mountains, and the tops of the low mountains.

And when she has thus carried [them] out, the goddess called Maiden-of-the-swift-opening,[76] who resides in the eight hundred meetings of the brine of the eight brine-currents, of the eight hundred currents of the brine of the fresh brine[77], will take them and swallow them down with gurgling sound.[78]

And when she has thus swallowed [them] down with gurgling sound, the god called the Lord-of-the-Breath-blowing-place who resides at the Breath-blowing-place[79], will take them and utterly blow them away with his breath into the Root-country, the Bottom-country[80].

And when he has thus blown [them] away, the goddess called the Maiden-of-Swift-Banishment[81], who resides in the

Root-country, the Bottom country, will take them and completely banish them and get rid of them.

And when they have been got rid of, it is to be expected that from this day onwards, there will be no offence which is called offence, in the four quarters of the region under heaven, especially with regard to all people of all offices who respectfully serve in the court of the Sovran:..........................

....and in this expectation, having led hither and put there a horse,[52] as a thing that hears with its ears pricked up to the Plain of High Heaven, [He] deigns to purify and deigns to cleanse[53] through the Great Purification, at the setting of the evening-sun on the last day of the watery moon[54] of this year."

[IV.] He says:

"You diviners of the four countries[55], leave and go away to the great river-way,[56] and carry away [the offences] by purification."

NOTES.

1   In the original 宣 is read *noru* by N. Motowori, Hirata and Haruyama, *nori-tamafu* by Mabuchi and Shikida. Like Satow I have adopted the view of Motowori. 'He' is the reader of the ritual, the Great Nakatomi (comp. note 51), and the word rendered by 'says' signifies that the speaker is supposed to be speaking the words of the Mikado (Satow, above, p. 23, note 1).

2   親王諸王 *Miko-tachi Oho-kimi-tachi* (*tachi* plural suffix). *Mi-ko*, lit. "august child," or rather its sinico-jap. equivalent 親王 *shinnō* "prince of the blood" is, according to the Keiji-Ryō (part of the Taihō-Ryō) the old Japanese designation of a son of the Mikado. Every other prince was styled *oho-kimi* "great lord," sinico-jap. 王, *ō*, *wō*, plural 諸王 sho-ō "many kings"=*Ohokimi-tachi* of our text. The distinction between *shinnō* and *sho-ō* seems to have been introduced during the reign of the Emperor Temmu, for it is first mentioned in the Nihongi in an Imperial edict dated the 15th day of the second month of the fourth year of this Emperor (16th March, 675). The brothers and sisters of the Emperor were also included in the term *shinnō*. Later on this title was applied only to those princes upon whom it was specially conferred by the Emperor. Comp. the present writer's commentary on the above mentioned passage of the Nihongi in his German translation, Book 29 page 10, note 19.

From the fact that a distinction probably first made under the reign of Emperor Temmu, is referred to in the opening words of our ritual, we are by no means entitled to conclude that the ritual was composed during or after the reign of this Emperor, for the bulk of this and several other rituals is no doubt very much older than Emperor Temmu's time. The truth is that up to the Engi period, the text of the Norito was probably subjected to various interpolations, of a character not perfectly congruous with the spirit and conditions of antiquity. I concur with Motowori Toyokahi in regarding the first clause of the present Norito as a later addition. The expression *momo no tsukasa* (百官) "the hundred offices" is, of course, only the Japanized rendering of a purely Chinese phrase.

3   The subject is not expressed, but must be supplied from the verbal forms *harahi-tamahi kiyome-tamafu* "deign to purify and deign to cleanse." I agree with

Motowori and the majority of the Japanese commentators in referring the honorific
—*tamafu* "deigns" to the sovran at whose command the ceremony of purification
is undertaken and who, therefore, figures so to say as the purifier himself. Arakida
Morikuni, however, in his Oho-harahi no Kotoba Shin-kai, refers *tamafu* to the Oho-
Nakatomi, the reader of the ritual, and explains therefore: "I (the Oho-Nakatomi)
purify and cleanse." He argues that the Nakatomi uses the honorific -*tamafu* with
regard to his own action, because it is undertaken for the benefit of such high persons as the princes of the blood etc., and points to the similar use of the phrase
mawoshi-tamahaku in two passages of the congratulatory address of the Chieftains
of Idzumo (Norito 27) where *Idzumo no kuni no kuni-no-miyatsuko nanigashi
kashikomi kashikomi mo mowoshi-tamahaku*, resp. *kamu-hogi no yogoto mawoshi-
tamahaku to mowosu* evidently mean: "I, the chieftain of the province of Idzumo,
of such and such a Kabane and name, *declare humbly to the Emperor* in reverence,
in reverence," resp. "I *declare humbly to the Emperor* the congratulatory words
of the divine congratulation; [thus] I declare."

The expression *harahi-tamahi kiyome-tamafu* occurs a second time in our ritual,
in the passage immediately preceding the mentioning of the goddess *Se-oritsu Hime*;
here again Motowori refers -*tamafu* to the Emperor, whilst Haruyama refers it to
the gods who carry away the sins. Motowori's interpretation seems preferable, for
the ceremony of the purification which is executed at the command of the Emperor
extends to the throwing away of the purification offerings into the water; only then
the action of the Gods, in carrying away the purification-offerings, the symbols of
the thrown-away sins, is supposed to begin.

4 *Ayamachi-okashikemu kusa-gusa no tsumi* 過犯ヶム雜々罪 I deviate
in the interpretation of this phrase from Dr. Weipert who takes it to mean only
"sins committed through inadvertency" and lays special stress on this meaning in his
note on page 375. I have, however, little doubt that my interpretation is the correct
one, *ayamatsu* (過) meaning "to do anything amiss, to fail through inadvertency,"
like the modern *shi-zokonau*, and *okasu* (犯) "to do anything or to transgress
deliberately, knowingly" (not simply "to commit" in its usual light sense; comp.
also its meaning in the phrases quoted notes 41—45), so that *ayamachi-okasu* is an
antithetical, not an attributive compound. Some of the best Japanese authorities
(Shikida, Haruyama, etc.) are of the same opinion. Satow, W. R. p. 53: Committed
in ignorance or out of negligence.

5 *Hire Kakuru Tomo-no-wo* "scarf-wearing attendants," i.e. *uneme* "court-
ladies," because the *uneme* wore a *hire* "scarf" hanging round the neck and shoulders
as an ornament. *Tomo-no-wo* signifies properly the "head of a company" (*tomo =
組 zumi, wo = wosa*) From the most ancient times to the end of the Tokugawa period
the Mikado was served only by women. Comp. Satow's note on *Oho-mi-ya-no-me*
above, p. 30. An illustration of the *hire* is given in Modzume's Daijirin.
By an Imperial decree of the 28th day, 3rd month, of the 11th year Temmu (10th
May, 682), mentioned in the Nihongi, the *uneme* were forbidden henceforth to
wear *scarfs*. By the same decree also, the stewards (see following note) were
forbidden to wear shoulder-straps.

6 *Tasuki kakuru Tomo-no-wo* "sash-wearing attendants," i.e. *kashihade* or
"(Imperial) stewards." The steward wore a *ta-suki* "hand-helper," i.e. a cord passed
over the shoulders and attached to the wrists, in order to assist the arms in supporting
a heavy tray. The modern *tasuki* worn by women to keep the sleeves out of the
way when working, is different from it. The wearing of *tasuki* was forbidden by
Imperial decree in 682 (see preceding note). When preparing the food for the
Emperor, the stewards wear to the present day a *fukumen* (= covering the face),
i.e. a mask of white paper fastened with a string behind the ears over the mouth, to
prevent their breath from touching and thereby polluting the food; they are also
not allowed to touch it with the hands, e. g. in cutting fish or meat, but must
seize the food with *hashi* "chopsticks" in the left hand, and cut with the knife in
the right hand. The same holds good with regard to the preparation of the offerings
placed in the Shintō shrine.

7 *Yugi ofu tomo-no-wo* "attendants who carry quivers on the back," and *tachi haku tomono-wo* "attendants who gird on swords," i.e. military officers (here perhaps more especially palaceguards). *Yugi* is the oldest word for "quiver;" in the middle ages it is called *yamaguhi* and still later *ebira.* It was always carried on the back (*ofu;* ep. also Manyōshū 20: *Masurao no yugi tori-ohite idete ikeba*), and its shape, at least of such quivers as were carried on ceremonial occasions, may be guessed from a passage in the 内宮長歴途官符 : "there were used 24 brocade [covered] quivers, length 2.4 feet, width above 6 inches, width below 4½ inches, mouth hole for the arrows 2.9 inches square; made of Hinoki wood, etc."

8 *Tomo-no-wo on ya-so tomo-no-wo,* i.e. all the attendants in the Mikado's court, among whom the above mentioned four classes of Tomo-no-wo are also included. *Ya-so* "eighty" means simply "many."

9 ......*wo hazimete*...... I have rendered this by "especially......and moreover......"; more literally it would have been: *beginning from* the [persons] serving........*down to* the people.

10 *Tsukasa-dzukasa ni tsukahe-matsuru hito-domo,* i.e. all officials of the country who do no direct service in the Imperial palace.

Section I and II being a *semmyō* (宣命) "Imperial message," from the introduction to the ritual proper which is contained in section III.

11 *Sumera-ga-mutsu kamurogi kamuromi,* see Satow above, p. 24, note 6. The mythical ancestors of the Emperor, viz. *Taka-mi-musubi no Kami* "the High-August-Producing Deity" and *Ama-terasu-oho-mi-kami* "the Heaven-Shining-Great-August-Deity," the Sun-goddess, are meant. *Sumera-ga* is contracted from *sumera aga* "sovran his," *aga* referring to the Grandchild.

12 *Mi-koto mochite* "by [their] angust word." See Satow above, p. 23, note 5.

13 Taka-mi-musubi and the Sun-goddess assembled the other gods in council, in the bed of the Tranquil River of Heaven, (the Milky Way) to consider which deity should be sent down from Heaven to subdue the uproarious deities then inhabiting Japan, (the descendants of Susa-no-wo no Mikoto) and thus prepare it for the peaceful rule of the Sun-goddess,' descendants. See Satow above, p. 93, note 8, and Chamberlain' Kojiki, Sect. 30-33.

14 The self deprecatory auxiliary verb—*matsuru* "to serve" is here used, because the mandate is given to an august person, the predecessor of the Japanese Emperors.

15 The *Sume-mi-ma no mikoto* "sovran (august) Grandchild's augustness" is the grandchild of the Sun-goddess, *Ama-tsu-hiko-Ho-no-nigi no Mikoto* "His Augustness Heaven's-Prince Rice-ear-Ruddy-Plenty," for whose fuller name see Kojiki, page 106, note 5. His descent and later experiences are described Kojiki, sect. 33 sequ. His father Oshi-ho-mi-mi no Mikoto was properly the son of Susa-no-wo no Mikoto and only adopted by the Sun-goddess as her son, therefore really her nephew. See Nihongi and Kojiki (sect. 13 sequ.)

16 I. e. Japan. See Satow above, p. 93, note 7.

17 *Kunuchi* (contracted from *kuni uchi*) *ni araburu kami-domo,* comp. Kojiki, sect. 30: *chihayaburu araburu kuni tsu kami-domo* "violent and savage Earthly Deities." The Earthly Deities were those born and dwelling in Japan, in contradistinction to the "Heavenly Deities" who either dwelt in Heaven, or had originally descended to Earth from Heaven. The subjugation of the savage Earthly Deities, and the silencing of the "rocks and trunks of trees and isolated leaves of the herbs that had spoken," and the subsequent conquest of Yamato by the Emperor Jimmu, are probably a legendary echo of the eastward invasion of the Japanese from Kyūshū, into the main island of Japan. The Earthly Deities seem to be the deified chieftains of tribes akin to the Japanese who immigrated into Japan before, and were subjugated by, them, whereas the "rocks and trunks of trees and isolated leaves of the herbs that had spoken" seem to refer to the original natives of Japan who lived in the forests and mountains, viz.the Ainu.

The pacification of these deities was undertaken by the two Gods *Take-mika-dzuchi no Kami* and *Futsu-nushi no Kami* (so the names according to the Nihongi; in the Kojiki, sect. 32 they are *Take-mika-dzuchi-no-wo no Kami* and *Tori-bune no Kami*).

18 *Kaki-ha* or *kaki-ba* presents some difficulty. It is mostly explained as equivalent to *kata-ha* .... "single or isolated leaves;" according to Shikida it is an abbreviation of *akaki ha* .... "red leaves." Satow above, p. 85 translates, "the least leaf."

19 I. e. his place in Heaven. *Iha* "rock" is considered to be merely an honorific.

20 This is related with nearly the same words in Kojiki, sect. 24.

21 [Omitted by author in original Ed. T. A. S. J.]

22 *Mi-ya* "august house" means indiscriminately the house of a chieftain, the tombs of the dead and the temples of the gods. Satow above, p. 31, note 29.

23 *Chigi* "cross-beams," i. e. the projecting ends of the rafters of the roof, Shintō temples built in the archaic style, as the temples of Ise, the Yasukuni shrine in Tōkyō etc. have preserved this peculiarity of the primeval Japanese house. See Satow's description of the architecture of Shintō temples, in vol. II of these Transactions [First Series] and his Handbook, 2nd edition, p. [65].

24 *Midzu no mi-araka* "fresh, i. e. beautiful august abode." *araka* is derived from *aru ka* "place where one lives.

25 This means that the house protects the Mikado from the weather and the heat of the sun. Satow above, p. 31, note 30.

26 *Ame no masu hito-ra* "the heavenly surplus-population" or "the heavenly increasing population," i.e. men. This expression has its origin, in an incident told with regard to the flight of Izanagi no Mikoto from Hades: Kojiki sect. 9, Aston's Nihongi p. 25. When Izanagi had reached the Even Pass of Hades, he was overtaken by his wife *Izanami* who pursued him. Izanagi blocked up the path between himself and her with a huge rock, and both standing opposite to one another, Izanagi pronounced the formula of divorce. 'Upon this,' continues the Nihongi, 'Izanami no Mikoto said: My dear Lord and husband, if thou sayest so, I will strangle to death the people of the country which thou dost govern, a thousand in one day. Then Izanagi no Mikoto replied, saying: My beloved younger sister, if thou sayest so, I will in one day cause to be born fifteen hundred.'

27 *Nori-wakete* from *nori-wakuru*: *nori* "announcing," where the character 法 *nori* is used phonetically in stead of 宣 *nori*, and *wakuru* "to distinguish." In the text the expression *ama tsu tsumi to* "as heavenly sins" is put twice, once before and then after the list of the heavenly sins, whereby the construction becomes a little cumbersome. Haruyama advises to supplement the word *idemu* "will be forthcoming" of the second list in meaning also to the first one; then the literal translation would be: "as heavenly sins a number of sins, [viz.] .... , distinguishing [them] expressly as heavenly sins, [will be forthcoming]."

28 In the Japanese order of words the term *kokodaku no tsumi* "a number of sins, many sins" follows the enumeration of the seven heavenly sins (*ama tsu tsu mi*), and farther on also, the enumeration of the earthly sins (*kuni tsu tsumi*). In taking *kokodaku no tsumi* as an apposition to what precedes, I agree with the generally accepted interpretation. The author of the Gogoshaku, Fujiwi, however thinks that *kokodaku no tsumi* must be connected with the preceding words by "and," so that the meaning would be: "there are expressly distinguished as heavenly sins: breaking down........*and* a number of [other similar] sins." As instances of other heavenly sins Fujiwi mentions: damaging the crop and pollution of pure (sacred) buildings (f. ex. temples, or any locality where religious rites are performed).

The so-called HEAVENLY SINS are in reality nothing else but those offences which, according to the mythological tradition, had already been *perpetrated by the unruly god Susa-no-wo "Impetuous-Male" in Heaven* (see Kojiki, sect. 15, Nihongi p. 40 sequ., and especially p. 48), whence the name *Susa-no-wo* is the mythical scapegoat to whom all crimes which the primitive Japanese considered as most heinous, are attributed; he is, so to say, the personified register of all deadly sins (i. e. sins against agriculture and ritual purity; see the remarks later on) committed by men. Compared with the various passages of the Nihongi, the list of Susa-no-wo's sins in the Norito is not quite complete. There are not mentioned the "letting loose in autumn, the Heavenly piebald colts and making them lie down in the midst of the rice-fields," and the "stretching division ropes round the rice-fields in autumn, when the grain was formed." The former was probably omitted from the Norito, because is admits of no generalization and could not possibly be enumerated as a crime perpetrated often by men; the latter because it was only an offence of lighter kind, a mere unlawful claim to the ownership of the land, which did not in itself interfere with the successful cultivation of the fields and the necessary food-supply of the people. The Kojiki, on the other hand, is even less explicit than the Norito: it omits the *hi-hanachi*, *kushi-sashi* and *shiki-maki*. The third recognized source of ancient Japanese mythology and history, however, the KOGOSHUI (compiled in 807 from traditions of the *Imibe* family), gives a list of *Susa-no-wo's* misdeeds which is perfectly identical with 'the list of the "heavenly sins" in the Norito. There is an evident connection between their statements, and I have no doubt but that *Imibe Hironari*, the Shintō priest and compiler of the KOGOSHUI, shaped his statement according to that of the OHO-HARAHE NO KOTOBA, which was, of course, well known to him.

The etymology of the word *kokodaku* is unknown. Mabuchi identifies the first part *koko* with *koko* in *kosoko* "here and there" and says that *koko* alone has already the signification "many;" *daku* is derived by him from *baku* (sic!) which he considers to be a contraction of *bakari*. Motowori is, of course, right in rejecting such a fanciful etymology. It occurs also often in the MANYOSHU as *kokota, kokoda, kokodaku* with the meaning "thus much, in this extent," e. g. *kokota tomoshiki* "thus rare," *kokodaku mo wa ga moru mono* "that which I guard to this extent." I am inclined to see in *koko* either the doubled demonstrative pronoun *ko* "this," or rather the compound *ko-ko* "this place," and in *ta, daku* an element which is akin to the modern *dake* "as much as, this much."

The so-called EARTHLY SINS enumerated after this are said to have been committed only since the time of Jimmu-tennō, and to be, therefore, of later origin than the heavenly sins. For anybody who is not a strict believer in the absolute truth of the ancient Japanese traditions, this view requires no refutation. Yet here is a hidden point in this assertion which deserves attention. No 1 to 5 of the heavenly sins constitute disturbances in the cultivation of the rice-fields, and endanger the food-supply of the people, so that we need not be astonished to see them condemned in the first place—as Dr. Weipert rightly puts it: what to-day appears to us to be hardly worse than a somewhat strong kind of rude misdemeanour (starke Art groben Unfugs), was then an execrable crime, since it threatened the basis of subsistence which even apart from that was probably only a poor one. The 6th and 7th in the list offend against the idea of *ritual purity*, the highest moral notion and watchword of Shintoism. The *heavenly sins* seem consequently to comprise all those trespasses, which the Japanese in their most primitive state of society considered as crimes perpetrated against the interests of the community, and apt to bring down upon them the wrath of the gods. The *earthly sins*, on the other hand, comprise trespasses against the life, welfare, and property of individual persons (cutting the living skin, bewitching people, killing the animals of other people), incest, bestiality, and several kinds of unusual calamity, which were considered to be a punishment of the offended gods. Only the "cutting of the dead skin," (desecration committed on corpses) might be enumerated as a direct offence against "purity," because every contact whatever with a corpse was, and is regarded by the Shintoits as polluting.

Satow, Westminster Review, p. 49 sequ., adopts the opinion of the Japanese commentators, who explain the distinction between heavenly, and earthly sins, as based on the myth, but gives also another interesting explanation of the way in which the division may have arisen: The so-called heavenly offences are chiefly such as would be possible only in an agricultural community, or to agriculturists

living in the midst of a population of hunters, and fishermen. Now, there is good
reason to believe that the immigrants from the continent of Asia, who originally
settled in the province of Izumo, the seat of the earliest Japanese civilisation, were
tillers of the ground. They conquered and ruled the aboriginal hunters, and
fishermen, but the two races, instead of amalgamating, for a long time separately
pursued their hereditary occupations. That men who apparently came from the sea
had in reality descended from heaven, was an idea easily accepted, and a celestial
origin being thus attributed to the superior part of the community, the world heavenly
would be adopted generally to express whatever was peculiar to their mode of life,
and in enumerating the offences of the whole people, was consequently applied to
offences which could only be committed by the agricultural class.

The "heavenly sins" and "earthly sins" constituted the regular list of sins in
the Oho-harahe no Kotoba, whether they had been actually committed or not. But
that is not all. Before the purification ceremony the Nakatomi heard the confession
of the other persons taking part in it, and enumerated the sins of which he had
been thus informed in the Norito, after having recited the regular list. (I have this
information from Motowori Toyokahi's lectures).

According to N. Motowori, *tsumi* "sin, offence" includes three categories, viz.
kegare "pollution," *ashiki waza* "ill-deeds," and *wazahahi* "calamities." That certain
kinds of *wazahahi* (see notes 46-48) were included in the notion of *tsumi*, shows
their being considered as divine judgments: they are injuries which come to us from
the unseen world. In this respect the sinico-jap. term *ten-kei-byō* (天刑病) "Heaven's-
punishment-disease," i. e. leprosy, deserves attention as corroborating our view.
Kuni-tsu-tsumi is literally "country-sins;" but in the archaic language, *kuni* had also
the wider meaning of "earth," especially where it is used in contrast with *ame*
"Heaven."

For curiosity's sake only, I will quote the etymology given by some scholars
for the word *tsumi*. They say: *tsumi* is properly *tsutsumi*, from the verb *tsutsumu* "to
cover, to conceal," and signifies generally anything bad which one would like to
conceal from other persons.

Whilst I am inclined to think that the ideas of offence (*ashiki waza*) and
pollution (*kegare*), both not clearly distinguished from one another, form the proper
meaning of the word *tsumi*, and that the idea of calamity (*wazahahi*) was included
into it only secondarily, because calamity was considered to be a divine punishment,
Satow in W. R. p. 51, takes a somewhat different view. He says: If the word
tsumi, which we are forced by its modern applications to render "offence," had from
the first possessed that signification and no other, it is difficult to see how it could
have come to be applied, as we have seen that it was, to a large class of occurrences
which were either unavoidable misfortunes, or at worst, the result of carelessness.
Moreover, the word *tsumi* itself conveyed at first no idea of guilt, but simply expressed
something that was disagreeable, whether in the acts or the appearance of men.
In fact, we have here one of those numerous cases discoverable by students of early
history, in which a word starting with a general, undefined, obscure signification, fully
corresponding to the vague notion of the men who use it, gradually becomes restricted
in its application, to one of the ideas which emerge out of the chaos, and thus
obtains a distinct and unequivocal meaning, while other new terms are adopted to
express the remaining products of the medley.

29 *A-hanachi,* from *a＝aze* (*aze* is a compound, whose latter part *ze* is＝*se*
"back"), the low, narrow dykes, which separate the rice-fields from another, and
hanatsu "to sever." By breaking down these divisions, the water is made to flow off
from the rice-fields and the rice-plants perish.

30 *Mizo-ume.* The *mizo* "channels, or drains" conduct the water to the rice-
fields.

31 *Hi-hanachi.* Water for the watering of the rice-fields is accumulated in
ponds, ditches etc., and the floodgates (*hi*) which keep it back, are of course only
opened when necessary. If they are mischievously opened, the precious fluid flows

out and is not available at the proper time, so that the fields dry up and the crop perishes.

32 *Shiki-maki* "sowing repeatedly, sowing seed over again," from *shiki* "repeatedly" (comp. the old adverb *shiku-ṣiku* "repeatedly.") and *maku* "to sow." Dr. Weipert attributes to it the meaning "sowing too densely (zu dichtes Besäen)" and explains: Sowing the seeds on the fields too copiously or repeatedly, is punished, because it brings about a deterioration in the quality of the rice. Taken in the abstract, *shikimaki* could have this sense; but the context in which it appears in the Norito, and especially in the Nihongi, shows clearly that its real meaning is: secretly and maliciously sowing seed over a field which has already been sown by its proprietor, so that the first seed is injured by the second one (probably tares) and the crop becomes illusory. It is a roguish trick, like the three preceding ones and the following, played by *Susa-no-wo* upon his sister,. the *Sun-goddess*. Comp. in the Nihongi (p, 40 sequ.) the narrative of his rude behaviour, especially in the third variant: Therefore, Susa-no-wo no Mikoto was jealous and destroyed his elder sister's rice-fields. *In spring,* he opened the floodgates of the sluices (Aston: he knocked away the pipes and troughs), filled up the channels and broke the divisions; *more over he sowed seed over again.* There cannot be the least doubt but that the composer of the Oho-harahe no Kotoba understood the term *shiki-maki* in the same sense as the popular legend reported in the above passage of the Nihongi.

The reader will probably have observed the parallelism between this and the parable told by Christ in St. Matthew, Chap. 13, verse 24 sequ.: The kingdom of heaven in likened unto a man which sowed good seed in his field: but while men slept, his enemy came and sowed tares among the wheat, and went his way. But when the blade was sprung up, and brought forth fruit, then appeared the tares also, etc.

33 *Kushi-sashi* (Nihongi, Chap. 6, Variant III of my edition, 挿籤, in the Norito 串刺). The passage of the Nihongi quoted in the preceding note continues the report of Susa-no-wo's misdeeds: In autumn, he set up pointed rods [in the rice-fields], and made horses lie down in the rice-fields. Whosoever has seen how the cultivation of the rice-fields is done, by wading about in the deep mud with naked feet, will easily understand that the hiding of pointed bamboo or other rods in the mud is a very bad practical joke, so bad that it may eventually prevent the peasant from stepping into the field and cultivating it or cutting the crop.

The term *kushi-sashi* allows of yet another interpretation which is accepted by Shikida, Ihida (Nihon-shoki-tsūshaku), etc., and is based on no less an authority than the KOGOUSHSI. The Kogoshūi says in a note: When the Sun-goddess was cultivating her rice-fields, Susa-no-wo went secretly to those fields, set up rods, and contended with her. From this some commentators infer that the setting up of rods and the four above-mentioned misdeeds of Susa-no-wo did not properly intend an injury to the rice-fields of the Sun-goddess, but a quarrel for their ownership. Also the NIHONGI-SHIKI (an old commentary, quoted by Aston in note 7, page 48) says that rods (Aston: combs) were stuck up in the rice-fields with words of incantation, so that if anyone wrongly claimed the fields he might be destroyed. The present custom of setting up rods in rice-fields whose ownership is disputed arose perhaps from this. According to this view the *kushi* are signs set up to indicate that one claims the ownership of the field, and are therefore called 田札 *ta-fuda* "field-placards." Nevertheless I cannot convince myself that this interpretation is better than the one adopted by me in the translation. The second variant of the account of Susa-no-wo's misbehaviour in the Nihongi runs: Now Susa-no-wo no Mikoto, in spring, filled up the channels and broke down the divisions, and in autumn, when the grain was formed, he forthwith stretched round them division-ropes [*aze-naha,* in token of his ownership]. The claim to the ownership of a field was therefore, in ancient times, made by stretching ropes round it, and unless it can be proved that the setting of *kushi* was equivalent to the stretching round of *aze-naha,* we are compelled to assume that *kushi-sashi* does not convey the meaning "setting up rods in token of ownership." I may also quote a passage of the Kojiki, sect. 15, which is rather in favour of my view. It runs: So, though he did this (viz. breaking down the divisions, filling up the ditches, strewing excrements in the palace), Amaterasu no Oho-mi-kami upbraided him not, but said: What looks like excrements must be something that His Augustness mine elder brother has vomited through drunkenness. Again, as to his breaking down the divisions of the rice-fields and filling up the ditches, it must be because he grudges the land [they occupy] that His Augustness mine elder brother acts thus." But notwithstanding *these apologetic words*, he still continued his evil acts, and was more and more [violent]. Nothing could show more clearly that the Sun-goddess regards Susa-no-wo's behaviour as rude, roguish tricks, and jealous vandalism, which, however, with genuine Japanese politeness, she ostensibly excuses with the above apologetic words as a sudden nausea and ill-directed zeal for the increase of the arable land now occupied with things, in his opinion, so useless as dykes and ditches. In the variant of this story (Nihongi, 2nd variant) which I quote in note 35, the Sun-goddess does not look at the same trick with the same Olympian calmness.

34   *Ike-hagi saka-hagi,* explained as "flaying a living animal in the direction from the tail to the head." Motowori remarks that flaying from the tail to the head was the usual way of flaying; it seems therefore advisable not to separate *ike-hage* "flaying alive" from *saka-hagi* "flaying backwards," as if both words were terms for different methods of flaying, but to treat them as a compound word expressing one action, =*ike-saka-hagi*. The repetition of the substantive *hagi* is no stumbling block in the way of this interpretation, for similar expressions are very frequent in the ancient poetic language. In stigmatizing "flaying alive and backwards" as a crime, the ancient Japanese will hardly have been guided, as Dr. Weipert remarks, by the motive of protecting animals against superfluous torture, since half-barbaric times do not shew such humane tendencies. It is rather to be supposed that this way of flaying was regarded as a pollution, probably in consequence of some superstitions ideas unknown to us.

Susa-no-wo committed this crime in a manner which aggravated the offence: when the Sun-goddess sat in her Weaving-Hall, he broke a hole in the top of the roof and flung through it a heavenly piebald colt which he had flayed alive with a backward flaying. The compound term *ike-hagi saka-hagi* does not occur either in the Kojiki or in the Nihongi, but by comparing the various readings it becomes clear that "flaying alive backwards" is meant. The Kojiki, sect. 15, has: "a heavenly piebald horse which he had flayed with a *backward flaying*" (*ame no fuchi-koma wo saka-hagi ni hagite*); the Nihongi in the chief text only: "he *flayed* a piebald colt of Heaven;" in the first variant: "flaying a piebald colt with a *backward flaying*" (*saka-hagi ni hagite*); in the second variant "*flaying alive* a piebald colt" (*ike-hagi ni hagite*). The information, however, which the Kojiki and Nihongi do not give directly, is supplied by a gloss in the KOGOSHUI: *ikitaru koma wo saka-hagi ni shite muro-nuchi ni nage-ire-tamafu* "he flayed backwards a living colt and flung it into the Hall."

Shikida argues at great length that the reading *ike-hagi*, which even Motowori has, instead of *ike-hagi* is wrong. Comp. also *ike-dori, ike-nihe, ikesu*, etc.

35   *Kuso-he*, from *kuso* "excrement," and *he*, a contracted from of *heri*, stem of the verb *heru* "to eject." In the more modern language *heru* has become *hiru* (*kuso wo hiru, he wo hiru*), but the form *heru* is still preserved in the compound *heri-tsukuru*, viz. *tamago wo heri-tsukuru* "to lay eggs," said of small insects. Shikida reads *kuso-be* and attacks the usual derivation of *he* from *heri*. The Chinese character in the text is 戸 *he* (used phonetically), which he says has the meaning 家 *he* "house," *kuro-be*="polluting by evacuating excrements in a house;" or if one gives to the character 戸 the reading *to*, 屎戸 would have been used phonetically instead of 屎處 *kuso-do* "excrement-place." I do not think this explanation is acceptable, though Shikida is certainly right in pointing out that in the WAMYOSHO (an ancient dictionary, compiled by Minamoto no Shitagō in the period Enchō, i. e. 923-920) there occur the expressions *Kuso-hiri* and *he-hiru*, but not *kuso-heri* or *he-heru*. The absence of these forms from the Wamyōshō is, however, no conclusive proof that they never existed, and the above mentioned *heri-tsukuru* as well as the

word *he* "breaking wind, fart," which is doubtless related to *hiru*, seem to justify our etymology.

The corresponding misdemeanour of Susa-no-wo is related most fully in the second variant of the Nihongi: When the time came for the Sun-goddess to celebrate the feast of first fruits (the Dai-jō-we festival), Susa-no-wo no Mikoto secretly voided excrement under her august seat in the New Palace (in which the festival was to be celebrated). The Sun-goddess, not knowing this, went straight there and took her seat. Accordingly the Sun-goddess drew herself up, and became sick. She therefore was enraged, and straightway took up her abode in the Rock-cave of Heaven, and fastened its Rock-door.

Mabuchi refers *kuso-he* only to the pollution of a place sacred to the gods, whilst Motowori gives it a wider scope.

36 Comp. note 28.

37 *Iki-hada-tachi*, i. e. wounding or killing. Wounding comprises all injuries to oneself or to others, especially when blood flows; for the flowing of blood means pollution. Thus, according to the strict regulation for a Shintoist (which are, however, no longer commonly observed), a person is forbidden to go to a shrine and worship (Jap. *sankei suru*): for 30 days, if he has wounded somebody; for the day on which he has accidentally injured himself, so that more than three drops of blood have flowed. If it was only 1 to 3 drops, he may *sankeisuru* on the same day but must take a bath beforehand (this purification by a bath is quite in analogy to the purification by water in the Oho-harahe ceremony itself). Similarly, for two days, after he has vomited blood or ejected blood through the anus; if he has an abscess, until it is perfectly cured; for seven days after the application of moxa; for three days in the case of the person who has applied it.

It seems to me that the ritual considers the *iki-hada-tachi* as a sin not so much for its being an unlawful injury to somebody's life or body, which is the stand-point of our penal codes, as for the reason that it causes pollution and seriously offends against ritual purity. At any rate this latter point of view plays a part in it. Comp. also Satow, W. R., p. 50. The shedding of blood was held to defile both the shedder and the person whose blood was shed, an idea which has left its indelible mark in the language, where the most common word for wound or hurt is *Kega* defilement," and a wounded person is called a "defilement-man."

38 *Shini-hada-tachi*, i.e. desecration committed on corpses. Any contact, even in the widest sense, with corpses pollutes, as will be seen from the following regulations:

Sankei (see note 37) is forbidden during the whole mourning period for parents or relatives.

Sankei is forbidden on the anniversaries of the dying-day of parents or consorts.

Sankei is forbidden for 100 days, if one has assisted at the funeral of a relative, for seven days, if at the funeral of somebody else.

Sankei is forbidden for three days, if one has entered a house where a dead person was lying.

If a man or animal has perished in a conflagration, everybody belonging to the house in question must stop *sankei* for 100 days.

Sankei is forbidden for three days, if one has eaten anything prepared in a house of mourning.

If somebody dies on the premises of a shrine (*Kei-nai*), no Matsuri (festival) can be celebrated there for 30 days afterwards; if only part of the dead body was lying on the premises, the forbidden time is limited to 7 days.

If a dog, horse, or other animal has died on the premises of a shrine, there can be no Matsuri for 5 days; if only part of the dead body (the head, a leg, etc) was lying on the compound, no Matsuri can be held for 3 days.

For other rules the KIFUKU-RYO, part of the TAIKO-RYO, may be consulted.

39 *Shira-hito* or *shiro-hito* "white men," according to Motowori, who quotes the Wamyōshō people who have white spots on the skin of the face or body, including the so-called *shiroko* or *shiro-tsu-ko*, i. e. people who are entirely white all over the

body, albinoes. Mabuchi following his master Kada Adzumamaro, gives the highly phantastical explanation that *shira-hito* (sic) means "people from Shiragi" (Shiragi is the name of an ancient Kingdom in Korea, Silla.) Instead of the following *kokumi* he reads *kokuri*, i. e. people from Kokuri" (Kokuri, or Korai, or Koma, is the name of another ancient Korean kingdom), and brings both these names into close connection with the list of the execrable crimes enumerated afterwards, saying that such crimes could not possibly have been committed by Japanese, but must have been committed by Koreans, people of Shiragi and Kokuri, settled in Japan. Certainly a patriotic view of the matter! The commentator's mind may have partly been directed to this interpretation by a passage of the Nihongi describing an incident of the year 612 (Aston II, 144). "This year a man emigrated from Pekche (a kingdom in Korea, called Kudara by the Japanese) whose face and body were all flecked with white, being perhaps affected with white ringworm (白 癩 *shira-hada* lit "white skin"). People disliking this extra-ordinary appearance, wished to cast him away on an island in the sea, etc., etc." Kubo in the Norito-ryakkai decides to understand *shira-hage* (白禿), a skin disease by which the head becomes pefectly bald, and *shira-katai* (白癩) white leprosy." For Shikida's entirely different view see the next note.

40 *Kokumi*, written only phonetically, probably because the meaning of the word was already doubtful at the time when the Norito were first committed to writing. *Kokumi* is, according to the *Wamyōshō*, identical in meaning with *amashishi*, which is contracted from *amari-shishi* "superfluous flesh, i. e. excrescence." Motozume's *Daiji-rin* enumerates under Kokumi: *ibo* "warts," *uwo no me* "corns or bunions," etc. Haruyama explains *Kokumi* as a contraction from *hakukumi* and says it is a kind of *Ko'bu fusube* "fleshly tumours and black spots." Satow, Westminister Review[n], p. 51: "That leprosy and proud flesh (Satow's rendering of *shira-hito* and *Kokumi*) should have continued to be regarded as unclean is no doubt owing to the intense feeling of disgust, stronger than pity in a barbaric race, which such diseases excite. Whatever may have been meant by proud flesh, leprosy at least was regarded as contagions, and the leper was held unfit to associate with the rest of mankind."

Shikida (Norito Bemmo 5,15) wishes to divide 白人胡久美 into *shira-hi toko-kumi* "cohabitation in clear day-light" (*shira* white, clear; *hi* day; *toko* bed; *kumu* to come together, embrace one another), pointing out that this has always been considered to be an impure action, even the Emperor being forbidden to cohabitate after the depth of the night is over. This interpretation is certainly an ingenious one, and not at all impossible, considering that the phonetically written *Kokumi* occurs only here, and that the writing 白人 *shira-hito* may be an old popular etymology, or may also be intended to give only the sounds. The tern *tokokumi* finds its analogy in the *Kojiki* and Nihongi. On the other hand, however, it must be observed that the expression *shira-hi* "bright daylight" is somewhat strange and cannot be illustrated by any quotation. As both the traditional interpretation, and that of Shikida have their weak points, I have thought it safer to adopt the former one, little satisfying as it is.

41 *Ono ga haha (wo) okaseru tsumi. Ono ga haha* "one's own mother;" *okaseru* attrib. from of *okaseri*, the preterite of *okasu* which means here "to have forbidden sexual intercourse, to abandon onesself to fornication."

42 *Ono ga ko (wo) okaseru tsumi. Ko* "child" means here the daughter.

43 *Haha to ko to okaseru tsumi*, lit. "fornication with the mother and [her female] child." This means, according to Haruyama, to marry a woman and abandon oneself to fornication with her daughter from a former marriage. *Okaseru* refers consequently not to *haha*, with whom the intercourse is legitimate, but to *Ko*, the step-daughter.

44 *Ko to haha to okaseru tsumi*, grammatically just the contrary of the former expression, *okaseru* referring to *haha*:—sexual intercourse with the child and the mother, i.e. with one's wife and her mother, one's mother-in-law.

These four terms (note. 41—44) correspond on the whole to our ideas of incest, viz. sexual intercourse between relatives (by blood and marriage) in the ascending line. It will be observed that the *incest between brother and sister* is not mentioned, and it appears probable that marriage between brother and sister was allowed in ancient Japan. The archaic language has also only *one* word for "wife" and "younger sister," viz. *imo*. But too much stress must not be laid upon the latter circumstance, as, in the classic time, the word *imo* "younger sister" was often applied as an endearing epithet to one's wife. The same is the case in the Shir-ha-shirim (the Song of Solomon), e. g. chapter 4, verse 9: "my sister, my spouse." More important for our hypothesis is the fact that, even in later times, marriages were allowed between children of one father by different mothers, though unions between children of the same mother were forbidden (a relic of matrimonial right).

45 *Kemono okaseru tsumi*, i.e. bestiality. The Kojiki, sect. 97, when mentioning, for the first time, the ceremony of the Great Purification of the country, which was performed after the death of the Emperor Chiū-ai (A. D. 200, according to the chronology of the Nihongi), enumerates in detail the various sorts of bestiality, viz. *uma-tahake* "marriages with horses," *ushi-tahake* "marriages with cattle," *tori-tahake* "marriages with fowls," *inu-tahake* "marriages with dogs." All these animals are kept in the house and are called *kemono*, which is said to be as much as *kahi-mono* "domestic animals" (from *kafu* to keep and feed animals, *mono* thing), and is to be distinguished from *kedamono* "beasts, wild animals." I have, however, some doubt whether this distinction between *kemono* and *kedamono* (probably from *ke-tsu-mono*, *tsu* genitive particle) be not merely an artificial one, and whether *ke* does not rather mean *ke* "hair."

Dr. Weipert draws attention to the fact that among these crimes against morality *pederasty* is not mentioned (though it is alleged to be, and to have been, very common. Quite a number of books exist on this subject in Japanese, like the Nanshoku-ōkagami etc.)

46 *Hafu mushi no wazahai.* For *wazahai* see end of note 28. *Hafu mushi* "crawling worms" are snakes, centipedes, etc. In ancient times the houses of the common people had neither ceilings nor floors made of wooden planks, as at present, and therefore accidents through being bitten by venomous snakes, centipedes, etc. were incomparably more frequent. Even the palace of the Emperor was originally nothing but a wooden hut, with its pillars planted directly in the ground (not erected on broad, flat stones as in modern time) and a *yuka*, "raised floor," which occupied only part of the interior, the rest of the space being a mud-floor. As thus the inmates of the palace were constantly exposed to the attacks of crawling worms,' a special service was celebrated to obtain the protection of the gods for the sovereign's abode, viz. the *Oho-tono-matsuri*, at which Norito No. 8 *Oho-tono-hogahi* (Satow above, pp. 81 sequ.) was recited. Comp. the following passage of this Norito: I repeat the names of the gods who tranquilly and peacefully watch so that the great House where he sits ruling, [as far as] the limit of the bottom-most rocks, may be free from the calamity of crawling worms [among] the lower cords [which tie it together, as far as the] limit of the blue clouds of the Plain of High-Heaven, may not have the calamity of birds flying in at the smoke-hole in the roof, etc.

47 *Taka-tsu-kami no wazahahi*, i.e. calamity sent by the *Thunder-god* (being struck by lightning) and the *Tengu*. The *Tengu* (two in number), lit. "heavenly dogs," are goblins with a red face, an enormous nose, claws and a pair of wings. They inhabit mountains and forests and often carry away people of both sexes into the desolate mountains. The Tengu belong, like *Inari, Hachiman, Dōryū*, etc. to the few Shintō deities whose statues are commonly found and used as objects of worship.

In the 大同類聚方一, (quoted in Shikida's Norito-bemmō) the term *mono-no-ke* "evil influence of a sprite" is explained by: *mojikori* "bewitchment," *kedamono no ke* "calamity from animals," and *taka-kami no ke* "calamity from the high gods." The last is identical with our *taka-tsu-kami no wazahahi*, *ke* being equivalent to *wazahahi*; the first corresponds to *mazimono seru tsumi* (note 49), but means the passive sufferance of bewitchment, whilst the Norito speaks of its active exercise; the second seems to include what is called *hafu mushi no wazahahi* and *taka-tsu-tori no wazahahi* in the Norito.

48 *Taka-tsu-tori no wazahahi.* See also the quotation from the 8th Norito in note 46. The roof of the ancient Japanese house was thatched, and perhaps had a gable at each end, with a hole to allow the smoke of the wood-fire to escape, so that it was possible for birds flying in and perching on the beams overhead, to defile the food, or the fire with which it was cooked (Satow above, p. 83.) The defiling things dropped by the birds are in the first line, their excrements which are believed to be poisonous, and secondarily dirty things dropped from their bills. Haruyama attributes to the term a still wider sense, viz., any damage done by birds, and mentions also the carrying away of babies by eagles and kites.

49 *Kemono-tafushi.* The above rendering follows Motowori's interpretation. He thinks that the people of old must have known and practised a peculiar art (*jutsu*) by which they injured or killed the animals of other people. He mentions also the popular superstition wiith regard to the existence of evil sprites which are able to make animals sick and make them die—the so-called *gyuba no ekijin* (牛馬 ノ 疫神) "cattle's and horses' pestilence-gods"—, but maintains that this does not come into consideration here, as foul tricks practised directly by men are to be understood. *Kemono-tafushi* belongs therefore, according to him, to the same category as the following *mazimono seru tsumi.*

Another noteworthy interpretation, however, and perhaps the better one, given by Mabuchi and accepted by Shikida, takes this and the following term as one: *kemono-tafushi-mazimono seru tsumi* "the sin of exercising witchcraft [by means] of killing animals." It is considered to be identical with a certain kind of sorcery called *inu-gami* (犬神) "dog deity," practised in Kyūshū and Shikoku to the present day, in which one pretends to be able to invoke evils on other persons through the spirit (*reikon*) of a slain dog. To come into possession of this witchcraft, one has to proceed in the following way: A hungry dog in chained up, and some food is laid before him, but so that he cannot reach and eat at it. While he stretches out his head to get at it, one cuts off his head. The head suddenly flies and swallows the food, whereupon it is seized, put into a box and worshipped. Henceforth it is a powerful means for exercising various kinds of witchcraft to the detriment of other people. the spirit of the dog being the medium (agent). The place of the dog can also be taken by a serpent, or in the province of Tosa by a *weasel* (*itachi*). See an article on *Inu-gami-mochi* in Fuzoku-gaho, fase. 6, p. 20. Mabuchi declares such sorcery as *inugami* not to be originally Japanese, but to have been imported into Japan by foreign barbarians *gwaiban*, i. e. Chinese and Koreans, for which reason it is found only in southwestern Japan. This imaginary foreign importation, in support of which he does not bring forth even the shadow of a proof, leads him to assert that the present Norito cannot be very old:—of course an entirely untenable view which is also rejected as absurd by Motowori. The latter scholar observes that he, too, was originally inclined to consider *kemono-tafushi mazimono seru tsumi* as one single expression, but that later on he changed his view.

50 *Mazi-mono seru tsumi.* Invoking evils on other persons plays still at present an important part in Japanese superstition. Comp. the preceding note.

51 *Oho-Nakatomi*, the chief of the whole Nakatomi family. *Nakatomi* is probably derived from *Naka-tsu-omi*, which etymology corresponds also to the meaning of the Chinese characters (中臣) "middle minister." Their duty was of a priestly character, they were considered as mediators between the kimi "sovereign" and the *kami* "gods," hence another etymology explains the name from *naka-tori-omi* (i.e. kimi to kami to no *naka* wo *tori* mochite kami ni yoroshiku mōshi-kō; Motowori and Haruyama), or *naka-torimochi* "mediator" Hirata).

They derive their origin from the god *Ame no Koyane no Mikoto* who played a conspicuous part in the ceremony arranged to entice the Sun-goddess from the Rock-cave. One of their members, the famous *Kamatari*, received the surname of *Fujihara* for his meritorious services under Emperor Tenji, thus becoming the founder of the

illustrious Fujihara family, while the rest retained their name of Nakatomi.
Ono-Nakatomi was adopted as a surname by Omi-maro, a son of first cousin of
Kamatari. The Fujihara family gave up the service of the gods, and devoted
themselves entirely to politics, while the Nakatomi still remained in the priesthood,
which explains the fact that so many of them were officials of the Jingi-kwan or
Ministry of Shintō religion (Satow, above, p. 42).

52 *Ama tsu miya-goto*, i.e. the ceremonies of the Great Purification performed
in the palace of the Sun-goddess Ama-terasu on the Plain of High Heaven. This
expression shows that the earthly Oho harahe was considered to be only the imitation
of an *Oho-harahe* long ago practised by the Gods in Heaven.

53 A similar expression is already used in Norito No. I with regard to
cutting the timber for the construction of the Imperial palace: because [the builders],
having cut the bases and ends of the big trees and little trees (*wo-gi*) which have
grown up in the distant mountains and the near mountains, etc. In both cases it
is intended to say that the lower and upper ends of the trees, as being of less value,
are cut off and thrown away, and only the middle and best part of the wood used
for the pillars or tables.

Kanagi 金木, translated by "young little trees" according to the usual interpretation, presents some difficulty. This view evidently considers 金 *kana* as a
phonetic element, (perhaps *ko* "child, small," *na* genitive particle, through vowel
harmony *ka-na* ?). Others, like Shikida, take 金 *kana* in its literal sense "metal,"
kana-gi then: wood as strong and hard as metal. Shikida quotes a passage from the
大同類聚方廿一, from which he infers that *kanagi* is 橿木, which again,
according to Giles No. 1223 is a name for the 萬年木 (ten thousand years tree)
everlasting wood, used (in China) for certain parts of carts.

54 *Chi-kura oki-kura*. *Okiku-ra* signifies a stand (*kura*) on which something
is put (*oku*). The first *kura* in the compound *chi-kura* is used as a numerative
(auxiliary numeral). *Chi* "thousand" indicates simply a very great number. A
similar expression, viz. *shi-kura-oki-do* (*do* = place) occurs in the Nihongi, in the
passage where it is reported that purification-offerings were demanded from Susa-no-
wo: after this (i.e. after the Sun-goddess had been enticed out of the Heavenly Rock-
cave) all the Gods put the blame on Susa-no-wo no Mikoto, and imposed on him a
fine of *one thousand tables* (*chi-kura-oki-do*), and so at length chastised him. They
also had his hair plucked out, and made him therewith expiate his guilt. It is also
said that they made him expiate it by plucking out the nails of his hands and feet.
When this was done, they at last banished him downwards.

55 *Suga-so* 菅曽; *suga* or *suge* "rush," *so* "fine strips" (the character 曽 is
used phonetically). Brinkley's Dictionary explains *suga-so* by "a kind of brush made
of rush, formerly used by a Kannushi to cleanse himself and the people who are
assembled in a shrine for prayer." Mabuchi considers *so* as a contraction of
saki "splitting," Motowori as a contraction of *sa-wo* (佐緒) "fine thread."
I have, however, not much confidence in either of these etymologies. There
is an archaic word *so* "hemp" (e. g. Manyōshū I, 29: *uchi-so Womi no oho-kimi*,
etc.) which we might have here; besides there is an adjective *suga*, "clear, pure"
always used as a prefix *sumu* (akin to the verb *sumu* "to be clear, to be pure and limpid").
Shikida takes *suga-so* indeed in this sense: 清麻 "pure hemp."

With regard to this passage, which he does not translate, Satow, W. R. p. 53,
has the following remark: The high priest then (i. e. after having enumerated the
offences) arranges the sacrifices, and, turning round to the assembled company, waves
before them a sort of broom made of grass, to symbolize the sweeping away of their
offences." This agrees with what Mabuchi remarks, viz. that the split *Suga* was
brandished as if sweeping away dust. I have no doubt that this *suga-so* is the
prototype of the *oho-nusa* (大麻) described in Introduction, chapter 8. The hypothesis
is supported by a remark of the commentator—Okubo who says that *asa* (hemp) took
later on the place of the *suga* (rush).

56 *Ya hari ni tori-sakite* 八針爾取辟底 Mabuchi's interpretation of 八 *ya*＝彌 *ya, iya* "more and more" is generally accepted: *ya hari ni* "more and more with the needle." Also Mabuchi's interpretation of *hari* by "needle" which the Chinese character 針 conveys, is universally acknowledged, except by Motowori, who considers 針 to be phonetical and ascribes to *hari* the meaning *suji* "stripe": splitting more and more in stripes.   Mabuchi's view deserves preference.

57 *Ama-tsu-norito no futo-norito-goto wo nore.*   There are divergent opinions with regard to the proper meaning of *ama-tsu-norito* "heavenly ritual." Hirata thinks that the so-called *Misogi no harahi no kotoba* "words accompanying the bodily purification" are meant; but these are, as Motowori Toyokahi remarks, only an abbreviation of the *Oho-harahe no kotoba,* our ritual, and are of later origin. Another commentator understands by *ama-tsu-morito* the sentence "*toho-kami emi-tame* you distant gods, deign to smile!" (*tama*＝*tamahe*) which is used in the method of divination from the cracks of the shoulder-blade of a deer scorched over a clear fire.

I think, however, that the nearest and simplest interpretation is, as usual, also here the correct one, viz. that *ama-tsu-norito* is nothing else but our present ritual, the Oho-harahe no kotoba itself. The differences in the views are partly due to the different interpretation of the verbal form *nore* "shall speak" which some consider to be the imperative, others the indicative＝*noru;* Fujiwi even declares *nore* to be a mistake for *nori.* There can be hardly any doubt but that the meaning conveyed is: Oho-Nakatomi is commanded by the Emperor, the successor of the Heavenly Grandchild, to perform such and such ceremonies and recite such and such words, as were performed and recited in the purification ceremony in Heaven, and were, therefore, also prescribed for the descendants of the Gods, the men on earth. *Nore* must be the imperative.

58 The gods residing on the Plain of High Heaven are contrasted with the gods dwelling on the earth. Lit. "country-gods."

59 I.e. the door, constructed of rocks, of their palace in Heaven. *Iha* "rock" is by some commentators taken only as an honorific.

60 短山 is read *hiki-yama* (*hiki*＝*hikui*) by Hirata, Haruyama and others, but the correct reading is *mizika-yama,* given by Motowori, Shikida, etc. The latter quotes quite a number of passages from ancient texts which show that the reading *mizika* alone is well founded.

61 *Ibori* or *ihori* "smoke," an ancient word, now *iburi* (verb *iburu* "to smoke"). The clouds and the mist hovering around the mountains are meant. The word *kemuri, keburi* "smoke" is probably a compound of *ke* (＝*ki, iki?*) and *iburi.*

62 There was an old tradition (according to Motowori Toyokahi) that the gods of Heaven and Earth come together at one place in order to hear the Norito.

63 What I have rendered by the words "it is to be expected that" is in the original the simple demonstrative particle *to* (....*arazi to*＝it is to be expected that ....will not be).

64 *Tsumi to ifu tsumi.* This curious expression occurs a second time further on.

65 The "sovran Grandchild" is properly, as already stated, *Ninigi no Mikoto;* but here the term is applied to the presently reigning Emperor, as successor of Ninigi. This is not the only instance of the kind: in the Suinin-ki of the Nihongi, 25th year, the term "sovran Grandchild" is used of the Emperor Suinin; in the Temmu-ki, 1st year, of the Emperor Temmu; and also in the Zoku-Nihon-kō-ki occurs a similar use of the word.

The word rendered by "court" is in the original the well-known *mi-kado,* which, does not (here) designate Emperor, but his court or palace. The etymology is uncertain: it may be *mi-kado* "august gate," which reminds us of the Sublime Porte, or *mika-to* "august place." There are many different ways of writing it with Chinese characters, e. g. in the Nihongi: 王室, 王宮, 天朝, 朝庭 (also used here in the ritual) etc., in the Manyōshū: 朝廷, 御朝廷, 御門 etc.

66 *Shinato no kaze* "the wind of Shinato," i.e. the wind produced by the wind-god Shinato. *Shinato* is an abbreviation of *Shinatobe no Mikoto* "the long-breathed maiden" (*shi* "wind," *na* apocopated form of *naga* "long," *to*=*tsu* the generic particle, *be*=*me* "woman"). In the service of the gods of wind at Tatsuta, the 4th Norito, two gods of wind are mentioned: *Shinatsu-hiko no Mikoto* "the long-breathed youth," and *Shinatobe no Mikoto,* also called *Shinatsu-hime no Mikoto.* For details see Satow, above, p. 58 sequ. Should it be possible that the feminine suffix *be* has been omitted in order to include both the male and female wind-god in the one name *Shinato?* The same phrase *Shinato no kaze* occurs also in a passage of the Genji-monogatari, chapter Asagao: Ana kokorou, sono mi no tsumi ha mina Shinato no kaze ni toguhe teki to notamafu. In later times Shinato has been used as a name for the north-west wind (Comp. Chamb. Kojiki, pag. 27, note 15).

67 *Ashita no mi-giri* (from *mi-kiri*). *Mi* is written with the character "august" which, however, in such compounds as *mi-giri, mi-yama, mi-yuki,* etc. must be translated by "deep" or "dense." Whether this *mi* "deep, dense" is etymologically identical with the honorifics *mi* and *ma,* or whether it is of different origin, it is difficult to decide.

68 *Oho-tsu-be* lit. "large harbour side."

69 大海原. Motowori reads *oho-umi no hara,* Hirata and Haruyama *oho-wata no hara,* Shikida *oho-una-bara.* The last reading seems to be the oldest, *wata* and *una* are both archaic words for "sea, ocean."

70 *Wochi-kata* "that side, yonder," used here with only very slight meaning, *wochi* is the contrary of *kochi* "here, this side"; both are often combined into *wochi-kochi* "here and there" (f. ex. Manyōshū 4 etc). *wochi-kata* corresponds in meaning to the modern *anata,* which is contracted from *ano kata* "that side," commonly used as a polite pronoun of the second person. Satow, W. R. p. 54 translates: the trunks of the forest trees, far and near.

71 *Yaki-kama no to-kama,* with the repetition of the substantive, so much in favour in the ancient poetic style, instead of saying simply "tempered sharp sickle." *To* is the stem contained in the adjective *toki* "sharp" and the verb *togu* "to whet;" *to kama* occurs also in the second book of the Kojiki (*to-kama ni sawataru kuhi*). *Yoki* is from the verb *yaku* "to burn, to roast," which means here "to harden by fire, to temper." An analogous expression *yaki-tachi* "tempered sword," is found in Manyōshū 18. Also in *yaki-ba* (*ha* edge) "tempered edge of a sword," *yaki* has the same meaning. The readings *yaki-kama* and *to-kama* are more correct than the nigoried forms *kaki-gama* and *to-gama.*

72 In the original only *koto* (事) "thing" which must be interpreted to mean *tsumi-koto* "sinful things, sins."

73 See note 3.

74 *Se-ori tsu Hime* (瀬織津比咩) is, according to the 倭姬世記, identical with *Ya-so-maga-tsu-bi no kami* "Wondrous-Deity-of-Eighty-Evils" who has born when Izanagi no Mikoto, on his return from Hades, went to the plain of Ahagi at Tachibana on the river Woto in the province of Himuka (now Kyūshū), and purified himself from the contracted filth in the middle reach of the stream. The Nihongi has only the name *Ya-so-maga-tsu-bi,* whilst the Kojiki mentions two distinct deities: *Ya-so-magatsu-bi no Kami* and *Oho-maga-tsu-bi no Kami* "Wondrous-Deity-of-Great-Evils." In my opinion *Ya-so-maga-tsu-bi* and *Oho-maga-tsu-bi* are only alternative names of one and the same deity, so that the more correct tradition would be on the side of the Nihongi. *Se-ori tsu Hime* signifies "Current-descending-Princess:" *se* "swift current, or a place in a river where the water is not deep;" 織 *ori* stands phonetically for 下 *ori* "descending."

75 *Sakunadari ni ochi-tagitsu.* The latter part is clear: *ochi* from *otsuru* "to fall," *tagitsu,* closely related to *tagiru,* "to boil, to foam" (*taki* "waterfall" belongs to the same root). The first part *sakunadari,* however, presents great difficulties. There are as many different opinions about it as there are commentators,

and the meaning of the word was probably already obscure at the time when the Norito was first committed to writing, for it is written only phonetically. I will pass in review the most prominent explanations:

a) *sa* honorific prefix, like *ma*; *kuna*=*kuda*, supposing a sound-change between *d* and *n*, which indeed sometimes occurs: *kuda* stem *kudaru* "to come down;" *tari* from *taru* (*tariru*) "to hang down, to drop down." *Sakuna-dari- ni*="in falling."

b) Shikida considers *sakunadari* to be a contraction of *saku-kuna-dari*. He gives *saku* the meaning 激 "fierce, violent" and quotes a poem from Manyōshū 14, where *saku-nami* is contrasted with *hira-se* "level current" and it must, in his opinion, mean "fierce waves." *kuna* would be an old word for 谷 "valley, ravine," the existence of which word he tries to prove by the name of the shrine 佐久奈度 神社 *Sakunado-jinja*, which ought to mean 激谷所 "fierce ravine-place," and by a passage of the Wamyōshō. In the Sarashina district of the province of Shinano there is a Sato called 小谷 which must be pronounced, according to the Wamyōshō, 乎宇奈 *wo-u-na*, and this *wo-u-na* is by Shikida considered to bo a transformation from wo-kuna 小谷.

c) Haruyama supposes the first word *saku* to mean 谷 "valley, ravine," and illustrates this by the place-name 宮谷村 *Miya-saka-mura* in the Yamabe district of the province of Kadzusa, and by orthographies like 長谷 *naga-zaku*, 越谷 *koye-saku*, etc., *nadari* is=*nadare* "gradual slope."

I think that Haruyama's hypothesis comes nearest to the truth. But *saku* might rather be an archaic form of *saka* "hill,, slope," just as we have the double form *waku* and *waka* "young," e. g. in the name *Waka-musubi* or *Waku-musubi*, *nadari is* the indefinite or stem form, used as a verbal substantive, of the verb *nadaru* "to slope or incline downwards;' it is the old form, whilst *nadare* is a more modern form of the substantive, derived form *nadaruru* (*nadareru*). If my explanation be correct, the literal meaning of *saku-nadari ni ochi-tagitsu haya-kaha* would be: "the rapid streams that fall boiling (foaming) down flow the gradual hill-slopes." I have, however, closely adapted my translation to Satow's rendering of a similar passage in the Hirose Oho-imi no Matsuri (Norito 3, above, p. 57: the water which the sovran gods deign to send boiling down the ravines *sakunadari ni kudashi-tamáfu midzu*). It would have been interesting to know Satow's view of the etymology, but unfortunately he has not appended a note.

76) *Haya-aki tsu Hime* 速開都比咩 (in the original the character 比 *hi* was wanting, but has been inserted by the various editors) signifies, according to the characters which are partly ideographic, partly phonetic "Swift-opening-princess," and is an offspring of Izanagi no Mikoto. It is, however, much disputed whether this is the real meaning of the name. The Kojiki and Nihongi agree in designating this deity as *minato no kami*, i.e. "Deity of the Water-doors," but the Kojiki (see Chamb. p. 26) enumerates two deities *Haya-aki-dzu-hiko* and *Haya-aki-dzu-hime*, writing *aki* with the character 秋 "autumn": Prince-of-Swift-Autumn" and "Princess of Swift Autumn;" whilst the Nihongi (Aston, p. 32) has only the name *Haya-aki-tsu-hi*, written 速秋津日 "Sun (i.e. Wondrous [Deity]-of-Swift-Autumn." which however must be taken in a plural sense, as it expressly says *minato no kami-tachi* "Gods of the Water-doors." It seems that *hi* "wondrous" is the neutral form, including *hi-ko* "wondrous child, prince" as well as *hi-me* "wondrous woman, princes." *Haya* is probably "swift," but could also mean "brilliant." *Aki* is explained as "clear, bright," and *tsu* as generic particle in Shida's Nihonshoki-tsūshaku; but Shikida interpretes it in his Nihongi-hyōchū: *aki* "open," *tsu* "port, harbour." According to the latter view the name of the goddess signifies "Swift-open-harbour-Princess." I prefer to consider *tsu* as the generic particle: "Swift-Opening-Princess" (die schnell sich öffnende Fürstin, as also Dr. Weipert puts it). This meaning agrees best with the part ascribed to her in the purification-ceremony: she resides in the great whirl-pool of the ocean, or rather *is* this whirlpool herself, and opens her mouth and swallows down the waters as well as everything floating in them. Satow, W. R. p. 54 translates her name by Maiden-of-the-Swift-cleansing. The goddess is also

identified with *Idzu-no-me-no-kami* "the Female-Deity-Idzu." Comp. Chamb. p. 41 note 17.

77 This pleonastic expression is highly characteristic of the solemn style of the ancient Japenese poetry. In rendering it I was really sorry I could not do so in German: die Salzflut-Allzusammenflusstelle der vielhundertströmigen vielen Salzflutströme der frischsalzflutigen Salzflut! In the original *ara-shiho no shiho no ya-ho-ji no ya-shiko-ji no shiho no ya-ho-ahi*. *Ara* is properly "rough" but according to Motowori Toyokahi it means here *dekitate* "fresh." *ya-ho* 800 = very many, all. *Ji* "way"=currents of the water. *ya-ho-ahi* "800 meetings" is that place of the ocean on the farthest border of the visible world where all the currents of the water come together and form the big whirlpool through which they rush down into the land of Hades. Through the same gorge the waters are also again spat out, and by this periodic swallowing down and spitting out are produced ebb-tide and flood tide Everything bad and impure in the world, is supposed to have come from Hades, and by the ceremony of the Oho-harahe it is again sent back to its birth-place.

78 In the original *ka-ka nomitemu* "will swallow down [with the sound] ka-ka." *Ka-ka* is an ancient onmatopoetic (in German "gluck-gluck," corresponding to the English verb to cluck), for which one now uses *gabu-gabu*.

79 *I-fuki-do* 氣吹戸 "breath-blowing-place:" *i-fuki* contracted from *iki-fuki* "breath-blow away;" the reading *ibuki* is not so good, as in shown by the Jimmei-shiki's (神名式) phonetic writing 意布伎 *i-fu-ki* in the name of the Shintō shrine Ifuki-jinja in the Kurimoto districts of the province of Afumi. 戸 *to* "door" is phonetic for 處 *to* "place." The Breath-blowing-place is the place where a special deity, and offspring of Izanagi no Mikoto, blows away by his breath all sins and pollutions into Hades. This god is therefore called *Ifuki-do-nushi* "Lord of the Breath-blowing-place." An authority identifies this god with *Kamu-naho-bi Oho-naho-bi no Kami* "Divine-Rectifying-Wondrous Great Rectifying-Wondrous Deity." The Kojiki and Nihongi, in the report of the lustration of Izanagi, make two gods of this: *Kamu-naho-bi no Kami* and *Oho-naho-bi no Kami*, I think that, as in the case of *Ya-so-maga-tsu-bi Oho-maga-tsu-bi* (comp. note 74), it is better to consider them as alternative names of one deity.

80 根國底國 *ne-no-kuni soko-no-kuni*. Hades, generally called *Yomi-tsu-kuni* or *Yomo-tsu-kuni*, is meant. The translation "Bottom-Country" gives the meaning of the Chinese characters; the real meaning is probably "distant country," from *so* "there, yonder," and *ko* "place": "das Jenseits" in German. Whether *ne* signifies "root" or not, it is in reality the name of a place, of an island, belonging to Idzumo, *Oho-ne-shima*. We find in the ancient traditions also *Yomi no Oho-ne-shima* "the island Great Ne of Yomi (Hades)," and *Ne no katasu kuni* "the border-land of Ne." *Yomi* "Hades" itself is the name of a place in the Shimane district of the province of Idzumo. The Even Pass of Hades, mentioned in the Nihongi and Kojiki, was, according to this latter authority, then called the *Ifuya-Pass* in the land of Idzumo. The name *Ifuya*, contracted into *Iya*, exists still in Idzumo. All these places I have mentioned, are not far distant from one another. There can hardly be any doubt that the ancient-Japanese located their Hades in one corner of the province of Idzumo! For further details I must refer the reader to my extensive commentary to the JINDAI-KI "Annals of the Age of the Gods (Book 1 and 2 of the Nihongi, especially chapter 4th, note 29).

81 *Haya-sasura-hime*, also called *Suseri-hime*, a daughter of Susa-no-wo no Mikoto. She is not mentioned, under the former name, in any other ancient text. Hirata identifies her, but without good reason, with *Susa-no-wo no Mikoto*. *Haya* signifies "swift" or "brilliant," and is only, as often, an honorific; *sasura-hime* seems to be contracted from *sasurahi-hime* according to the rule that the same syllable should not occur twice successively; *sasurafu* means either "to wander about aimlessly or in exile," or, as Modzume's Daijirin explains it, "to make" (length-ened form of *sasuru*, from *suru*). The compound verb *mochi-sasurahi-ushinafu*,

rendered by "take them and completely banish them and get rid of them," is by Moto-wori explained to mean: "to lose something so that one does not know whither it has come." Toyokahi gives to *ushinafu* the signification *shōmetsu suru*, i.e. "to make disappear."

In the above notes (74, 76, 79, 81) I have pointed out that the four Deities of Purification (*harahe no kami-sama*) mentioned in the ritual, are identified, by the Japanese commentators, with certain other gods mentioned in the Kojiki and Nihongi. We saw that only one of the four names is actually mentioned in the ancient records and annals; the identification in the other cases is more or less problematical. It seems therefore advisable not to lay too much stress on this question and to be, on the whole, content with Mabuchi's view that the four deities are personifications of the successive places and actions in the process of purification.

82   According to the view of Mabuchi and nearly all the later commentators, the horse acts a symbolical part in the ceremony of purification. It is regarded to be an animal especially quick of hearing, and therefore its presence symbolizes the desire that the Gods of Heaven and Gods of Earth may hear, and act upon, the words of the ritual, as quickly as a horse hears with its ears pricked up. Such a horse is called *harahe no uma* "purification-horse." In ancient times the number of the *harahe-no-uma* was six, according to the reports of the Sei-gū-ki. Hoku-zan-shō and Kōke-shidai, and four or five sheaves of rice in the ear were placed beside them. The Imperial edict of the 5th year Temmu, 8th month, 16th day (28th September, 676) commands the Kuni no Miyatsuko of each province to furnish one horse for the ceremony (performed in their respective provinces); the same is required by the Jingi-Ryō, etc.

83   The freer translation we (or I) purify and cleanse in the name of the Sovran would perhaps be preferable.

84   *Minazuki*, sixth month, from *mi* "water," *na* Gen. particle (cp. *mi-na-to* "water-door, harbour"), *tsuki* "month." The interpretation "waterless month" (*na*= stem-form of *naki* "is not"), which is sometimes given, is wrong.

85   Motowori, Hirata, etc. read 四國 *ko-kuni* "four countries or provinces" and understand the provinces *Idzu, Iki,* and *Tsushima,* the latter being counted as two provinces by counting especially its two districts Kami-tsu-agata and Shimo-tsu-agata and Shimo-tsu-agata. Others, as Motowori Toyokahi, consider *U-kyō,* the right division of Kyōto, as the fourth country. The former view is to be preferred, because it is reported that there were five diviners (*urabe*) in Idzu, five in Iki, five in Kami-tsu-agata and five in Shimo-tsu-agata of Tsushima. The original text has the character 毛 *mo* after 四, which has been suppressed by Motowori, etc., being considered as a later interpolation. Shikida, however, restores it and reads *yo-mo no kuni,* taking 毛 as a phonetic writing of 方 *mo* "side, quarter of the compass," so that the meaning would be: the diviners of the countries of the four sides, i.e. of all the countries.

The duty of the diviner (*urabe*) is to carry the purification offerings to the river, after the Oho-Nakatomi has finished the recital of the ritual, and throw them away into the water.

86   *Oho-kaha-ji.* The word *ji* "way" is added to *kaha,* because the river is the road by which the thrown away objects are carried into the sea. As in ancient times the capital was frequently removed from one place, and even from one province, to another, different rivers came, of course, to be used for the ceremony by which the court-officials were purified. At the time when Kyōto was the capital, the Kamo River was probably used for the purpose, says Haruyama.

The last clause is, by the commentators, also styled a Semmyō.

THE REVIVAL OF PURE SHIÑ-TAU*

BY ERNEST SATOW.

By 'pure Shiñ-tau' is meant the religious belief of the Japanese people previous to the introduction of Buddhism and the Confucian philosophy into Japan, and by its revival the attempt which a modern school of writers has made to eliminate these extraneous influences, and to present Shiñ-tau in its original form. The very name of Shiñ-tau is repudiated by this school, on the ground that the word was never applied to the ancient religious belief until the introduction of Buddhism and Confucianism rendered its employment necessary for the sake of distinction, and the argument that, because this belief is called by a Chinese name, it must therefore be of Chinese origin, is of no value whatever.

The statement that the study of the Chinese classics was introduced in the year 285 A. D., though received without mistrust by European writers on the authority of native historians, may certainly be questioned. The earliest extant account of historical events (the Ko-zhi-ki) dates only from the year 711 of our era, while no attempt whatever of the kind is recorded to have been made earlier than the 5th century; and yet the Ni-hoñ-gi (720 A. D.) affects to give the precise dates, even to the day of the month, of events that are ascribed to the seventh century B. C., or fifteen centuries back. An even stronger ground for disbelieving the accuracy of the early chronology is the extraordinary longevity assigned by it to the early Mikados. Of the fifteen Mikados from Zhiñ-mu Teñ-wau down to Ou-zhiñ Teñ-wau's predecessor, eleven are said to have lived considerably over one hundred years. One of them, Suwi-niñ Teñ-wau, reached the age of one hundred and forty-one years, and his successor Kei-kau Teñ-wau lived to the age of one hundred and forty-three, while to Ou-zhiñ Teñ-wau and his successor Niñtoku

*Revised by the author, 1882. Reprinted from the Transactions of the Asiatic Society of Japan, First Series, Vol. III.

Teñ-wau are given one hundred and eleven and one hundred and twenty-three years respectively. They are, however, surpassed in longevity by the famous Take-uchi no Sukune, who is reported to have died in A. D. 390 at the age of three hundred and fifty-six years. A further reason for doubting the statement is that the Ko-zhi-ki names the "Thousand character Composition" (Señ-zhi moñ) as one of the books brought over in A. D. 285, although it is certain that it could not have reached Japan much earlier than the middle of the 5th century.[1] All that can safely be said is that Confucianism probably preceded Buddhism.

The first Buddhist images and Sûtras were brought to Japan from Korea in the year 552, if we can believe the Ni-hoñ-gi, but it was long before the religion obtained much hold on the people. In the beginning of the ninth century the priest Kuukai (b. 774, d. 835, better known by his posthumous name of Kou-bofu Dai-shi) compounded out of Buddhism, Confucianism and Shiñ-tau a system of doctrine called Riyaubu Shiñ-tau. Its most prominent characteristic was the theory that Shiñ-tau deities were nothing more than transmigrations of Buddhist divinities, and Kuu-kai is accused of perpetrating various forgeries in order to obtain credit for his teaching. The alliance thus effected between the native belief and the foreign religion enabled the latter to obtain the ascendancy to which it was entitled on account of its superior adaptation to man's sense of his own shortcomings and longing for perfection. Buddhism became the religion of the whole nation, from the Mikado down to the lowest of his subjects, and continued to hold that position until the period of the Tokugaha Shiyauguñs, when it was supplanted in the intellects of the educated class by the moral philosophy of Choo He. The practise of pure Shiñ-tau was kept alive for one or two centuries at the Mikado's court, and at a few Shiñ-tau temples which might be counted on one's fingers, but finally degenerated into a mere thing of forms, the meaning of which was forgotten, while the forms themselves were perverted.

In addition to the Riyau-bu Shiñ-tau there arose at least three other schools; namely the Yuwi-itsu Shiñ-tau invented by

[1] Ko-zhi-ki Deñ, vol. xxxiii., f. 27.

Yoshido Kanetomi about the end of the 15th century, that of
Deguchi Nobuyoshi, *Kaññushi* of the *Ge-kuu* temple in Ise, about
1660, and the Suwi-ga Shiñ-tau of Yamazaki Añ-sai (b. 1618,
d. 1682). The first of these is chiefly founded on the Buddhism
of the Shiñ-goñ-shiu, the second explains the phenomena of the
divine age by means of the Book of Changes (*Yeki* or *I-king*);
the third is a combination of the Yoshida Shiñ-tau and Choo
He's philosophy.[2]

From these few remarks it may be inferred that the successive waves of Buddhist and Chinese doctrine which had passed
over Japan during a period of more than a thousand years had
considerably transformed the belief of the people, and if the
only means of discovering its original nature were an analysis
of the teaching of the above-mentioned sects, and the rejection
of whatever bore traces of a foreign origin, the task would
necessitate a wide knowledge of Buddhism in both India and
China, as well as of the Confucian philosophy, and perhaps of
Taouism. But fortunately, there exist independently in the
Ko-zhi-ki, the Mañ-yefu-shifu, the Ni-hoñ-gi, the Ko-go-shifu-wi
and the Norito, abundant materials for the student of the divine
age, and it was to these books that Mabuchi, Motowori and
Hirata devoted their attention. Together with Kada they from
the revivalist school of pure Shiñtau. I propose to give some
account of their lives and works, and the views held by them as
to the essence of Shiñ-tau.

During the long period amounting to nearly three hundred years which elapsed between the downfall of the Hou-deu
family in 1334, and the final establishment of the Togugaha family
as *de facto* rulers of Japan after the death of Hideyoshi (Taico-
sama) in the end of the 16th century, Japan had been the scene
of constant civil war and rebellions. The Ashikaga family,
which established itself at Kiyau-to with a branch in the Kuwañ-
tou, was utterly unable to control its unruly vassals, and the
capital of the Mikado was frequently delivered up to fire and
sword. In 1467 and during the six following years, it became
the battle-field of the rival retainers of the Ashikaga family, and
the greater part of the city was twice burnt to the ground. The

[2] Zoku-Shiñ-tau Tai-i, vol. iv., f. 5.

loss to Japanese literature by the destruction of books is said to have been immense. Apart from the immediate effects of civil war, learning must necessarily have decayed during a period when the profession of the soldier was the only honourable calling, and every man was obliged to be constantly under arms for defence or attack. Nobunaga, it is true, restored peace at the capital and in the surrounding provinces, but civil wars still went on in the more remote parts of the country, and he had to be perpetually in the field against rival chiefs. Hideyoshi, who succeeded him as the chief military leader, did much to facilitate the pacification of the Empire. He broke the power of the Mouri family, conquered the turbulent *dai-miyau* of Kiu-shiu, annihilated the Wodahara Hou-deu who ruled over the Kwañ-tou, and then despatched his warriors to fight and die in Korea.

The fruits of these efforts were reaped by Iheyasu, whose power was virtually rendered absolute by the victory of Sekigahara, and who became Shiyauguñ in 1603. During the remainder of his life, with the exception of the two short campaigns against Hideyori's partizans in 1614 and 1615, he lived tranquilly at Suñ-pu in Suruga, the modern Shidzu-woka. His chief pursuit seems to have been the collection of old manuscripts, and it is chiefly owing to his exertions that what remains of the ancient literature has been preserved. The Suñ-pu-ki, quoted by Hirata,[3] mentioned a large number of works brought to him from various parts of the country, some from Kiyau-to, and others from Kamakura, and a few from the monastery of Minobu Sañ in Kafu-shiu. Before his death he gave directions that the library of Japanese and Chinese books which he had formed at Suñ-pu should be divided between his eighth son, the prince of Wohari, and his ninth son, the prince of Ki-shiu. The former received the greater part of the Japanese books, the latter the Chinese books. Under the direction of the Prince of Wohari were composed the Zhiñ-gi-hofu-teñ and Ruwi-zhiu Ni-hoñ-gi. One of Iheyasu's grandsons, the famous second Prince of Mito (1622-1700), known variously as Mito no Kuwau-moñ Sama, and Mito no Gi-kou (Mitsukuni was his *nanori*), also collected a vast library by purchasing old books from Shiñ-tau and Buddhist

---

" Tamadasuki, vol. ii., t. 58.

temples and from the people. With the aid of a number of scholars, amongst whom tradition says were several learned Chinese who had fled to Japan to escape from the tyranny of the Manchu conquerors, he composed the Dai-Ni-hoñ-shi, or History of Great Japan, in two hundred and forty books. This books is the standard history of Japan to this day, and all sub-sequent writers on the same subject have taken it as their guide. He also compiled a work on the ceremonies of the Imperial Court, consisting of more than five hundred volumes, to which the Mikado condescended to give the title of Rei-gi Ruwi-teñ. To defray the cost of producing these two magnificent works the Prince of Mito set aside at least 30,000 *koku* of rice per annum (some accounts say 50,000, others 70,000 *koku*).

While the study of ancient history thus received powerful impulse from men of high position, there manifested itself amongst the lower ranks an equal desire to cultivate the native literature. Two of the earliest who turned their attention to this subject were the Buddhist priest Kei-chiyun and the Shiñ-tau priest Kada no Adzuma-maro.

Kei-chiyuu was the son of a *samurahi* in the service of Awoyama, the *dai-miyau* of Ama-ga-saki in Setsutsu. He was born in 1640, and early distinguished himself by an excellent memory for poetry, having, as it is said, committed the Hiyaku-niñ shiu to memory in the space of ten days, when he was only five years of age. At the age of eleven he became a neophyte at the monastery of Meu-hofu-zhi at Imasato near Ohozaka, much against the inclination of his parents. Two years later he shaved his head and removed to the famous monastery of Kau-ya-sañ in Ki-shiu. In 1662 he became an inmate of a monastery near Ikudama at Ohozaka, but finding its proximity to the city dis-agreeable, he absconded, leaving a verse behind on the wall. From this time he travelled much in the central parts of Japan, studying Buddhism, Sanscrit, Chinese literature and poetry, and Japanese history; but his favourite occupation was the study of Japanese poetry. In 1680 his former teacher, the abbot of Meu-hofu-zhi, died, and left directions that he should be succeeded by Kei-chiyuu, who accepted the charge simply for the sake of his mother, who was living at Imasato. About this time the Prince of Mito above alluded to invited him to Yedo in order to com-

plete a commentary on the Mañ-yefu-shifu which had been commenced by Shimokahabe Chiyau-riu. He declined the invitation,
but pleased with the Prince's love for ancient learning, compiled
a similar work for him called Mañ-yefu-dai-shiyau-ki in twenty
volumes, with a supplement in two volumes. After the death of
his mother he left the monastery, and retired into private life
in a small cottage in the neighbourhood of Ohozaki, whence the
repeated invitations of the Prince of Mito failed to draw him.
He died in the year 1701. His published works relating to poetry
and general literature number sixteen, and he is said to have left
a quantity of unfinished manuscript behind him.[4]

Besides Kei-chiyuu and Shimokahabe Chiyau-riu (1622-
1684) Hirata mentions Nashimoto Mo-suwi[5] as one of the
first who vindicated the style of the Mañ-yefu-shifu against that
of the modern school. His works are extremely rare. The
efforts of these three men were, however, confined to the department of poetry, and the credit of having founded the modern
school of pure Shiñ-tau belongs to Kada.

I.

Kada Adzuma-maro, as he is most commonly styled, was
born in 1669 near Kiyau-to, his father being the warden of the
temple of Inari between Kiyau-to and Fushimi. From his boy-
hood up he was fond of study, and devoted himself to antiquarian
investigation. He thus acquired an accurate knowledge of the
ancient national records, the old laws, of which only fragments
have been preserved, the early prose and poetry and the
chronicles of the noble families. Though absolutely without any
one to point out the way to him in these researches, he was
neverthless enabled to make many valuable discoveries. When
considerably over sixty years of age he went to Yedo, where his
reputation came to the ears of the government, and he received
a commission from it to revise and edit the ancient text. After
residing at Yedo for some years he returned to Kiyau-to, and
the governor of Fushimi presented him with a considerable sum
of money as a reward for his labours. It is said that the commission came in the first place from the Mikado, who was obliged

---

[4] *Ki-zhiñ Deñ, San-zhifu-roku Ka-shifu Riyaku-deñ.*
[5] *Tamadasuki,* vol. ix., f. 2.

to communicate with his subjects through the Shiyau-guñ, and that the money-reward came from the same source, but there is no documentary evidence of this.

Kada had long cherished a scheme for the establishment of a school for the study of Japanese language and literature, and he sent in a memorial on the subject to the authorities at Kiyau-to, probably to the *machi-bu-giyau,* or to the Shiyau-guñ's Resident (*shiyo-shi-dai*). But he died soon after (in 1736), and the project was never carried out. The Ki-zhiñ Deñ indeed says that the necessary sanction had been given, and that Kada had already selected a spot near the burial-place of the Higashi Hoñ-guwañ-zhi, but Hirata (in the Tamadasuki) thinks that this so-called sanction, if ever given, was not formal and official. Kada's memorial has lately been published in a separate form by Hirata Kanetane and can easily be obtained. It is a most vigorous protest against the utter neglect of Japanese learning for Chinese, which had up to that time been almost universal.

It is usually stated that Kada, shortly before his death, gave orders to his pupils to destroy all his manuscripts, on the ground that they must contain many errors, and be therefore calculated to mislead students, while the good which might be in them could easily be discovered without their aid. Hirata Atsutane repeats this story, but it is stated, on the authority of Atsutane's son Kanetane, that the Kada family still possess several boxes full of unpublished writings of Adzuma-maro. It may be doubted, however, whether they are of much actual value, seeing that their author was the first who attempted to elucidate the meaning of the ancient books, and as Atsutane says, 'we can see from the works which Kada published during his life-time, such as his commentaries on the Mañ-yefu-shifu and Zhiñ-dai no Maki, that he had good reason to be dissatisfied with the conclusions which he had reached.'

Kada's views may be briefly stated as follows: "Learning is a matter in which the highest interests of the empire are involved, and no man ought to be vain enough to imagine that he is able by himself to develope it thoroughly. Nor should the student blindly adhere to the opinions of his teacher. Any one who desires to study Japanese literature should first acquire a good knowledge of Chinese, and then pass over to the Mañ-yefu-

shifu, from which he may discover the ancient principles of the
divine age.   If he resolve bravely to love and admire antiquity,
there is no reason why he should fail to acquire the ancient style
in poetry as well as in other things.   In ancient times, as the
poet expressed only the genuine sentiments of his heart, his style
was naturally straight-forward, but since the practice of writing
upon· subjects chosen by lot has come into vogue, the language
of poetry has become ornate and the ideas forced, thus producing a laboured appearance.   The expression of fictitious sentiment about the relations of the sexes and miscellaneous subjects,
is not genuine poetry."⁶   Kada, true to his own principles, never
wrote a line of amatory poetry.   We can readily understand his
contempt for the modern versifiers, when we recall the picture
of licentiousness which some of the verses in the popular collection called *Hiyaku-niñ shiu* present.   What in English has to
be disguised under the name of love was too often mere sensual
passion indulged in at the expense of the most sacred domestic
relations.   During the middle ages it seems to have been the
practice for persons skilled in the trifling art of making stanzas
of thirty-one syllables to assemble at drinking parties, and to
draw lots for subjects to write about.   The 67th stanza of this
collection contains an allusion to this custom.

Atsutane has a note in the Tamadasuki, the object of which
is to refute the common notion that Kei-chiyuu, Motowori and
Mabuchi ought to be considered the ancestors of the antiquarian
school, to the exclusion of Kada.   The cause of this notion is that
the men who entertain it are merely versifiers and take verse-
making to be an essential part of the labours of the antiquarians.
Kei-chiyuu, who was a Buddhist priest, certainly did some
service in editing the Mañ-yefu-shifu, but to praise Mabuchi and
Motowori for their poetry alone is to misapprehend the real
character of the work they performed.   This consisted in the
revival of Shiñ-tau, and poetry was merely secondary with them.
Kada's memorial proves that he was the founder of the school
of Pure Shiñ-tau.   Mabuchi was his pupil, and Motowori in his
turn the pupil of Mabuchi.

⁶ Preface of Nobuyoshi to the collection of Kada's verses entitled Shiyuñ-yefu-
shifu, quoted in the Tamadasuki, vol· ix., p. 6.

Kada had no children of his own, and adopted his nephew Arimaro (1706-1751). Arimaro came to Yedo, and taught his uncle's views with some success. He was particularly learned in that branch of Japanese archæology which deals with the ancient system of government under the Mikados, and having attracted the notice of Tayasu Kiñgo (1715-1771), the first of the name, who took great interest in the subject, he entered the service of that Prince. A dispute subsequently took place, on account of which Arimaro resigned, but he continued to take pupils at his own house. There is a notice of his life and works in the Ki-zhiñ Deñ.

When Arimaro quitted the service of Tayasu Kiñ-go, he recommended a certain Mabuchi in his stead.

II.

Mabuchi was a man of ancient lineage, being descended from Taketsunumi no mikoto, the demi-god who took the form of a gigantic crow and acted as guide to Zhiñ-mu Teñ-wau in his invasion of Yamashiro, as related in the Ni-hoñ-gi.[7]

About the middle of the 13th century there was a *Shin-tau* priest of one of the lesser shrine of Kami-gamo near Kiyau-to, whose daughter, one of the Emperor's women, received a gift of 500 koku of land at Wokabe near Hamamatsu in Towotafumi. With these lands she endowed a shrine to the gods of Kamo and made her brother Michi-hisa chief warden of it. The living, if it may be so called, became hereditary in the family of his younger brother and heir, and three generations later the name of the village was adopted as the family surname. In the end of the 17th century the wardenship was held by Wokabe Zhi-rau-za-we-moñ, and Mabuchi, who was his nephew, was born at Wokabe in 1697.

His biographer says that at one period he was desirous of entering the Buddhist priesthood, but his parents refused their consent, and he thereupon quitted their roof for that of the chief innkeeper at Hamamatsu, whose daughter he married. Amongst his friends were two *Shiñ-tau* priests, Sugiura Shinano no Kami and Mori Miñ-bu no Seu-fu, both pupils of Kada. Sugiura's

---

[7] Vide Klaproth's introduction to the "Annales des Dairi," which contains a fairly good translation of vol. iii. of the Ni-hoñ-gi.

wife was a niece of Kada, who on his way to and from Yedo used to stop with his relations, and Mabuchi thus made his acquaintance. It was about this time that he changed his previous name of Masa-fuji for that of Mabuchi, by which he is generally known.[8]

In 1733, at the age of thirty-six, he went up to Kiyau-to and became one of Kada's pupils, but as Kada died in 1736, he only profited by his teacher's lessons for a comparatively short period. Nevertheless, he made excellent use of his time, as is shown by the fact that he alone of all those who studied under Kada, surpassed his master in learning. In 1738 he removed to Yedo, where he passed the remainder of his life. Having established his reputation as a scholar, he entered the service of Tayasu Kiñ-go in 1746, with whom he remained fourteen years, until old age compelled his retirement. He died in the end of 1769 at the age of 72, and was buried at the Buddhist monastery of Tou-dai-zhi at Shinagaha.

Motowori in his Tamagatsuma,[9] under the heading "Agatawi[10] no ushi's claim to be considered the founder of ancient learning" says: "The branch of study which consists of investigating the ancient language and modes of thought with a mind perfectly freed from Chinese influences was initiated by Mabuchi. Before his time the usual studies were confined to the Ko-kiñ-shifu and later collections. The Mañ-yefu-shifu was considered obscure and unintelligible. No one was capable of appreciating its merits or of distinguishing between the more ancient and modern poems which it contains, and no one ever attempted to acquire the language of the Mañ-yefu-shifu, so as to wield it as his own. The power of acquiring this ancient language so as to employ it with perfect ease, of composing poetry in the style of the Mañ-yefu-shifu and of writing prose in the ancient manner, which some have attained to in later times, is owing to the teachings of Mabuchi. The Moderns may imagine that they have made this acquisition by their own efforts, but there is no one who does not stand in debt to him. Every one knows

---

[8] Previous to this he had either received or chosen five other names in turn at different periods of his life.

[9] Vol. i., f. 8v.

[10] Name adopted by Mabuchi for his place of abode.

now that in order to understand the ancient texts, such as the Ko-zhi-ki and Ni-hoñ-shiyo-ki,[11] it is necessary to avoid being misled by Chinese notions, to study antiquity and to be guided by ancient ideas, but the knowledge of these truths is the very spirit of Mabuchi's teaching of the Mañ-yefu. The service which he performed in founding a branch of learning which has such high claims to veneration as the study of antiquity, is one of incalculable value to mankind."

Ka-tou Chikage, who for many years was a pupil of Mabuchi, is the best authority for biographical and literary details. He says: "From a very early age I lived in Mabuchi's service, and I was both a constant spectator of his mode of life and an auditor of his words. He was very different in appearance from ordinary men. From his looks he might be taken to be a person of small acuteness and slow in thinking, but sometimes the true heart of a Japanese burst forth in his language, which was then distinguished by the most perfect eloquence. That his hand-writing resembled that of ancient manuscripts, was no doubt the effect of his unwearied and long continued diligence in the study of antiquity. His house and furniture were both formed upon ancient models, and he neither lent ear to nor bestowed attention on anything modern. In this way his mind naturally acquired an old-fashioned mould, and all its productions, whether written or verbal, were pervaded by the same tint.

"In composing poetry he worked most conscientiously. Every stanza was the subject of much consideration and frequent correction. Three separate styles are to be distinguished in his compositions. The first was imitated from Kada no Adzumamaro, and is elegant and feminine in form. The second is entirely his own; polished, musical, and yet manly. In his later years his range of thought was higher, and his language was natural and simple to a degree not to be attained by ordinary persons."[12] Mabuchi's chief aim was to carry out the idea originated by Kada, namely to illustrate the prehistoric age. For this purpose he considered that it was necessary to begin by

[11] Another name for the Ni-hoñ-gi.
[12] From the preface to a collection of Mabuchi's prose and poetical works, entitled Agatawi Kamo no Ka-shifu, quoted by Hirata.

explaining the Mañ-yefu-shifu. Poetry was with him only the means to an end. At the only interview which ever took place between Mabuchi and Motowori, the latter spoke of his own project of writing a commentary on the *Ko-zhi-ki*. Mabuchi replied that he also had wished to explain the sacred writings, but in order to do this it was first necessary to get rid of the effects of Chinese philosophy, and discover the genuine beliefs of antiquity. The first step towards their elucidation was to recover the ancient language, which could only be done by studying the Mañ-yefu-shifu. This preliminary task he had himself accomplished, and he urged Motowori, who was yet young, to apply himself diligently to the study of the *Ko-zhi-ki*.

It appears that some writers have accused Motowori of inventing these views for Mabuchi, but the writings of the latter are evidence of his having held these opinions. In his Nihimanabi (quoted in the Tamadasuki) he says: "The Moderns have held the erroneous opinion that the Mañ-yefu-shifu contains nothing but poetry, which is fit only for women to amuse themselves with, and many shallow fools, who cannot understand the ancient poetry and are ignorant of the ancient books, have made attempts to explain the divine age according to ideas derived from Chinese literature. Thus their utterances are mere sophistry, utterly opposed to the ancient Japanese 'way.'"

Mabuchi then proceeds to lay down the course of study which should be followed in order that the 'way' of the gods and ancient emperors may be thoroughly comprehended. The old poetry is to be taken at the commencement, namely the collection entitled the Mañ-yefu-shifu, and the *Norito,* as being the earliest specimens of prose, should come next. Next follow the *Ko-zhi-ki, Ni-hoñ-ki* (also called *Ni-hoñ-shiyo-ki*), *Shiyoku Ni-hoñ-gi,* and other ancient histories. After this the books which treat of rites and ceremonies, such as the *Yeñ-gi Shiki,* the *Seikiu-seu,* the *Hoku-gañ-seu, Gau-ka Shi-dai,* etc., must be carefully read in proper order, and the *Monogatari,*[13] or earliest writings in syllabic characters (*kana*), must be studied for the sake of the traces which they contain of the archaic language.

---

[13] A list of the chief *Monogatari* is given in the third volume of the bibliographical work called *Guñ-shiyo ichi-rañ.* The Heike-monogatari does not really belong to this class, as has been erroneously supposed by some students.

Mabuchi was a very voluminous writer. A list of his works is given at the end of the notice of his life in the *Sañ-zhifu-roku Ka-shifu Riyaku-deñ*. Many of them have been superseded by the writings of subsequent authors, but a considerable number are still worthy of being studied. These are the *Mañ-yefu-kau*, or commentary on the Mañ-yefu-shifu, and its supplement, *the Ko-kiñ-shifu Uchi-giki*, commentary on the collection called *Ko-kiñ-shifu, Hiyaku-niñ-shiu Ko-setsu* and *Hiyaku-niñ-shiu uhima-nabi*, commentaries on the collection of verses called *Hiyaku-niñ-shiu; Kuwañ-zhi-kau*, a lexilogus of *Makura kotoba, Ise-Mono-gatari Ko-i* and *Tai-i;* and the *Geñ-zhi Monogatari Shiñ-shiyaku* (new comments on), besides those which are noticed below.

In the *Koku-i-kau* we have Mabuchi's views upon the worth-lessness of the Chinese philosophy. He asks: "Wherein lies the value of a rule of conduct? In its conducing to the good order of the state." He argues that 'while the Chinese for ages past have had a succession of different dynasties to rule over them, Japan has been faithful to one uninterrupted line of sovereigns. Every Chinese dynasty was founded upon rebellion and parricide. Sometimes a powerful ruler was able to transmit his authority to his son and grandson, but they in their turn were inevitably deposed and murdered, and the country was in a perpetual state of civil war. A philosophy which produced such effects must be founded on a false system.

'When Confucianism was first introduced into Japan, the simple-minded natives, deceived by its plausible appearance, accepted it with eagerness, and allowed it to spread its influence everywhere. The consequence was the civil war which broke out immediately after the death of Teñ-ji Teñ-wau in 671 between that emperor's brother and son, which only came to an end in 672 by the suicide of the latter. In the 8th century the Chinese costume and etiquette were adopted by the Court. This foreign pomp and splendour covered the rapid depravation of men's hearts, and created a wide gulf between the Mikado and his people. So long as the sovereign maintains a simple style of living, the people are contented with their own hard lot. Their wants are few and they are easily ruled. But if the sovereign has a magnificent palace, gorgeous clothing, and crowds of finely-dressed women to wait on him, the sight

of these things must cause in others a desire to possess themselves of the same luxuries; or if they are not strong
enough to take them by force, it excites their envy. If the
Mikado had continued to live in a house roofed with shingles,
and whose walls were of mud, to wear hempen clothes, to carry
his sword in a scabbard wound round with the tendrils of some
creeping plant, and to go to the chase carrying his bow and
arrows, as was the ancient custom, the present state of things
would never have come about. But since the introduction of
Chinese manners, the sovereign, while occupying a highly
dignified place, has been degraded to the intellectual level of a
woman. The power fell into the hands of servants, and although
they never actually assumed the title, they were sovereigns in
fact, while the Mikado became an utter nullity.'

Some one had observed to Mabuchi that it was owing to
the Chinese system of morals that the practice of marriage between brothers and sisters was discontinued. He explains in
reply that 'according to ancient Japanese custom the children of
the same mother were alone regarded as united by the fraternal
tie; that it was not considered in any way objectionable for
children of the same father by different mothers to intermarry.
The Chinese forbid marriages between persons who bear the
same surname, and it was the adoption of this ridiculously strict
rule that led to the gradual disuse of the ancient practice, which
was in itself quite harmless.

'In ancient times when men's dispositions were straight-
forward, a complicated system of morals was unnecessary.
It would naturally happen that bad acts might occasionally
be committed, but the straightforwardness of men's dispositions
would prevent the evil from being concealed and growing in
extent. So that in those days it was unnecessary to have a
doctrine of right and wrong. But the Chinese, being bad at
heart, in spite of the teaching which they got, were only good
on the outside, and their bad acts became of such magnitude
that society was thrown into disorder. The Japanese being
straightforward could do without teaching. It is said on the
other side that as the Japanese had no names for benevolence,
righteousness, propriety, sagacity and truth, they must have been
without those principles. To this Mabuchi replies that they

exist in every country, in the same way as the four seasons
which make their annual rounds. In the spring the weather does
not become mild all at once, nor the summer hot. Nature proceeds by gradual steps. According to the Chinese view it is
not spring or summer unless it becomes mild or hot all of a
sudden. Their principles sound very plausible, but are un-
practical.'

Mabuchi rendered a great service to the study of Shiñ-tau
by the pains which he took to illustrate the *Norito* in a commentary entitled Norito Kau (1768). The *Norito* consists of a
selection of the liturgies used at certain of the more important
Shiñ-tau festivals, and together with those parts of the *Jiyau-*
guwañ Gi-shiki and *Yeñ-gi Shiki* which contain directions for
the celebration of such festivals, afford the most authentic information as to the native religious ceremonies. Some of them
contain passages of remarkable beauty, especially those which are
considered to be most ancient in their origin, such as the *Oho-*
harahi no Kotobo and *Toshigohi no Matsuri no Kotoba.* The
festival of the "General Purification" (*Ohobarahi*) is first mentioned in the Kozhi-ki as having been celebrated after the death
of Chiyuu-ai Teñ-wau (200 A. D. according to the native
chronology), but is supposed to have been instituted as far back
as the time of Izanagi no mikoto. Mabuchi, who may be taken
as a pretty safe guide in such matters, attributes the liturgy as
it is preserved in the Yeñ-gi Shiki to the reign of Teñ-mu Teñ-
wau (673-686), by which period the words, in the earliest times
composed by the Nakatomi on each occasion, had assumed a
definite form consecrated by precedent. The *Yeñ-gi Shiki,*
however, belongs to the 10th century, and therefore the date at
which the *Norito* are actually known to have been committed
to writing is two centuries later than that of the *Ko-zhi-ki* and
Ni-hoñ-gi. Still more ancient than the *Ohobarahi no Kotoba* is
said to be the *Idzumo Kuni no Miyatsuko Kamu yogoto,* which
Mabuchi assigns to the reign of Zhiyo-mei Teñ-wau (629-641),
though the origin of the ceremony at which it was used is
evidently far back in the prehistoric age. The Toshigohi,
Hirose and Tatsuta *Norito* are later again than the *Ohobarahi.*
By a fortunate coincidence the study of pure Shiñ-tau cannot be
successfully prosecuted at first hand, without a previous acquain-

tance with ancient forms of the language, and the result has a natural tendency towards a combined devotion to the two subjects, which is explanatory of the wide meaning of the term *Koku-gaku*, 'national learning,' sometime erroneously used to signify the study of poetry alone.

This notice of Mabuchi's writings is unavoidably deficient, owing to the difficulty of procuring copies of his works in the book-shops. Even the public library, recently removed to Asakusa, does not possess three volumes by this author which relate to the Ko-zhi-ki, and it is much to be regretted that the means should therefore be wanting in order to form an estimate of what he accomplished towards the elucidation of this most important and ancient Shiñ-tau monument.

III.

The mantle of Mabuchi fell upon the shoulders of Motowori Norinaga. This remarkable scholar and critic was born in 1730 at Matsuzaka in Ise, a town belonging to the Prince of Ki-shiu. At the age of ten years he lost his father, and his mother was left in straitened circumstances. Motowori displayed an ardent taste for learning from his earliest childhood, and read every book, Chinese or Japanese, which came in his way. In 1752 he went to Kiyau-to, where he studied Chinese under Hori Kei-zañ and medicine under Takegaha Hofu-gañ, in accordance with his mother's wish that he should become a doctor. During his stay at the capital of the Mikado he became acquainted with the works of Kei-chiyuu, and read them with avidity. Previous to this his notions of poetry had been the same as those of the later versifiers, but from Kei-chiyuu he learnt the principles of correct style. In 1757 he returned to his birth-place and set up in practice as a children's physician.

Shortly after his return, a person who was passing through from Yedo lent him a copy of Mabuchi's work on the *makura kotoba*, which had just been published. A first perusal failed either to interest or convince him, but after repeated readings he was compelled to acknowledge the justice of the author's views, and their superiority over those of Kei-chiyuu. It was this book which inspired him with his love for the study of Japanese antiquity. In the year 1761 he had an opportunity of making the acquaintance of Mabuchi, when the conversation before quoted took place, and he continued to correspond with him and to profit by his lessons until the death of the elder scholar.[14]

The *Ko-zhi-ki Deñ*, which is an edition of the Ko-zhi-ki with an elaborate commentary, unquestionably his greatest work, was commenced in 1764, but the first part, which contains the commentary on the first book of the *Ko-zhi-ki*, was not completed until 1786. It must have at once established his reputation, and one of his biographers states that his fame drew nearly five hundred students from all parts of the country. The second part was finished in 1792. Three years later he was invited to Wakayama by the Prince of Ki-shiu, for whose sake he refused a pension of 300 *koku* annually, which had been offered to him by another *ḍai-miyau*. The concluding part of the commentary was completed in 1796. The printing of the work was begun in 1789 and finished in 1822.

In 1801, at the request of a number of his admirers, he again visited Kiyau-to, where crowds flocked together to hear his lectures. The princes of the blood and many of the Court nobles sought instruction from him in matters relating to the early history of Japan. He died in the autumn of the same year, and was buried in a tomb which he had previously caused to be constructed at the monastery of Meu-raku-zhi near Matsuzaka.

This seems a fitting place in which to give some account of the earliest extant historical records of the Japanese, and of those of which only brief notices have been preserved, taking for our authority the first volume of the *Ko-zhi-ki Deñ*.

The *Ni-hoñ-gi* states that in the year 403 (4th of Ri-chiyuu Teñ-wau) "historiographers were appointed for the first time to all the provinces, to record words and events," from which it may be inferred that such officials had existed at the Court before that date. The latter probably also had records of what was known of the earlier ages, which would account for the existence of numerous independent chronicles, such as are quoted in the *Ni-hoñ-gi*, especially in the first two books called the *Zhiñ-dai-no-maki.* The *Ni-hoñ-gi* also says that in the year 620

---

[14] Tamagatsuma, vol. ii., p. 35, et infra.

(28th of the Empress Suwi-ko Teñ-wau) Shiyau-toku Taishi and Soga no Umako [began to] compile by their joint efforts "A Record of the Mikado, a Record of the Country, and records of the *Omi, Murazhi, Tomo-no-miyatsuko, Kuni no miyatsuko,* of the chiefs of the Mikado's followers, and of the people." This is the first mention of any records of the court. Teñ-mu Teñ-wau also commanded Prince Kahashima and eleven others in 681 to compile a history of the Mikados and an account of ancient matters. Neither of these collections has been preserved. In the 9th month of the year 711 the Empress Geñ-miyau Teñ-wau commanded the minister Yasumaro to commit the Ko-zhi-ki to writing, and he presented it in a finished state in the first month of the following year, as is stated in the preface. This is therefore the earliest of the extant records. The Shiyoku-Ni-hoñ-gi says that the Ni-hoñ-gi was completed in the year 720, the 6th of the Empress Geñ-shiyau Teñ-wau, and it so far superseded the Ko-zhi-ki that the latter was almost forgotten. The cause of this was no doubt the general adoption of Chinese ideas, and the consequent preference of a work written in Chinese style to one of which the chief object was to preserve the form and spirit of Japanese antiquity. In 714 Kiyohito and Fujimaro were instructed to prepare a national history, but either they never completed the work at all, or it must have been looked on as a failure, for no further mention of it occurs anywhere.

The preface to the Ko-zhi-ki is the only authority for the accepted account of its origin. The Emperor Teñ-mu, at what portion of his reign is not mentioned, lamenting that the records possessed by the chief families contained many errors, resolved to take steps to preserve the true traditions from oblivion. He therefore had the records carefully examined, compared and weeded of their faults. There happened to be in his household a person of marvellous memory named Hiyeda no Are, who could repeat without a mistake the contents of any document he had ever seen, and never forgot anything that he heard. Teñmu Teñ-wau took the pains to instruct this person in the genuine traditions and 'old language of former ages,' and to make him repeat them until he had the whole by heart. "Before the undertaking was completed," which probably means before it could be committed to writing, the Emperor died, and for twenty-five years Are's memory was the sole depository of what afterwards received the title of *Ko-zhi-ki* or *Furu-koto-bumi,* as it is read by Motowori. At the end of this interval the Empress Geñmiyau ordered Yasumaro to write it down from the mouth of Are, which accounts for the completion of the manuscript in so short a time as four months and a half. Are's age at this date is not stated, but as he was twenty-eight years of age some time in the reign of Teñ-mu Teñ-wau, it could not possibly have been more than sixty-eight, while taking into account the previous order of Teñ-mu Teñ-wau in 681 for the compilation of a history, and the statement that he was engaged on the composition of the Ko-zhi-ki at the time of his death in 686, it would not be unreasonable to conclude that it belongs to about the last year of his reign, in which case Are was only fifty-three in 711.[15]

Apart from the fact that all European writers who have dealt with Shiñ-tau obtained their information from natives who were acquainted with its impure forms alone, another source of error has been the too ready recognition of the Ni-hoñ-gi as the only authority for the native cosmogony and the ancient legends. It is not difficult, however, by the aid of a comparison between the Ni-hoñ-gi and the Ko-zhi-ki, to show that the former contains numerous traces of direct Chinese influence, and this is also what we should be led to expect from the fact of its having been composed in a language which is intended to represent the Chinese idiom as nearly as possible, while the Ko-zhi-ki is to a very large extent pure Japanese. Motowori has devoted several pages to the discussion of the book in question, and I think that it will be useful to take note of his observations.

'The very commencement of the Ni-hoñ-gi affords an example. Its first words, are "Anciently, before heaven and earth separated and the Negative and Positive Essences were parted, chaos was like a fowl's egg; and subsequently deity came into existence in the midst thereof." It then proceeds to state, "now it is said that in the beginning of heaven and earth, the soil

---

[15] Hirata in his Ko-shi Chiyou, vol. i., gives reasons for supposing that Are was a woman, and that the compilation of a history attributed to the year 681 and the project of the Ko-zhi-ki were identical.

floated about like a fish floating on the surface of water." This passage is the real Japanese account of the beginning of the world, and what precedes the words "Now it is said" is an addition taken from Chinese books.

'In the next passage the existence of the first three male deities is attributed to the working of the Heavenly Mode by itself, and the production of four pairs of male and female deities to the joint working of the Heavenly and Earthly Modes. The Negative and Positive Essences, and the Heavenly and Earthly Modes were philosophic terms utterly unknown to the ancient Japanese, and are the inventions of ignorant men, who instead of accepting with faith the true traditions which have been handed down from the beginning of time, endeavour to discover explanations for what man with his limited intelligence can never comprehend.   The deities referred to as having been produced by the working of the Heavenly and Earthly Modes, came into existence by the spirits of Takami-musubi no kami and Kami-musubi no kami.   What the process was is beyond our ken; we have only to accept the fact.   To call Izanagi no kami the "Positive Deity," and Izanami no kami "Negative Deity," as the Ni-hoñ-gi does, is to make use of terms which are entirely foreign to the Japanese language, which would have called them the "Male Deity" and "Female Deity."   The effect of the Chinese phraseology is to cause men to believe that Izanagi no kami and Izanami no kami are abstract principles, whereas they are living powers. A proof that the terms "Positive Essence" and "Negative Essence" were imported from abroad, if one were needed, lies in the fact that the sun-deity is female and the moon-deity male according to the ancient native traditions, which is in diametrical opposition to the Chinese theory, according to which the sun is Male or Positive and the moon Female or Negative.   Most of the speeches in the Ni-hoñ-gi, attributed to Zhiñ-mu Teñ-wau, Suu-zhiñ Teñ-wau and other ancient Mikados, contain passages which in their meaning and form are wholly Chinese, and cannot therefore be regarded as otherwise than fictitious.   The Shiyoku-Ni-hoñ-gi contains speeches of the Mikados in both Chinese and native style, and if the speeches made in the 8th century contained so few traces of Chinese expression, it is pretty certain that those which were

spoken fourteen centuries earlier must have been purely
Japanese. Zhiñ-mu Teñ-wau is represented as making use of
such expressions as the following: "It is the part of a good
general not to be haughty after conquering in battle," and, "I am
the descendant of the sun-deity, and to march in the sun's face
to conquer barbarians is contrary to Heaven's way," and, "Rely-
ing on the prestige of supreme Heaven, the evil horde has been
cut to pieces"; in all of which the true Chinese ring is clearly
heard. All reference to Heaven as an intelligent acting power
is of Chinese origin, while in Japan heaven is merely the region
where the heavenly gods have their abode. In the same way
the allusions to eating beef in the Book of Zhiñ-mu, to divination by means of a tortoise's shell in the Book of Suu-zhiñ, and
to the use of such weapons as battle-axes in the Book of Kei-kau,
are borrowed from the Chinese, as is also the title of *Kuwau-
tai-kou,* applied to the consort of Suwi-zei (B.C. 581-549?).'
Motowori has by no means exhausted his criticisms upon the
Ni-hoñ-gi, but is of opinion that he has said enough to show
that it must be read with careful discrimination.

There is another book, of considerable age, which professes
to give an original account of the divine age and of the early
history down to Suwi-ko Teñwau (593-628). It is called the *Ku-
zhi-ki,* and its authorship is attributed to Shiyau-toku Tai-shi
and Soga no Umako, and the preface by the latter states that it
was completed in 622; it purports, in fact, to be the non-extant
compilation already mentioned. Motowori condemns it as a
forgery, compiled at a much later date, chiefly from the *Ko-zhi-ki*
and *Ni-hoñ-gi.* It further contains passages from the *Ko-go-
zhi-fu-wi,* composed in 807, and even mentions Saga Teñ-wau,
who reigned as late as 810-823. Parts of it, however, seem to
be based upon other sources than those above mentioned, and
are of considerable value.

Motowori speaks of two editions of the Ko-zhi-ki which
were in existence when he commenced his own. One which was
printed in the period Kuwañ-yei (1624-1644), contains many
omissions, erroneous readings, and numerous faults in the
kana transcription. The second was published later in the same
century by Deguchi Nobuyoshi, who corrected most of the omissions and errors of the older edition, but took upon himself to

make some unnecessary alterations in the text, thus diminishing to a considerable extent the value of his work. Besides these two printed editions Motowori obtained after much search an old manuscript copy, unfortunately disfigured by a multitude of mistakes, a copy of a manuscript with insertions by Nobuyoshi, an old copy belonging to a Kiyau-to resident named Murawi, and a copy of an ancient manuscript belonging to the monastery of Shiñ-puku-zhi at Nagoya in Wohari, all more or less incorrect, but useful for comparison.

The *Ko-zhi-ki Deñ* consists of forty-four large volumes of clear print, of which two are devoted to prolegomena, three to indexes arranged chronologically and alphabetically, and one contains a tract on the Cosmogony by Hatori Nakatsune, one of Motowori's pupils.

The earliest work of Motowori upon Shiñ-tau was the tract entitled *Nahobi no Mitama,* or the "Spirit of Straightening," which forms part of the first volume of the Ko-zhi-ki Deñ, and was written in the year 1771, about seven years after the commentary was commenced. It may be summarized as follows:

'Japan is the country which gave birth to the goddess of the Sun, Amaterasu-oho-mikami, which fact proves its superiority over all other countries which also enjoy her favours. The goddess, having endowed her grandson Ninigi no Mikoto with the three sacred treasures, proclaimed him sovereign of Japan for ever and ever. His descendants shall continue to rule it as long as the heavens and earth endure. Being invested with this complete authority, all the gods under heaven and all mankind submitted to him, with the exception of a few wretches who were quickly subdued.

'To the end of time each Mikado is the goddess' son. His mind is in perfect harmony of thought and feeling with hers. He does not seek out new inventions, but rules in accordance with precedents which date from the age of the gods, and if he is ever in doubt, he has resort to divination, which reveals to him the mind of the great goddess. In this way the age of the gods and the present age are not two ages, but one, for not only the Mikado, but his Ministers and people also, act up to the tradition of the divine age. Hence, in ancient times the idea of *michi* or way (ethics) was never broached. The word was only applied to ordinary thoroughfares, and its application to systems of philosophy, government, morals, religion and so forth, is a foreign notion.

'As foreign countries (China and India, particularly the former) are not the special domain of the sun-goddess, they have no permanent rulers, and evil spirits, having found a field of action, have corrupted mankind. In those countries any bad man who could manage to seize on the power became a sovereign. Those who had the upper hand were constantly scheming to maintain their positions, while their inferiors were as constantly on the watch for opportunities to oust them. The most powerful and cunning of these rulers succeeded in taming their subjects, and having secured their position, became an example for others to imitate. In China the name of *Sei-zhiñ* (translated "Holy Men" by Meadows) has been given to these men. But it is an error to look upon these so-called Holy Men as in themselves supernatural and good beings, as superior to the rest of the world as are the gods. The principles which they established are called *michi* (ethics), and may be reduced to two simple rules, namely to take other people's territory, and to keep fast hold of it.

'The Chinese "Holy Men" also invented the "Book of Changes" (*Yeki*, or *I-king*), by which they pretended to discover the workings of the universe, a vain attempt, since it is impossible for man with his limited intelligence to find out the principles which govern the acts of the gods. In imitation of them the Chinese nation has since given itself up to philosophizing, to which are to be attributed its constant internal dissensions. When things go right of themselves it is best to leave them alone. In ancient times, although there was no prosy system of doctrine in Japan, there were no popular disturbances, and the empire was peacefully ruled. It is because the Japanese were truly moral in their practice that they required no theory of morals, and the fuss made by the Chinese about theoretical morals is owing to their laxity in practice. It is not wonderful that students of Chinese literature should despise their own country for being without a system of morals, but that Japanese who were acquainted with their own ancient literature should have pretended that Japan also had such a system, simply out of a feeling of envy, is ridiculous.

'When Chinese literature was imported into Japan, the people adopted many Chinese ideas, laws, customs and practices, which they so mixed up with their own that it became necessary to adopt a special name for the ancient native customs, which were in consequence called *Kami no michi* or *Shiñ-tau*, the word *michi* being applied in the same sense as the Chinese *tau* (*tao*), and *Kami* because of their divine origin. These native customs only survived in the ceremonies with which the native gods are worshipped.

'Every event in the universe is the act of the gods. They direct the changes of the seasons, the wind and the rain, the good and bad fortune of states and individual men. Some of the gods are good, others bad, and their acts partake of their own natures. Buddhists attribute events to "retribution" (*iñ-guwa*), while the Chinese ascribe them to the "decree of heaven" (*teñ-mei* or *t'ieñ-ming*). This latter is a phrase invented by the so-called "Holy Men" to justify murdering sovereigns and seizing their dominions. As neither heaven nor earth have minds, they cannot issue decrees. If heaven really could issue decrees it would certainly protect the good rulers and take care to prevent bad men from seizing the power, and in general, while the good would prosper, the bad would suffer misfortune. But in reality we find many instances of the reverse.

'Whenever anything goes wrong in the world it is to be attributed to the action of the evil gods called *Magatsubi no kami* (gods of crookedness) whose power is so great that the sun-goddess and the creator god are sometimes unable to restrain them; much less are human beings able to resist their influence. The prosperity of the wicked and the misfortunes of the good, which seem opposed to ordinary justice, are their doing. The Chinese, not possessing the traditions of the divine age, were ignorant of this truth, and were driven to invent the theory of "Heaven's decrees."

'The eternal endurance of the dynasty of the Mikados is a complete proof that the 'way' called *Kami no michi* or *Shiñ-tau* infinitely surpasses the systems of all other countries.

'The "Holy Men" of China were merely successful rebels.

The Mikado is the sovereign appointed by the pair of deities, Izanagi and Izanami, who created this country. The Sun-goddess never said, 'Disobey the Mikado if he be bad,' and therefore, whether he be good or bad, no one attempts to deprive him of his authority. He is the immovable ruler who must endure to the end of time, as long as the sun and moon continue to shine. In ancient language the Mikado was called a god, and that is his real character. Duty therefore consists in obeying him implicitly, without questioning his acts. During the middle ages such men as Hou-deu Yoshitoki, Hou-deu Yasutoki, Ashikaga Taka-uji and others violated this duty (*michi*), and took up arms against him. Their disobedience to the Mikado is attributable to the influence of Chinese learning.

'This "way" was established by Izanagi and Izanami, and delivered by them to the Sun-goddess, who handed it down, and this is why it is called the "way of the gods." The nature of this "way" is to be learnt by studying the *Ko-zhi-ki* and ancient writings, but mankind have been turned aside from it by the Spirits of Crookedness to Buddhism and Chinese philosophy.

'The various doctrines taught under the name of *Shiñ-tau* are without authority.

'Human beings having been produced by the spirit of the two Creative Deities, are naturally endowed with the knowledge of what they ought to do and what they ought to refrain from. It is unnecessary for them to trouble their heads with systems of morality. If a system of morals were necessary, men would be inferior to animals, of all whom are endowed with the knowledge of what, they ought to do, only in an inferior degree to men. If what the Chinese call Benevolence (*Zhiñ*), Righteousness (*Gi*), Propriety (*Rei*), Retiringness (*Zhiyau*), Filial Piety (*Kau*), Brotherly Love (*Tei*), Fidelity (*Chiyuu*) and Truth (*Shiñ*) really constituted the duty of man, they would be so recognized and practised without any teaching, but as they were invented by the so-called "Holy Men" as instruments for ruling a viciously-inclined population, it became necessary to insist on more than the actual duty of man. Consequently, although plenty of men profess these doctrines, the number of those who practise them is very small. Violations of this teaching were attributed to human lusts. As human lusts are a part of man's nature, they must be a part of the harmony of the universe, and cannot be wrong according to the Chinese theory. It was the vicious nature of the Chinese that necessitated such strict rules, as for instance that persons descended from a common ancestor, no matter how distantly related, should not intermarry. These rules not being founded on the harmony of the universe, were not in accordance with human feelings, and were therefore seldom obeyed.

'In ancient times Japanese refrained only from intermarriage among children of the same mother,[16] but the distance between noble and mean was duly preserved. Thus the country was spontaneously well-governed, in accordance with the "way" established by the gods.

'Just as the Mikado worshipped the gods of heaven and earth, so his people prayed to the good gods in order to avert their displeasure. If they committed crimes or defiled themselves, they employed the usual methods of purifications taught them by their own hearts. As there are bad as well as good gods, it is necessary to propitiate them with offerings of agreeable food, playing the harp, blowing the flute, singing and dancing and whatever else is likely to put them in a good humour.

'It has been asked whether the *kami no michi* is not the same as the Taoism of Laotzu. Laotzu hated the vain conceits of the Chinese scholars, and honoured naturalness, from which a resemblance may be argued; but as he was born in a dirty country not under the special protection of the Sun-goddess, he had only heard the theories of the succession of so-called Holy Men, and what he believed to be naturalness was simply what they called natural. He did not know that the gods are the authors of every human action, and this ignorance constituted a cause of radical difference.

'To have acquired the knowledge that there is no *michi* (ethics) to be learnt and practised is really to have learnt to practise the 'way' of the gods.'

This attack on the current Chinese philosophy was resented

---

[16] This was allowed among the Jews and by Solon (v. Lubbock's Origin of Civilization, p. 124). It was probably the result of polygamy. Although a distinction is made between the wife and concubines at the present day, that is probably of Chinese origin, for in more ancient times they were classed together as 'women.'

by a scholar named Ichikaha Tatsumaro, who in a pamphlet entitled Magano-hire begins by saying: "A certain man having abandoned himself to the study of the Kozhi-ki, Ni-hoñ-gi, Mañ-yefu-shifu and other books of the kind, until he had thoroughly masticated the old fables about which later ages can know nothing, and acquired an extensive acquaintance with them, the modern verse-makers have sounded his praises as a great teacher. It seems however that he had fancied the "naturalness" expounded by Laotzu to be a good thing, and he has violently abused the Holy Men. I have now undertaken to refute him."

Ichikaha starts by laying down the principle that 'unwritten traditions can never be accepted with implicit belief on account of the difficulties which stand in the way of their being handed down correctly, and the most incredible stories are those which have the best chance of being preserved. Now, even allowing that the Chinese system of writing was introduced in the reign of Ou-zhiñ Teñ-wau, the documents which Hiyeda no Are committed to memory must have been produced after that time, and for the period of about a thousand years which is calculated to have elapsed between Zhiñ-mu and Ou-zhiñ and the immense period called the "age of the gods" which preceded Zhiñ-mu's reign, no written records can have existed at all, since there was no native system of writing in use in ancient times.[17] The stories told us about the earlier ages must have been invented by the Mikados. The name of Amaterasu is probably a posthumous title conferred at a later period. If the sun-goddess is the real sun in heaven, it must have been quite dark before she was born; and yet it is stated that before she was born there were trees and plants, clothing, weapons, boats and buildings. If all these things existed before her birth, it seems probable that both sun and moon likewise preceded that event. It is curious that the stars are not mentioned in the Zhiñ-dai-no-maki. To say that the sun was born in Japan is a fiction which was probably invented by the earlier Mikados in order to support the assertion that this country is the root and all other countries only branches. The gods in heaven make no difference between different races of mankind, who are formed into separate nations by the seas and

---

[17] Hirata Atsutane has made an attempt to prove the genuine character of the zhiñ-dai no mo-zhi, which will be noticed further no.

mountain ranges which divide them off from each other, and the sun shines equally over all.

'During the thousand years or so which are said to have elapsed between the reigns of Zhiñ-mu and Ou-zhiñ there were no written characters, and no cyclical signs by which time could be measured and its lapse recorded. Men knew that it was spring by the blossoming of the flowers, and that autumn had arrived by the leaves falling from the trees. The statement that a thousand years did actually elapse cannot be accepted with confidence.

'The Japanese word *kami* was simply a title of honour, but in consequence of its having been used to translate the Chinese character *shiñ* (shên), a meaning has come to be attached to it which it did not originally possess. The ancestors of the Mikados were not gods but men, and were no doubt worthy to be reverenced for their virtues, but their acts were not miraculous or supernatural. If the ancestors of living men were not human beings, they are more likely to have been birds or beasts than gods.'

This is but a short summary of fifty-four pages of close print, a great part of which is occupied with the defence of the "Holy Men" and the Chinese philosophy. Some of the arguments remind us somewhat of the early deistical writers of Europe who maintained that religion was invented by priests with interested motives. It is not improbable that the author was indebted in some measure to the *Ko-shi-tsuu* of Ara-wi Haku-seki, a rationalistic work composed about the year 1716.

Motowori replied to Ichikaha in a book called Kuzuhana, written in 1780. In reply to the accusation of being an admirer of Laotzu, he says that it by no means follows that because that philosopher attacked the "Holy Men," all others who attacked them must be his followers. It is quite possible to have a bad opinion of both Taoism and Confucianism. To maintain the contrary is to resemble certain people who seeing a party of gamblers arrive first at the scene of a fire, and work hard to put it out, believed some honest villagers who came later, and aided in the good work, to be gamblers also. The teaching of the "Holy Men" is like a fire burning a house, Laotzu is the gambler who first tried to extinguish it, and Motowori's own work the Nahobi no Mitama is the honest villager.

With regard to the first argument put forth by Ichikaha, he argues that 'before the invention of writing the want of it could not have been felt in the same way as it would, if we were now deprived of a medium of recording facts on which for ages past we have been accustomed to depend almost entirely. It is an acknowledged fact, however, that we still find ourselves obliged to have recourse to oral language in matters of delicacy or detail which cannot be conveniently committed to writing, and it is probable that the ancient traditions, which were preserved by exercise of memory, have for this very reason come down to us in greater detail than if they had been recorded in documents. Besides, men must have had much stronger memories in the days before they acquired the habit of trusting to written characters for facts which they wished to remember, as is shown to the present day in the case of the illiterate, who have to depend on memory alone.

'The facts that the sacred mirror bestowed by Amaterasu upon Ninigi no Mikoto is still preserved at the Nai-kuu temple in Ise; that the sword "Grass-cutter" is to this day at the temple of Atsuta in Wohari; that remains which date from the divine age are even now to be found in various provinces; that the sepulchres of the Mikados from Zhiñ-mu downwards exist in parts of the Ki-nai; that numerous relics of the divine age remain in the possession of the Court, and that the Nakatomi, Imibe and Ohotomo families have transmitted the functions which they exercised in the age of the gods in unbroken succession to their descendants of later times, vindicate beyond the possibility of a doubt the truth of the old traditions.

'In reply to the argument that if Amaterasu and the sun be identical, there must have been perpetual night before she was born, which is inconsistent with the fact of trees and plants being in existence before her birth; and that therefore the sun must have been previously hanging in the sky, he reiterates the statement that the goddess and the sun are one and the same. For although she will continue to shine as long as heaven and earth endure, she was born in Japan, and her descendants to this day rule over the empire. The difficulty of reconciling the statements that the world was plunged into darkness when she retired into the cavern, and that darkness did not exist before she was born is one that would strike even a child's intelligence. The critic need not make so much fuss about this point, as if it were entirely a new discovery of his own. The very inconsistency is the proof of the authenticity of the record, for who would have gone out of his way to invent a story apparently so ridiculous and incredible. The acts of the gods are not to be explained by ordinary principles. Man's intelligence is limited, and there are many things which transcend it.

'If we reflect that Izanagi had to kindle a light when he visited the nether world, because of the darkness which reigned there, while the opposite was the case in the upper world, although the sun-goddess had not yet come into being, it will be clear that there was some cause, which we cannot explain, for the darkness of the nether world, and for light existing on the earth. Some principle was evidently at work with which we are unacquainted. After the birth of the sun-goddess, no light could be obtained except from her brightness,[18] as she had been appointed to illuminate the space between heaven and earth, which accounts for night covering the earth when she went into the cave.

'Many other miracles occurred in the age of the gods, the truth of which was not disputed until men were taught by Chinese philosophy to analyse the acts of the god by the aid of their own feeble intelligence. The reason assigned for disbelieving in miracles is that they cannot be explained, but in fact although the age of the gods has passed away, wondrous miracles surround us on all sides. For instance, is the earth suspended in space or does it rest upon something else? If it be said that the earth rests upon something else, then what is it that supports that something else? According to one Chinese theory the earth is a globe, suspended in space with the heavens revolving round it. But even if we suppose the heavens to be full of air, no ordinary principles will account for the land and sea being suspended in space without moving. The explanation offered is

[18] The parallel between the creation of light and the vegetable world before the sun, as given in the I. Chapter of Genesis and the Japanese account is very curious; it might be useful to those who think that the Japanese are the descendants of the lost tribes.

as miraculous as the supposition previously made. It seems plausible enough to say that the heavens are merely air, and are without any definite form. If this be true there is nothing but air outside the earth, and this air must be either infinite or finite in extent. If it is infinite in extent, we cannot fix on any points as its centre, so that it is impossible to understand why the earth should be at rest; for if it be not in the centre it cannot be at rest. If it be finite, what causes the air to condense in one particular spot, and what position shall we assign to it? In any case, all these things are miraculous and strange. How absurd to take these miracles for granted, and at the same time to disbelieve in the wonders of the divine age. Think again of the human body. Seeing with the eyes, hearing with the ears, speaking with the mouth, walking on the feet and performing all manner of acts with the hands are strange things; so also the flight of birds and insects through the air, the blossoming of plants and trees, the ripening of their seeds and fruits are strange; and the strangest of all is the transformation of the fox and *tanuki* into human form. If rats, weasels and certain birds can see in the dark, why should the gods not have been endowed with a similar faculty?'

In reply to an observation of Ichikaha's that "to obey and revere a sovereign, no matter whether he be good or bad, is. the part of women," after an argument intended to prove that it is not safe to allow subjects to criticise the acts of their prince, Motowori says: "Thus, even if the prince be bad, to venerate, respect and obey him in all things, though it may seem like a woman's duty, is the right way of action, which does not allow of the obligations of a subject towards his prince ever being violated."

'All the moral ideas which man requires are implanted in his bosom by the gods, and are of the same nature as the instincts which impel him to eat when he is hungry and to drink when he is thirsty. But the morals inculcated by the Chinese philosophers are inventions, and contain something more in addition to natural morality.

'The facts that many of the gods are invisible now, and have never been visible, furnish no argument against their existence. Existences can be made known to us by other senses than those of sight, such as odours and sound; while the wind,[19] which is neither seen, heard nor smelt, is recognized by the impression which it makes on our bodies. The gods of the divine age are indeed no longer visible, but in that age they were visible. The sun-goddess must be excepted, for she is visible to all men even now. And as for the gods whose existence was never perceived by the eyes of men, they are known by their special modes of action upon men. All our knowledge comes to us in fact by our senses. We thus know that fire is hot and water cold, but of the nature of heat and cold we can discover nothing.

There is a tradition in China that the left and right eyes of Puanku became the sun and moon, which is, however, usually discredited because the natives of that country, being admirers of false knowledge, assign the origin of these two luminaries to the Positive and Negative Essences. The real truth is that the sun and moon were produced when Izanagi no kami washed his eyes after returning from his search after Izanami no kami in the nether world. The tradition has evidently travelled to China, and assumed the perverted form in which we find it there, during the lapse of ages.'

Motowori disclaims any intention of endeavouring to resuscitate pure Shiñ-tau so far as to make it the rule of life in the present day. His only object is to present the age of the gods in its real form. All that comes to pass in the world, whether good or bad in its nature, is the act of the gods and men have generally little influence over the course of events. To insist on practising the ancient "way of the gods," in opposition to the customs of the present age, would be rebellion against that "way," and equivalent to trying to excel it. If men in their daily practice obey the laws made from time to time by the authorities, and act in accordance with general custom, they are practising *Shiñ-tau*. It was with this reservation that he vindicated the ancient practice of inter-marriage among children of the same father by different mothers, and not in order to recommend its revival.

The *Keñ-kayau-zhiñ*, or "The madman thrust into an iron

---

[19] He probably means 'air.'

collar," is likewise a controversial work in reply to the *Shiyou-kou-hatsu*, which was apparently an attack upon the ancient records. The latter is a rare book, and we have not been able to procure a copy, but to judge from the short quotations contained in the *Keñ-kiyau-zhiñ* the points in dispute have no direct bearing upon the essential principles of Shiñ-tau.

From the central truth that the Mikado is the direct descendant of the gods, the tenet that Japan ranks far above all other countries is a natural consequence. No other nation is entitled to equality with her, and all are bound to do homage to the Japanese Sovereign and pay tribute to him. These truths are enlarged upon in great detail by Motowori in a work entitled *Giyo-zhiyuu Gai-geñ*, "Indignant words about Ruling the Barbarians," written in 1778. It takes the form of a review of the relations between Japan and other countries from the earliest period down to the time of Iheyasu, as recorded in the histories of both countries, but does not touch upon the subject of the intercourse with Christian states in the 16th and 17th centuries, probably because Christianity was a forbidden question.

'That on the earliest occasion when the Mikado exchanged letters and envoys with the Chinese Sovereign, the first step should have been taken by the former is a source of deep annoyance to Motowori. This deplorable event occurred in the year 707 under the Empress Suwi-ko, when an envoy was sent to China to fetch a Buddhist Sûtra which Shiyau-toku Tai-shi remembered to have possessed during a previous state of existence, when he was studying the sacred mysteries in that country. It is true that the Chinese histories contain notices of tribute bearers from Japan much earlier than this date, but these envoys, whatever may have been their character, certainly were not commissioned by the sovereign. As for their paying tribute, the statement is due to the inordinate vanity of the Chinese, who fancy themselves superior to all surrounding nations, whereas they are no better than barbarians themselves, and are bound to acknowledge the supremacy of Japan. The Ni-hoñ-gi speaks also of the despatch of Japanese to China in 464 and 468, but Motowori thinks that they were not accredited to any Chinese sovereign. One of the Chinese histories has an account of the mission sent by Suwi-ko, and gives what purports to be a letter from that Empress, in which appears the famous phrase, "The Teñ-shi (son of Heaven) of the place where the sun rises sends a letter to the Teñ-shi of the place where the sun sets." 'If the Empress Suwi-go really sent such a letter, she treated the Chinese sovereign with far too much civility, and if she had addressed him with some such phrase as, "The Heavenly Emperor notifies (chiyoku) to the king of 'Go (Wu)," he ought to have been filled with gratitude, instead of which he is represented by the Chinese historiographer as having been offended at being treated as an equal. But the truth is that Suwi-ko Teñ-wau wanted to get something from him, and therefore condescended to flatter his vanity.' The Ni-hoñ-gi relates that this Empress showered civilities upon the envoy who brought the Chinese Emperor's answer, but Motowori does not care to dwell on this fact.

Uninterrupted intercourse seems to have continued between the two Courts for about two centuries, and then to have ceased during a period of about thirty years. 'It was unworthy of Japan to enter into relations with a base barbarian state, whatever might be the benefits which she expected to obtain. It resulted in too many cases in the shipwreck of the vessels and the profitless deaths of the envoys by drowning. Had the Chinese ruler paid due reverence to the Mikado as a being infinitely superior to himself, the objection would have been less.' After the end of the tenth century the Mikados appear to have ceased sending envoys to China, and Motowori remarks that "so long as Japan wanted anything from China, she overlooked the insolent pretensions of the Chinese sovereigns, but now being no longer in a position to gain by the interchange of courtesies, she rejected all further overtures of friendship."

The failure of the expeditions sent against Japan by Kublai Khan and the Tai-kafu's conquest of Korea of course afford much matter for reflections of a gratifying nature, which are only clouded by the disgraceful conduct of the Shiyau-guñ Ashikaga Yoshi-mitsu, who in writing to the Ming sovereign addresses him as Your Majesty (hei-ka), and in one of his letters uses the title 'King' (koku-wau) in speaking of himself, of the Shíyau-guñ Yoshihisa, in sending envoys to ask for money (such sums as 50,000 and 100,000 strings of cash[20] at a time), and by the unfortunately obsequious language used by the Tai-kafu and some of his generals in writing to the Chinese officials about the negotiations for peace. 'But the responsibility in these last cases lay with the priests, who being the only men in those days with the slightest tincture of learning, had charge of the correspondence.'

The most remarkable point about this long tirade against China is that Japan was indebted to her for all the arts and sciences that make life better than nonentity, for a complete system of government and laws, and even for the very art of writing which enabled the writer to record his arrogant and spiteful feelings.

Of Motowori's other works relating to Shiñ-tau the most important are his commentaries on the *Oho-barahi no kotoba* (1795) and the *Idzumo Kuni-no-miyatsuko Kamuyogoto* (1793), the *Zhiñ-dai Udzu no Yama-kage*, which is a development of his criticisms on the first two books of the *Ni-hoñ-gi* called the *Zhiñ-dai no maki*, and the *Zhiñ-dai Shiyau-go* (1789). This last is a compilation from those parts of the *Ko-zhi-ki* and *Ni-hoñ-gi* which describe the age of the gods and certain other ancient books, written in the mixture of Chinese characters and *Hira-gana* called *Kana-mazhiri*, with a few explanatory notes. It is intended to give a clearer account of the ancient traditions than either of the original works on which it is based, by eliminating the Chinese order of characters, and substituting purely Japanese sentences. To these may be added the *Teñ-so to-zhiyau Beñ-beñ* (1767), a reply to two writers, one of whom had tried to prove that the capital of Amaterasu was at Nakatsu in Bu-zeñ, the other that it was in the province of Yamato, and the *Ise Ni-guu Sakitake no Beñ*, the object of which is to refute the heretical notion that Amaterasu is not the sun, and to show that the deity of the Ge-kuu, who is identified by some writers with Ame-no-mi-naka-nushi, by others with Kuni-no-toko-tachi, is in reality Uke-mochi no kami, the goddess of food.

The *Reki-teu Seu-shi kai*, in six volumes, published two years after his death, is of great value to the student of ancient

---

[20] The string of cash was probably worth about a dollar.

Japanese history. It contains an amended text of all the *mi-koto-nori*, or Imperial messages, which are recorded in the *Shiyoku-Ni-hoñ-gi* during the period which elapsed from the abdication of Ji-dou Teñ-wau in 696, down to 791, the 10th year of Kuwañ-mu Teñ-wau. These messages were delivered on various occasions, such as the recognition of the heir-apparent, the abdication of the Sovereign, the creation of an Empress, the punishment of criminals of rank, the outbreak of rebellions, the granting of lands to distinguished subjects, and several were pronounced in connection with the execution of a new kind of dance by the Princess who afterwards became Kau-keñ Teñ-wau. Another was composed for a thanksgiving service for the discovery of gold in Japan, celebrated in 749 at the temple of Tou-dai-zhi in Nara, when the Empress Kau-keñ was present with her whole court, and worshipped the great image commonly called *Dai-butsu*. The style is in many cases pure Japanese, and these messages together with the *norito* preserved in the *Yeñ-gi Shiki*, form the only native prose compositions which are of older date than the 9th century.

Like the other members of this Pure Shiñ-tau School, Moto-wori devoted a great deal of attention to the study of the ancient language, and composed numerous works of great value in this department of learning. Mr. Aston has given the titles of several of these in the list appended to his Grammar of the Written Language, to which may be added th *Ko-kiñ-shifu Towokagami*, a commentary on the collection of poetry entitled *Ko-kiñ-shifu*, notes on the *Geñ-zhi Monogatari* under the title *G.M. Tana no Wogushi*, the *Chi-mei Zhi-oñ Teñ-you-rei*, on the etymology of local names, the *Mañ-yefu Tama no Wo-goto* and *Mañ-yefu-shifu hai-kuñ*, and the *Uhi-yama-bumi*, a general introduction to Japanese studies. The *Tama-kushige* is a highly interesting work on the philosophy of government written in 1687, in which the abuses that were even then beginning to sap the foundations of the feudal system are laid bare with an unsparing hand. A summary of its contents might be of value to those who are interested in modern Japanese politics, but would be foreign to the scope of this paper.

Motowori's style, less ornate than that of Mabuchi, is clear and correct, though sometimes wanting in terseness, and his con-

troversial writings give evidence of his logical powers in dealing
with his own premises. He may be said almost to have created
the modern literary Japanese language, and the influence of his
example is seen even in the lighter literature of the present day.
The violence of his prejudices in favour of everything native
and antique is probably due to a reaction against the dominion
of Chinese ideas and forms of expression, which at the time he
thought and wrote bade fair to extinguish every trace of
Japanese nationality. No author can be studied to such advantage by those who wish to acquire a mastery of written Japanese.

IV.

Hirata Atsutane, the fourth in chronological order of those
scholars whom I have named as the founders of this school, was
born in 1776 at the town of Kubota in Deha, the capital of that
remote district in the north of Japan commonly called Akita.
His father was Ohowada Seibei, a *samurai* of the Satake family,
who traced back his descent to the sun-goddess through Kuwañ-
mu Teñ-wau, the fiftieth *Mikado* from Zhiñ-mu, and enjoyed a hereditary pension of a hundred *koku* of rice. Atsutane
was the fourth son of a family of eight children. At the age
of eight he entered the school of a professor of Chinese named
Nakayama Sei-ga, and three years later commenced the study
of medicine under his uncle Ohowada Riu-geñ. Up to his
twentieth year he chiefly devoted himself to Chinese studies, and
practised fencing under various teachers, but he longed to distinguish himself in some way more worthy of his abilities, and
in the beginning of 1795 he suddenly quitted his father's house,
leaving a letter behind him bidding farewell to his relations.
He had chosen the 8th of the month for his departure, apparently
on account of the popular belief that a person who leaves home
on that day never returns. With a *riyau* in his purse he started
for Yedo, where, after his arrival, avoiding the society of his
fellow-clansmen and friends, he sought on all sides for a virtuous
and learned teacher. Sometimes he obtained employment as an
under-teacher, and in his worst extremity was reduced to seeking
a livelihood by manual labour. In this manner he passed four
or five years, suffering great hardship and privation. In 1800,
at the age of twenty-five, he became the adopted heir of Hirata

Fujibei, a retainer of the *daimiyau* of Matsuyama in Bi-chiyuu, and took up his residence in the *yashiki* of Hoñda Shiu-ri on Kagura-zaka in Yedo.

It was in the following year that Atsutane first became acquainted with the writings of Motowori, and was seized with an enthusiastic love for the study of Japanese antiquity. In the seventh month he formally enrolled himself among Motowori's pupils, about two months before the death of the elder scholar. His first essay in the new branch of learning to which he had devoted himself was an attack upon the writings of Dai-zai Shiyuñ-tai (b. 1680, d. 1747), in a book entitled *Ka-bau-shiyo*, which he wrote in 1803, and in the following year he began to take pupils. It was in 1804 that he drew up a table of Chinese characters relating to the practise of the five virtues. These he enumerates as Reverence, Righteousness, Benevolence, Wisdom and Valour, and nineteen characters are included under each heading. It is a more curious than valuable production.

The *Ki-zhiñ Shiñ-roñ*, completed first in 1805 and revised for publication in 1820, is intended to prove that the ordinary Chinese philosophers have misunderstood the teachings of Confucius with regard to supernatural beings, and to show by quotations from the Confucian Analects and other writings that he believed in their actual existence. Hirata in this work refutes the opinions of Chinese and Japanese scholars with regard to the non-existence of gods, and demonstrates the correctness of the opposite view. We have not time to analyze the work more minutely, and have had recourse to the bibliographical list of Hirata's writings printed at the end of the *Nifu-gaku Moñ-dafu* for this brief notice of it.

In 1807 he resumed practice as a physician, and the study of medicine. During this year he commenced the compilation of the Chishima Shira-nami, or White Waves of the Kurile Islands, which contains an account of the incursions of the Russians under Davidoff and Chwostoff against the Japanese possessions in Sagalien and Itorup in the previous year. It was intended also to be a manual of the way to 'restrain barbarians' and of maritime defence. It is to be regretted that this interesting work still remains unprinted.

The year 1811 was an extremely fruitful one. Early in

the spring he began to revise the lectures on Shiñ-tau, Chinese philosophy and Buddhism which during the two previous years he had delivered to his pupils, and produced in succession the *Ko-dau Tai-i*, Summary of the Ancient Way; *Zoku-Shin-tau Tai-i*, Summary of the Vulgar Shiñ-tau; *Kañ-gaku Tai-i*, Summary of Chinese Learning, the same as that which was afterwards published under the title of *Sai-zhiyaku Gai-roñ;* the *Butsu-dau Tai-i*, Summary of Buddhism, subsequently renamed *Go-dau Beñ; I-dau Tai-i*, Summary of the Medical Art, printed under the title of *Shidzu no Ihaya;* the *Ka-dau Tai-i*, Summary of the Art of Poetry, and the *Tama-dasuki*, which he rewrote from beginning to end some years later. Of the works in this list the first, second and last are alone of interest to the student of Shiñ-tau, but as the *Zoku Shiñ-tau Tai-i* is a hostile criticism of the sects comprehended by the author under the name of vulgar Shiñ-tau I shall not ask my readers to go through a summary of its contents. It will be more useful to consider it on some future occasion in connection with the works of the writers against whom it is directed.

The Summary of the Ancient Way treats of the following subjects: firstly, the reason why the subject-matter of his teaching is called the Ancient Learning (*Ko-gaku*); secondly, the origin of this study, with a brief account of those who founded it and spread it abroad in the world; thirdly, the foundations upon which it is based; fourthly, the age of the gods; fifthly, the reasons why the gods are entitled to the gratitude of mankind; sixthly, why Japan is "the country of the gods"; seventhly, how it is certain beyond a doubt that every Japanese is a descendant of the gods; eighthly, the uninterrupted continuance of the imperial line from the beginning of the world, together with proofs of the superiority of Japan over all other countries in the world, both materially and morally; ninthly, the truth that the Japanese, being natives of 'the country of the gods,' are born with a naturally perfect and true disposition, which from the most ancient times has been called *Yamato-damashihi* or *Yamato-gokoro*,[21] and tenthly, how the traditions of the Age of the Gods, and of their actions, appear to the ordinary man to

---

[21] *Yamato*, one of the old names of Japan; *tamashishi*, spirit; *kokoro*, heart.

be mysterious and difficult of belief; and the refutation of this error;—in the course of which exposition the real 'way' will be disclosed.

Japanese learning may be divided into several branches, firstly, the Way of the Gods; secondly, poetry; thirdly, law; fourthly, romances; fifthly, history; and sixthly, archæology. Under these there are subdivisions, such as the various schools of what is commonly called Shiñ-tau, and two or three schools of poetry. Chinese learning also has many subdivisions, and in Buddhism there are the doctrines of the numerous sects, besides the Learning of the Heart,[22] which is an offshoot of Buddhism. Then we have astronomy and physical geography, the learning of the Hollanders, and medicine, which is divided into three schools, the ancient, the modern and the Dutch. But Japanese learning is the chief of all these. A man passes for a good Chinese scholar if he has learnt to read the Four Books and the Five Classics, or, according to another enumeration, the Thirteen Classics, has run hastily through half a dozen other works, and can compose Chinese prose and what they have a trick of calling poetry. There is nothing very difficult in all this. The Buddhist priests have a much larger task. Their canon (which Hirata here says he has read) consists of some five thousand volumes, seven or eight horse-loads, a tenth part of which is far more than the sinologue has to study; and to make the work harder the priests have to study Chinese as well as their own religious books, or else they could not read the latter. And owing to the strange manner in which Buddhist and Chinese notions have been mixed up with Japanese learning (*Shiñ-tau*), the student of the latter must possess all the knowledge of the sinologue and the priest that he may be able to separate the wheat from the chaff, and he must know all the possible arguments which his opponents may have at their command in order to refute them. Besides, if a Japanese studies foreign learning he will be able to select whatever good things there are in it, and turn them to the service of his country. From this point of view Chinese, Indian and even Dutch studies may be looked upon as Japanese learning.

---

[22] This is the form of doctrine taught in the *Kiu-wou Dau-wa, Shiñ-gaku Michi no Hanashi, Te-zhima Dau-wa* and similar works.

'In the first place it is necessary to state that the reason why this teaching is called the "study of the ancient way" is because it aims at explaining the facts which begin with the origin of heaven and earth, by means of the ancient ways of thinking and the ancient tongue, such as they were before the introduction of the Chinese and Buddhist "ways," and at demonstrating, that in those facts is embodied the whole of the true "way."

Having disposed of his first heading in this manner, Hirata proceeds to deal with the second, namely the founders of the school to which he himself belongs. A summary of what he has said about them in the second and ninth volumes of his *Tamadasuki*, has already been given in the former part of this paper.

The foundations upon which the Ancient Learning is based are the writings in which the Imperial Court has recorded the facts of antiquity. Most people are wont to suppose that the only way to attain to a knowledge of right conduct is to read books full of precepts, but they labour under a mistake. Precept is far inferior to example, for it only arises in the absence of example, while it is unnecessary when example exists. As Laotzŭ says, "When the Great Way decayed, humanity and Righteousness arose."[23] In order to spur on a warrior to valient deeds, rather than show him a book which says, "When you go to battle strive to be first, do not lag behind others," show him a book in which are written the facts about ancient heroes' who led the way, fought bravely and achieved renown. The facts will sink deeply into his heart, and he will say to himself, "When the occasion arises, I will distinguish myself like such an one of antiquity," but the mere exhortation will scarcely stir his emotions. The story of Ohoishi Kuranosuke and the forty-seven faithful retainers, who underwent a thousand hardships and perils in order to slay Kira Kaudzuke no suke, the enemy of their lord Asano Takumi no kami, will do far more to keep alive the flame of loyalty than any simple precepts about the duty of avenging a master. The ethical writings of the T'ang dynasty

---

[23] Taôtê-king, chap. xviii. Julien translates: Quand la grande voie eut dépéri, on vit paraitre l'humanité et la justice. That is, according to the commentator whom he follows, when the way decayed, the absence of affection and the existence of disobedience brought humanity and justice into prominence.

are full of the most admirable teachings of this kind, but when we find that the authors were themselves guilty of murdering their sovereigns and of treason, their words lose all their effect.

As has already been said, the real principles of conduct are not to be taught by precept, and we must go to the books to find the facts from which the real ancient way is to be learnt. The most important of these is the Ko-zhi-ki. Most Japanese, including those who profess to be students of the way of the gods, hold the Ni-hoñ-shiyo-ki in great honour. Its first two books are printed separately under the title of *Zhiñ-dai-no-maki*, and the common teachers of Shiñ-tau have written various so-called commentaries thereon. They even assert that these books are the only authorities about the beginning of the world and the age of the gods. Motowori in the first volume of the Ko-zhi-ki Deñ pointed out the erroneousness of this opinion. Part of the cosmogony given in the Zhiñ-dai-no-maki can be actually traced to ancient Chinese writing, from which it has been taken almost word for word. But on the other hand the Ni-hoñ-shiyo-ki, or, as it should properly be called, the Ni-hoñ-gi, has great merits of its own, which ought not to be passed over. In addition to the main text of the first two books, it quotes a number of other parallel passages from documents then extant, which often throw much light on the received traditions of the divine age, and it gives much fuller details of the history of the Mikados from Zhiñ-mu Teñ-wau downwards than the Ko-zhi-ki does. When the ornamental Chinese phraseology has been eliminated there remains a great treasure of truth, and the Ni-hoñ-gi therefore does really deserve the first place among the sacred books.

It is most lamentable that so much ignorance should prevail as to the evidences of the two fundamental doctrines, that Japan is the country of the Gods and her inhabitants the descendants of the Gods. Between the Japanese people and the Chinese, Hindoos, Russians, Dutch, Siamese, Cambodians and other nations of the world there is a difference of kind, rather than of degree. It was not out of vain-glory that the inhabitants of this country called it the land of the gods (*Shiñ-koku, kami no kuni*). The gods who created all countries belonged without exception to the Divine Age, and were all born in Japan, so that

Japan is their native country, and all the world acknowledges the appropriateness of the title. The Koreans were the first to become acquainted with this truth, and from them it was gradually diffused through the globe, and accepted by every one.

Before the origin of things there was infinite space (*ohosora*); neither heaven nor earth, nor the sun, nor moon, nor anything else existed. In infinite space were Ame-no-mi-naka-nushi no kami,[24] and next Taka-mi-musu-bi no kami and Kamu-mi-musu-bi no kami, by whose miraculous power a thing whose shape cannot be described in words came into existence in the midst of space. This thing floated (or, was suspended) in space like a cloud, without any support. From it came forth something sprouting like a horn, or like the young sprout of the rush called *kaya;* but as to its nature there is no tradition. It may however be conjectured that it was pure, translucent and bright, for it afterwards became the sun, and from the time when Ama-terasu-oho-mi kami became its ruler, the brightness of her august body has shone through it. As this thing grew upwards it widened out infinitely, just as a cloud rising from the top of a mountain looks like a rush sprouting, but afterwards becomes immensely extended. This is what in the Divine Age was called *Ama-tsu-kuni* (the kingdom of heaven), *Taka-ma-no-hara* (the high plain of heaven), and sometimes simply *Ame* (heaven). In a similar manner there grew downwards a something, which afterwards separated and became the moon. During the double process fourteen other gods came into being, of whom the last were Izanagi no kami and Izanami no kami. They are the parents of the deities of the sun and moon and the progenitors of all the other gods.

As to the signification of the word *kami;*[25]—it is applied in the first place to all the *kami* of heaven and earth who are mentioned in the ancient records, as well as to their spirits which reside in the temples where they are worshipped. Fur-

---

[24] The Lord of the Middle of Heaven. *Taka* and *kamu* are explained as honorifics; *mi* has the same force. *Musu* means to beget; this word enters into composition with *ko* and *me* to produce *musuko* and *musume*, son and daughter. *Bi* is the same as *hi*, an archaic word applied to whatever is wonderful, miraculous and ineffably worthy of honour, and to the sun *par excellence*.

[25] This passage is copied by Hirata almost word for word from vol. iii. of the Ko-zhi-ki Deñ, without any acknowledgment.

ther, not only human beings, but also birds, beasts, plants and trees, seas and mountains, and all other things whatsoever which possess powers of an extraordinary and eminent character, or deserve to be revered and dreaded, are called *kami*. Eminent does not mean solely worthy of honour, good or distinguished by great deeds, but is applied also to the *kami* who are to be dreaded on account of their evil character or miraculous nature. Amongst human beings who are at the same time *kami* are to be classed the successive Mikados, who in the Mañ-yefu-shifu and other ancient poetry are called *towo-tsu-kami* (distant gods) on account of their being far removed from ordinary men, as well as many other men, some who are revered as *kami* by the whole Empire, and those whose sphere is limited to a single province, department, village or family. The *kami* of the Divine Age were mostly human beings, who yet resembled *kami*, and that is why we give that name to the period in which they existed. Beside human beings, the thunder is called the 'sounding god' (*naru-kami*). The dragon goblins, (*ten-gu*) and the fox are also *kami*, for they are likewise eminently miraculous and dreadful creatures. In the Ni-hoñ-gi and in the Mañ-yefu-shifu the tiger and the wolf[26] are spoken of as *kami*. Izanagi gave the name of Oho-kamu-dzu-mi no mikoto to the fruit of the peach-tree, and the jewels which he wore on his neck were called Mi-kura-tama no mikoto. In the *Zhiñ-dai-no-maki* and the *Oho-barahi no kotoba*, rocks, stumps of trees, leaves of plants and so forth are said to have spoken in the Divine Age; these also were *kami*. There are many cases of the term being applied to seas and mountains. It was not a spirit that was meant, but the term was used directly of the particular sea or mountain; of the sea on account of its depth and the difficulty of crossing it, of the mountain on account of its loftiness.[27]

[26] *Oho-kami*, literally, great god.

[27] *Kami*, god, is evidently the same word as *kami* applied to a superior, as to a master by his servant or to the sovereign' by his subjects, to the chief officer of a sub-department of the administration, and in ancient times to the governor of a province. Its primary meaning is 'that which is above,' and hence 'chief.' So that Izanagi no Oho kami would mean Great Chief Izanagi. *Mikoto*, which is a title applied to gods, and forms part of the word *Sumera-mikoto*, the ancient name of the sovereigns of Japan, is composed of the honorific *mi* and *koto*, word, and hence, thing. It might be rendered augustness, and Izanagi no mikoto would mean His Augustness Izanagi.

Izanagi and Izanami, after descending by command of the Heavenly Gods upon Onogoro-zhima, begot the eight islands of Japan, namely, what are now called Ahaji, Shi-koku, Oki, Kiushiu, Iki, Tsushima, Sado and the main island. They begot a number of gods, and their posterity gradually increased. Amongst the descendants of their child Susanowo no kami was Oho-na-muji no kami, a god of surpassing powers. For a long time he was subjected to great annoyance at the hands of his numerous brothers, but having taken a journey to the nether world (the moon) to consult his ancestor, he was enabled, by following the advice he then received, to overcome his rebellious brethren, and establish himself as the ruler of this country. One of his many names is Oho-kuni-nushi no kami, which means the 'great lord of the country.' The seat of his government was in the province of Idzumo. He had many children, the eldest of whom was Koto-shiro-nushi no kami, one of the eight gods worshipped in the Zhiñ-gi-kuwañ; second was Aji-suki-taka-hiko-ne no kami, the god of Kami-gamo near Kiyau-to, and another was Take-mi-na-gata no mikoto, the god of Kami no Suwa in Shinano. Oho-na-muji is a corruption of Oho-na-mochi, the Great Possessor of Names, a title given to him because of the numerous names which he possessed. In conjunction with Sukuna-bikona no kami, the eldest son of the two creators, he completed the work begun by Izanagi and Izanami, and civilized the country. To these two gods are ascribed the discovery of medicine and the invention of divination.

Amaterasu oho-mi-kami, having been appointed Queen of the sun by Izanagi, shares the government of the world with the two creators. She in turn desired to make a son of her own ruler over the terrestrial world. This was Oshi-ho-mimi no mikoto, a god who was produced from the goddess' necklace; he was married to Tama-yori-hime no mikoto, a grand-daughter of the two creators. The offspring of this pair was Ninigi no mikoto, who was therefore the grandson of Amaterasu, and the title Sume-mi-ma no mikoto (Sublime Grandchild) applied to him expresses this relationship. Ninigi no mikoto replaced his father as sovereign-designate of the world, but as Oho-na-muji who was in actual possession could hardly be expected to surrender peacefully, a council was held of all the gods. By the

advice of the most sagacious of the gods, one of the other
children of Amaterasu, named Ame-no-hohi no mikoto, was sent
on an embassy to the world, to persuade Oho-na-muji to give up
his rights. The envoy remained away three years, and as no
result had yet been obtained, a second envoy was despatched,
who was to induce Oho-na-muji to submit by a display of military force. The second envoy, however, fell in love with Shita-
teru-hime, a daughter of Oho-na-muji, and failed to perform his
errand. He even slew a messenger who was sent to stimulate
him to accomplish his mission. Upon this an expedition was
started under two warlike gods named Take-mika-dzuchi and
Futsu-nushi, who in joint action with Ame-no-hohi no mikoto
succeeded at last in obtaining from Oho-na-muji a renunciation
of his sovereignty over Japan in favour of the Sublime Grandchild. The only conditions which he exacted were that he should
have a temple built for his residence where proper services might
be performed in his honour, and that the Unseen (*kakuri-goto*)
should be placed under his charge. This arrangement was
ratified by Amaterasu and the two creators. The temple of Oho-
yashiro in Idzumo, which exists to this day, was built for Ohonamuji; and Ame-no-hohi, from whom sprang the family of the
Idzumo-no-kuni no miyatsuko, at first hereditary governors of
the province, and afterwards priests of the temple, became his
servant.

It now became possible for Ninigi-no-mikoto to descend
and take possession of his realm. Before starting from the sun
he received from the goddess, his grandmother, the three divine
insignia, called *Kusanagi-no-tsurugi* (a sword, which is enshrined
at Atsuta in Wohari), the *Yasakani-no-maga-tama* (a stone)
and the mirror which is worshipped at the Nai-kuu in Ise as the
representative of the goddess of the sun. Accompanied by a
number of inferior gods, he descended on the *Ama no uki-hashi,*
or floating bridge of heaven, to Taka-chi-ho no mine, now called
Kirishima yama, which lies on the boundary between Hiuga and
Ohosumi in Kiu-shiu. On this occasion grains of rice were
thrown broadcast in the air to dispel the darkness which covered
the sky, and it is said that rice grows wild on Kirishima yama
to this day.

The *Ama no uki-hashi* was a thing by which communication

took place between heaven and earth in those days. It floated in the air, and was also called *Ama no iha-fune*, literally, the rock-boat. It was on this that Izanagi and Izanami took their stand when they stirred about with the sacred spear to find land. There are still remains of the *hashi-date*, lofty mounds by which the *uki-hashi* was reached, in the provinces of Harima and Tañ-go. After the descent of the Sublime Grandchild, the sun and the earth, which had already receded from each other to a considerable distance, gradually became further separated, and communication by the floating bridge ceased. The *hashi-date* fell down, and have since lain on their longest side: that near Miyadzu in Tañ-go measures twenty-two thousand two hundred and ninety feet in length.

The sun having thus ascended, became fixed in the centre of space, where it constantly revolves on its axis from left to right. The earth is far removed from it in space, and moves round it from right to left, one revolution being called a year. At the same time the earth revolving on itself, produces the phenomena of day and night. The moon which split off from the earth about the same period revolves round the earth in a little over twenty nine days and a half, waxing and waning as it goes. The process by which the sun, earth and moon were thus produced resembles the separation of the umbilical cord and the placenta at the birth of a child, or the detachment of a ripened seed from the capsule. It is not merely a fortuitous resemblance, but the processes are identical in all three cases.

As it was Japan which lay directly opposite to the sun when it had sprouted upwards and separated from the earth, it is quite clear that Japan lies on the summit of the globe. It is equally evident that all other countries were formed at a much later period by the spontaneous consolidation of the foam of the sea and the collection of mud in various localities, when Izanagi and Izanami brought forth the eight islands of Japan, and separated the land from the water. Foreign countries were of course produced by the power of the creator gods, but they were not begotten by Izanagi and Izanami, nor did they give birth to the goddess of the sun, which is the cause of their inferiority. The traditions about the origin of the world which are preserved in foreign countries are naturally incorrect, just as the accounts of an event which has happened at the capital become distorted when they travel to a province, and it finally comes to be believed that the province was the actual scene of the event. The fact is patent that the Mikado is the true Son of Heaven, who is entitled to reign over the four seas and the ten thousand countries.

People who have been misled by their foreign studies are wont to say that Japan is a little country, as if extent of territory were any criterion of the importance or rank of a state; and they also point to her tardy civilisation. But every one knows that great minds develope late; for example Ota Nobunaga, who was commonly called *Baka dono* (Lord Idiot) until he was past the age of twenty, and the same was the case with the famous Oho-ishi Kura-no-suke, whose fame will endure to the end of time. Animals and birds know how to pick up and eat grain and insects as soon as they are born, and some have offspring when they are only two or three months old. If man were to be judged by such a standard, what a helpless. good-for-nothing creature he would be. But his slow development is a proof of his superiority, and the same holds good with regard to the development of nations.

A common but extremely erroneous phrase which has obtained currency, is the "Seven Generations of Celestial Gods and the Five Generations of Terrestrial Gods." In the first place neither the Ko-zhi-ki nor the Ni-hoñ-gi, although they speak of the succession of gods beginning with Kuni-no-toko-dachi and ending with Izanagi and Izanami as seven generations of the Divine Age, call them Celestial Gods; the reason being that all these gods came into existence on the earth. The Ko-zhi-ki gives the name of Celestial Gods to Ame-no-mi-naka-nushi, the two creator gods, Umashi-ashi-kabi-hiko-ji and Ame-no-toko-dachi. The term Terrestrial Gods was given to the gods of this country after the time of Ninigi no mikoto, to distinguish them from the Celestial Gods. It is a huge error to call the succession of gods beginning with Amaterasu and ending with the father of Zhiñ-mu Teñ-wau the Five generations of Terrestrial Gods, for in the first place Amaterasu, though born on the earth, was made ruler over the sun, and is therefore distinctly a Celestial God; and secondly Oshi-ho-mimi and Ninigi were both born in heaven;

neither was the title Terrestrial Gods ever applied to their descendants. The inventor of the phrase was Imibe no Masanori, the author of the *Zhiñ-dai no Maki no Ku-ketsu*, who wrote about the middle of the fourteen century. There exists no hard and fast line between the age of the gods and the present age, and there is no justification whatever for drawing one, as the Ni-hoñ-gi does, betweeh U-kaya-fuki-ahezu arid Zhiñ-mu Teñ-wau.

The descendants of the gods who accompanied Ninigi no mikoto, as well as the offspring of the successive Mikados, who entered the ranks of the subjects of the Mikados with the surnames of Tahira, Minamoto, and so forth, have gradually increased and multiplied. Although numbers of Japanese cannot state with any certainty from what gods they are descended, all of them have tribal names (*kabane*) which were originally bestowed by the Mikados, and those who make it their province to study genealogies can tell from a man's ordinary surname who his remotest ancestor must have been.

From the fact of the divine descent of the Japanese people proceeds their immeasurable superiority to the natives of other countries in courage and intelligence.

It is not necessary to quote the opinions of foreigners in order to prove that the heavens are immovable and that the earth revolves, for these facts are clear enough from ancient traditions, but as the westerners have elaborated astronomy and physical geography to a very high degree of minuteness, their account of the matter is more easily comprehended. It will be unnecessary to follow Hirata in the exposition which he here gives of the formation of the earth and its division into five continents, since he is candid enough to acknowledge the source from which it is taken. It is only fair to say that he praises the Dutch very warmly for their achievements in natural science, and accords to them a much higher place among philosophers than to the Chinese, whom he regards as empty visionaries. He also mentions Kæmpfer, and gives a summary of his "History of Japan." There exists a book called *I-zhiñ-kiyou-fu Deñ*, or the Way to Terrify Barbarians, which takes for its text that part of the "History of Japan" in which Kæmpfer gives his reasons for approving of the policy of excluding foreigners. It is difficult not to suppose that Kæmpfer's account of the dangers which have to be encountered in navigating the Japanese seas, and his statement that Nagasaki was the only port into which a good-sized vessel could enter, were prompted by a desire to serve Dutch interests. The story of the seizure by Japanese of the Dutch governor Nuits on the island of Formosa is quoted with much satisfaction by Hirata, as ' an illustration of the superior valour of his countrymen.

In the 12th month of the same year, which would about correspond to January 1812, he started off secretly to Fu-chiyuu (now called Shidzuwoka) in Suruga, where he quartered himself in the house of a friend, and began the composition of the *Ko-shi Sei-buñ,* or 'Complete Text of the Ancient Record.' After offering up a prayer[28] to all the gods for their aid he set to work on the 5th, and finished his labours at the end of the month. As a proof of his remarkable memory, it is said that he composed the three volumes of the Text and several volumes of the prolegomena, entitled *Ko-shi-chiyou,* without making a single reference to the works from which his materials were drawn. The *Ko-shi Sei-buñ* was apparently intended to have been brought far down into what is usually called the historical period, but the part which relates to the Divine Age is all that has at present appeared. It is a compilation founded on the texts of the Ko-zhi-ki, Ni-hoñ-gi, Ko-go-zhifu-wi, Fu-do-ki, Ku-zhi-ki, Norito and several other of the ancient books, with some slight conjectural additions of his own, and is written in the style of the Ko-zhi-ki. Many native scholars are of opinion that he has gone too far in altering the ancient texts, and prefer the originals, inconsistent and contradictory as they sometimes are, but this is a matter on which I have not had time to form an opinion. Those who care to investigate the subject will find in the last six volumes of the Ko-shi-chiyou[29] the grounds on which he adopted the text of each of the hundred and sixty-five sections into which the Ko-shi Sei-buñ is divided. In the course of the same year he began to work at the commentary, entitled Ko-shi

[28] This prayer is given at the end of the supplement to vol. i. of the *Ko-shi-chiyou.*

[29] The Ko-shi-chiyou was originally entitled *Ko-shi Waku-moñ,* and the Ko-shi sei-buñ simply *Ko-shi.* It is necessary to be aware of this, because he sometimes quotes these works by their earlier titles.

Deñ. It was to have extended to about one hundred volumes, but only twenty-eight have as yet been printed; they cover the first one hundred and forty-three sections. The *Kai-dai-ki,* or introduction to the Ko-shi-chiyou, in five volumes, was begun in 1819 and printed shortly afterwards. Besides discussions on the authority and relative value of all the ancient records, it contains a great deal of information relative to the introduction of Buddhism, and the gradual substitution of Chinese political institutions for those of native growth. Amongst other matters of interest to the historical student, it is proved that the *hou-keñ,* or feudal system, the destruction of which only a few years back was hailed as a 'return to the ancient régime,' was the original form of government in Japan, and that a central power, ruling by means of a council of state, ministries and local prefects, was an innovation derived from China.

Hirata's next work of importance was the *Tama no Mi-hashira,* completed early in the year 1813. It is of similar character to the *Sañ-dai-kau,* already named as forming a supplemental volume to the Ko-zhi-ki Deñ. The peculiar feature of the Sañ-dai-kau is that it for the first time identifies the sun with *Ame,* usually interpreted 'heaven,' and *yomi no kuni,* the region of darkness, which Motowori had explained as the abode of departed spirits, with the moon. According to this new view, Amaterasu oho-mi-kami, instead of being the ruler of heaven, is the ruler of the sun, and Tsuku-yomi no mikoto is the ruler of the moon and not the moon itself. In the Ko-zhi-ki Deñ Motowori had defined *Ame* as a region above the sky, in which the celestial gods have their abode, and Takama-no-hara as merely another name for it. In several places in the same work he speaks of the sun as being identical with Amaterasu oho-mi-kami, and his comments on the passage of the text in which the origination of this goddess and Tsuku-yomi no mikoto from the eyes of Izanagi is related, are "the sun and moon originated from this washing" (*i.e.* of the god's eyes), and "the sun and moon did not exist before this." He makes the same statement in the *Nahobi no Mitama* and in the *Teñ-so To-zhiyau Beñ-beñ,* and although the passage in the *Sakitake no Beñ,* "*Amaterasu, oho-mi-kami** ima mo yo wo terashi-tamafu ama-tsu-hi no kami ni mashimasu nari*" might at first sight appear to imply that the goddess is the deity of the sun, this view is negatived by a sentence which follows on the very next page to the effect that "this great deity actually is the sun in heaven, which even now illuminates the world before our eyes, a fact which is extremely clear from the divine writings." It is true that the expression *ni mashimasu* used in this place may mean either 'exists in' or 'is,' but the use of *sunahachi* (actually) favours the latter rendering, which is also supported by the other passages in Motowori's writings to which we have alluded. The Sañ-dai-kau was written in 1791, ten years before Motowori's death, by his favourite pupil Hatori Nakatsune, certainly with Motowori's knowledge, for at the end of it is a laudatory notice by the master. It is possible therefore that Motowori changed his opinion on this important point towards the end of his life, but was not willing to give more than an indirect sanction to the theory, and this supposition has given rise to the belief that the Sañ-dai-kau, although published under the name of another, was in reality his own work. It is somewhat strange that, seeing that the Sañ-dai-kau forms a supplement to Vol. XVII. of the Ko-zhi-ki Deñ, he should repeat on p. 35 of the following volume the statement that Amaterasu is the sun. Hirata has interwoven into the text of the Tama no Mi-hashira a great part of the Sañ-dai-kau, as he acknowledges in his preface, but in the body of his work he frequently quotes Hatori almost verbatim, without any special indication that he is using the words of another. A careful comparison is therefore necessary in order to distinguish between the theories which are the particular property of each writer. The following extract from Hatori's preface exhibits the vein of prejudice which was common to both.

"The accounts given in other countries, whether by Buddhism or Chinese philosophy, of the form of the heavens and earth and the manner in which they came into existence, are all of them inventions of men, who exercised all their ingenuity over the problem, and inferred that such things must actually be the case. As for the Indian account, it is only nonsense fit to deceive women and children, and I do not think it worthy of refutation. The Chinese theories, on the other hand, are based upon profound philosophical speculations, and sound extremely plausible, but what they call the absolute and infinite, the positive and negative essences, the eight diagrams and the five elements are not real existences, but are fictitious names invented by the philosophers and freely applied in every direction. They say that the whole universe was produced by agencies, and that nothing exists which is independent of them. But all these statements are nonsense.

"The principles which animate the universe are beyond the power of analysis, nor can they be fathomed by the human intelligence, and all statements founded upon pretended explanations of them are to be rejected. All that man can think out and know is limited by the powers of sight, feeling and calculation, and what goes beyond these powers cannot be known by any amount of thinking.

"How is it then possible for men who were born hundreds and thousands of myriads of years after the origin of the universe, to know how it originated and the successive steps by which it assumed its present form? Our country, owing to the facts that it was begotten by the two gods Izanagi and Izanami, was the birth-place of Amaterasu oho-mi-kami, and is ruled by her Sublime Descendants for ever and ever, as long as the universe shall endure, is infinitely superior to other countries, whose chief and head it is; its people are honest and upright of heart, and are not given to useless theorizing and falsehoods like other nations, and thus it possesses correct and true information with regard to the origin of the universe. This information has descended to us unaltered from the age of the gods, and unmixed, even in the slightest degree, with unsupported notions of individuals. This indeed is the genuine and true tradition. The Chinese accounts sound as if based on profound principles, and one fancies that they must be right, while the Japanese accounts sound shallow and utterly unfounded in reason. But the former are lies, while the latter are the truth, so that as time goes on, and thought attains greater accuracy, the erroneous nature of these falsehoods becomes ever more apparent, while the true tradition remains intact. My reason for this observation is that in modern times men from countries lying far off in the west have voyaged all round the seas as their inclinations prompted them, and have ascertained the

actual shape of the earth. They have discovered that the earth
is round, and that the sun and moon revolve round it in a vertical
direction, and it may thus be conjectured how full of errors are
all the ancient Chinese accounts, and how impossible it is to
believe anything that professes to be determined à priori. But
when we come to compare our ancient traditions, as to the
origination of a thing in the midst of space and its subsequent
development, with what has been ascertained to be the actual
shape of the earth, we find that there is not the slightest error,
and this result confirms the truth of our ancient traditions. But
although accurate discoveries made by the men of the far west
as to the actual shape of the earth and its position in space infinitely surpass the theories of the Chinese, still that is only a
matter of calculation, and there are many other things actually
known to exist which cannot be solved by that means; and still
less is it possible to solve the question of how the earth, sun and
moon came to assume their form.   Probably those countries
possess theories of their own, but whatever they may be, they
can but be guesses after the event, and probably resemble the
Indian and Chinese theories."

The plan adopted by both writers is to give a series of
diagrams representing the gradual formation of the sun, earth
and moon, together with the evidence by which each diagram is
supported, followed by a commentary. Hatori quotes from the
Ko-zhi-ki and Ni-hoñ-gi, while Hirata relies for his proofs on
the text of the *Ko-shi*, which he had just completed. A minute
examination of this work would probably show that it contains
deviations from the ancient authorities, prompted by a desire
to harmonize revelation and science. It appears that he had
acquired a slight degree of knowledge of astronomy, either from
some of his countrymen who were acquainted with the Dutch
language, or from translations of Dutch books. He had thus
learnt and admitted as a fact, that the earth moves round
the sun, and was therefore considerably ahead of Hatori, who
preferred to believe what he saw with his eyes, and only cursorily
mentions the theory of the earth's movement as a matter of
indifference to his views of the cosmogony. Hirata of course
assumed the truth of all ancient Japanese traditions, but saw
that they were sometimes inconsistent with each other and with

actual fact, and he hoped by reconciling these contradictions to
prove that Shiñ-tau contains all the knowledge necessary to man.
He is therefore not to be implicitly depended on for a correct
view of the ancient belief about the origin of things.

Diagram 1 in both books is a large circle containing three
black spots in its upper part. This is intended to represent the
existence of Ame-no-mi-naka-nushi, Taka-mi-musu-bi and Kamu-
mi-musu-bi in space, before the sun, earth and moon were
formed. The circle means nothing; it is merely introduced to
give the reader a definite idea of what is meant by space, but
as it is dispensed with in the third and succeeding Diagrams,
when the reader is requested to look on the blank part of the
page as representing space, it seems hardly necessary even here.
Hatori quotes the Ko-zhi-ki, which says that these three gods
came into existence in *Takama no hara* in the beginning of
heaven and earth (*ame tsuchi*), while Hirata quotes his own
Ko-shi to the effect that they 'came into being in Heaven's Sky'
(*Ama-tsu- mi sora*). At a later period, in publishing his commentary entitled Ko-shi Deñ, he reverted to the old reading
Takama no hara. A great deal of ingenuity has been expended
by the expounders of Pure Shiñ-tau to prove that Takama no
hara does not mean 'the plain of high heaven,' as its evident
etymology would suggest. Motowori is perhaps not unreasonable in explaining it to mean a region above the sky. Hatori
says that "*Takama no hara* did not exist at this period which
was antecedent to all material existence, but the region wherein
these three gods originated afterwards became *Takama no hara*."
The theory that this name signifies 'space' is derived from
one of the parallel passages in the Ni-hoñ-gi, where the Chinese
characters *kiyo-chiyuu* (emptiness) occur instead of *Takama
no hara ni*. But this would scarcely be sufficient to prove that
the ancient Japanese possessed the highly abstract idea of 'space,'
and it is more natural to suppose that they meant the blue sky
which they saw over their heads. Hirata has a fanciful theory
about Ame-no-mi-naka-nushi and the other two gods inhabiting
the Pole star, which is not usually accepted by other teachers of
Shiñ-tau. In the *Ko-shi Deñ*, on the authority of a parallel
passage in the Ni-hoñ-gi, he substitutes the word "existed"
(*mashiki*) for "originated" (*narimaseru*), and draws thence the

inference that these gods never had a beginning, but the passage from which the word *masu* is taken refers not to Ame-no-mi-naka-nushi and the other two gods, but to Umashi-ashi-kabi-hiko-ji and deities of later origin. The difficulty of supposing that *Ame* could ever have meant the sun, lies in the fact that it certainly signifies the sky or heaven, in which sense it is employed in forming the name of the primeval god, as Hirata himself states. Hirata says that the upper part of heaven is the pole star, which must therefore have been the location of the three gods. Heaven is limited on the outside, as is proved by the statement that Susanowo no mikoto made the circuit of its boundary. *Kami,* translated by 'god,' is the same as *kabi,* compounded of the demonstrative root *ka* and *bi,* or *hi,* a word applied to whatever is miraculous and supernatural, which is seen in *musu-bi,* termination of the names of the creator and creatrix.[30] In the Tama no Mi-hashira he derives *kami* from *kabimoye,* 'sprouting growing,' but later he became convinced that this etymology was erroneous. *Kamurogi* and *Kamuromi,* which are titles of the creator and creatrix, he derives from the continuative form of the root *Kami,* *ro* a particle, and *gi* and *mi* which are used in forming the names of male and female deities. Motowori has suggested that *gi* is a contraction of *wo-gimi,* male prince, and *mi* of *me-gimi,* female prince, but nothing can be safely asserted on this point. With respect to the statement that these three gods 'concealed their bodies,' Motowori's suggestion that it signifies their incorporeality is not to be admitted, for Takami-musu-bi no kami is represented as saying that Sukuna-bikona no kami "passed between his fingers," and if he had a hand, he must have had a body, so that the tradition must be accepted in all its literal meaning.

Diagram 2 in both works represents space bounded by a circle, with three black spots as in diagram 1, and underneath them a smaller circle inscribed '*ichi-motsu,*' or Thing. Hatori supports this by the following quotations from the Ni-hoñ-gi: "In the beginning of heaven and earth, there was a Thing in the great sky, whose shape cannot be described." "Before heaven and earth had originated a thing originated in the midst, like

---

[30] Ko-shi Deñ, vol. i. f. 7v.

as it were a floating cloud on the sea, without any point of attachment." "In the beginning of heaven[31] and earth, a thing like the sprout of a rush originated in the great sky"; again "a thing like floating fat originated in the great sky." Hirata quotes from his own compilation a similar passage, without any reference to the rush-sprout. Hatori ascribes the origin of this Thing to the creator and creatrix, who gradually formed the sun, earth and moon out of it, and brought various gods into existence at different stages. The fact of these creative acts being performed by the two deities named is known from a revelation made by the god of the moon, who in the year 487 entered into the body of a man, and declared to one Abe no Omi Kotoshiro that "his ancestor Takami-musu-bi no kami created heaven and earth. People and lands must consequently be presented to him." And in the same year the sun goddess made a similar revelation to the same Abe no Omi, in which she declared that Takami-musu-bi no kami was her progenitor. The comparison of the Thing to floating fat and floating cloud simply refers to its indefinite position, and involves no statement as to its composition, which was probably a mixture of the natures of the sun, earth and moon.

In diagram 3 the Thing is presented in the form of a dumb-bell, with the smaller end upper-most. In Hatori's diagram there is a small projection depending from the bottom of the Thing, probably intended to indicate the budding-out of the moon. The ancient books quoted here say that 'from the thing which floated in space something sprouted up like the shoot of a rush, in which there originated two gods named Umashi-ashi-kabi-hiko-ji no kami and Ame-no-toko-tachi no kami, both of whom, like the previous three, were single gods, and hid their Bodies.'

From the name of the second god who is here mentioned it is inferred that the thing which sprouted up afterwards became *Ame,* or the sun, according to Hatori and Hirata, and according to Motowori, heaven. This is nowhere explicitly stated, either in the Ko-zhi-ki or in the Ni-hoñ-gi, but is inferred from the name of the second god, *toko* being the same as *soko,* bottom,

---

[31] Or 'the sun,' if we accept the theory that *ame* signifies the sun.

and *tachi*, to stand. Hatori supposes the nature of *ame* to have been of the essence of fire, but Hirata repudiates this as a Chinese notion, and conjectures that it was clear and bright, like crystal. The name of the first god is derived from *umashi*, pleasant, *ashi-kabi*, rush-sprout, *hiko*, an honorific term applied to males, and *ji*, another honorific, seen in the word *woji*, old man. He is identified by Hirata with Suku-na-bi-kona, a diminutive god who afterwards aided Ohokuni-nushi to civilize the country. The five deities who have now been named are entitled the *Amatsu-kami*, or 'Celestial gods.'

Diagram 4 in the *Tamano Mi-hashira*, represents three globes of gradually diminishing sizes, connected by short necks, the largest being uppermost, and labelled *Ame*. The five celestial gods are represented therein by the same number of black spots. How the three earliest of them found their way into this particular portion of space is not explained, and their being here somewhat favours the original explanation that *Ame* is heaven. It was probably in order get out of this difficulty that Hirata suggested in the *Ko-shi Deñ*, that they are located in the pole-star. The central globe, which is of medium size, is marked earth,' and contains five small circles arranged in pairs. Underneath is the third globe, marked *Yomi*, and containing two black spots to represent a pair of invisible deities; *Yomi* is shaded with black, to express the fact that it is in darkness, owing to the interception of the sun's light by the earth. In the Sañ-dai-kau the diagram is similar, but the globes are not perfectly round, and the two black spots placed by Hirata in *Yomi*, are placed above the five pairs of circles in the earth.

Hatori acknowledges that neither the Ko-zhi-ki nor the Ni-hoñ-gi contain any tradition as to the formation of *Yomi*, but that probably something grew downwards from the underside of the Thing, which developed into *Yomi*, just as from its upper surface something had sprouted up which became *Ame*.

Hirata, however, finding in one of the parallel passages quoted in the Ni-hoñ-gi, the sentence "Next there was a Thing like floating fat, which came into existence in the sky, from which a god originated named Kuni-no-toko-tachi no kami," converts this into "Next, [from the root of the Thing which was drifting about like a floating cloud], a Thing came into existence. The

name of the god who originated from this thing was Kuni-no-
soko-tachi no kami." It may be observed that the original text
does not connect the second Thing with the first, from which
the Ame is supposed to have been formed, and in the *Ko-shi Sei-
buñ* he afterwards omitted the sentence enclosed between
brackets. To this he added part of a passage from the *Ko-zhi-ki,*
which speaks of Toyo-kumu-nu no kami. These two gods were
single gods, and were invisible, for which reason they are
represented in the diagram by black spots. They were succeeded
by five pairs of deities, Uhi-jini and Suhi-jini, Tsunu-guhi and
Iku-guhi, Oho-to-no-ji and Oho-to-no-be, Omo-daru and Aya-
kashiko-ne, Izanagi and Izanami. The word *imo,* which means
either sister or wife, is prefixed to the name of the second
of each of these pairs, and each pair counts as one generation,
making, with the two single gods previously named, the seven
Generations of the Divine period (*kami-yo nana-yo*). The title
kami is given to each, but I have omitted it to save space, as
I shall continue to do henceforth in the case of all other gods.
Uhi-jini signifies 'first mud,' *Suhi-jini* 'sand and mud.' The
names of the next pair are said to be derived from *tsumu,* a germ
in which the hands and feet, head and tail are yet undistingush-
able, *guhi,* the same as *kamu,* to integrate, and *iku,* which
signifies the commencement of life, and is the same as *ikiru,* to
breathe. The names of the next pair are interpreted to mean
'man and woman of the great place,' pointing to the fact that
solid land was formed. *Omo-daru* is 'complete perfection,' and
Aya-kashiko-ne is 'awful one,' *aya* being an ejaculation of awe
(from which come *ayashi,* strange, and *ayaushi,* perilous), and
kashiko, an adjectival root meaning awful. The name of the
female is said to express the sentiment which filled her when
she looked at the male. *Iza* in the names of the last part is
supposed to be the radical of *izanafu,* to invite, and to allude to
their invitation to each other to join in begetting the earth; *gi*
and *mi* are the same as in *Kamurogi* and *Kamuromi,* the titles
already mentioned as being given to the creator and creatrix.
It appears from these etymologies that a gradual progress in
development is here indicated, and Hirata suggests that the first
four pairs are not distinct deities, but merely names descriptive
of the various stages through which Izanagi and Izanami passed

before arriving at the perfection of existence. As it seems certain that they were never worshipped in any known period of history, this theory is accepted by many modern writers on Shiñ-tau.

The globe called *Yomi* is identified by both Hatori and Hirata with Yomo-tsu-kuni or Yomi no kuni, the region whither Izanami betakes herself after the birth of Homusubi, the god of fire. Other names for it are *Ne no kuni*, literally the 'root-region,' because of its being at the root of the earth, *Soko no kuni*, or the 'bottom region,' *Shita-tsu-kuni*, or the 'under region,' and *Ne-no-katasu-kuni* from *katasumi*, one corner, used in the sense of lowermost or most distant. *Yomi* is explained to mean darkness. The reasons for identifying *Yomi no kuni* with the moon are several. In the first place the element *Yomi* in the name *Tsuku-yomi no mikoto* is evidently the same as *Yomi*, 'the kingdom of darkness,' whither Susanowo no mikoto finally proceeded. Secondly, although in the Ko-zhi-ki the rule of the sea is given to the latter god, one of the parallel passages of the Ni-hoñ-gi speaks of Tsuku-yomi no mikoto as being appointed ruler over the multitudinous salt-waters. The murder of the goddess of food is attributed to the former by the *Ko-zhi-ki*, to the latter by the *Ni-hoñ-gi*.[32] The fact that the tides of the sea actually follow the moon's movements is another reason for assuming these two gods to have been one. As the whole region pervaded by the light of the sun was called *hiru*, or day, the expression *yoru no wosu kuni*, 'the realm of night,' over which the Ko-zhi-ki says Tsuku-yomi was appointed to rule, would be extremely appropriate to *yomi*, from which the sun's light would be intercepted by the earth.[33] Hirata further points out that the notion of *yomi* being the abode of the dead is comparatively modern, and that the few gods who are spoken of in the ancient records as having gone thither, were still in the body when they did so.

Diagram 5 exhibits a marked difference between the two writers in their theories as to the subsequent development of the system of the three bodies. In Hatori's diagrams the sun continues to be attached to the earth until after the descent of

---

[32] *Ko-zhi-ki Deñ*, vol. ix. f. 9.
[33] *Sañ-dai-kau*, ff. 15 ad 16.

Ninigi no mikoto, while Hirata places the separation at some time antecedent to the descent of Izanagi and Izanami. This divergence is owing to the different explanations given by them of the *ama no uki-hashi* (literally, heaven's floating bridge) which Hatori represents as an axis connecting the sun with the earth, which is ever growing longer and consequently thinner, while Hirata interprets it to mean some kind of huge boat, in which the gods went backwards and forwards between the two bodies.[34] He argues that the phrase "this floating region" used of the earth by the celestial gods in commanding Izanagi and Izanami to form and harden it, can only be interpreted on this theory, for if the separation had not taken place the term "floating" could not have been applied to the earth alone. He consequently represents the sun detached, and to the right of the earth above it. The spear (*nuboko*) which was given to this pair for the purpose of forming the earth is supposed by him to have been of iron in the form of the lingam, and *nu*, which is interpreted to signify *tama*, a ball, has a profound signification if this view be adopted.[35] The passage quoted here by Hirata from the *Ko-shi* says that "The two gods, setting forth on the *ama-no-uki-hashi*, pushed down the spear and stirred the plain of the green sea.[36] When they drew it up after stirring it round and round, the drops which fell from its end, spontaneously consolidated and became an island. This was Ono-goro-zhima." This name was given to it on account of its 'spontaneous consolidation,' and to distinguish it from the other islands of Japan, which were begotten by Izanagi and Izanami in the ordinary manner. They descended on to this island, and planting the *nuboko* in the ground point downwards, built a palace round it, taking it for the central pillar which was to support their roof. The point of the spear became the axis of the earth. Ono-goro-zhima is identified by the author of the *Zhiñ-dai Ku-ketsu* with a small island at the north-west corner of Ahaji in the eastern part of the inland sea, called Ye-shima.[37] Close by is another

---

[34] *Tama no Mi-hashira*, vol. ii, f. 26.

[35] *Koshi Deñ*, vol. ii, f. 23, note.

[36] This is a literal rendering of *awo-una-bara*. Hirata, however, assumes the term to mean the appearance of the semi-fluid earth as it was seen from heaven, and rejects the common explanation.

[37] *Ko-shi Deñ*, vol. ii, f. 46.

island called Seki-rei-shima (Wagtail island), and there
are many other traces of the ancient tradition in the neighbourhood. The motion imparted to the fluid mass of the earth by
the stirring with the *nuboko* was the origin of its daily revolu-
tions.[38] Ono-goro-zhima was thus originally at the north pole,
but subsequently removed to its present position. In what manner
this happened we are not told. Nevertheless, Japan continues
to be on the summit of the terrestrial globe. It appears that
some one having objected that, if Japan were on the top of the
world and opposite to the sun, the sun would be in the zenith
at the equinoxes, Hatori was puzzled and referred the point to
Motowori, who replied that as the sun and moon move round
from East to West, and not from North to South, it is evident
that the globe, in spite of its being round, may be said to have
sides, that is, top, bottom, right, left, back and front. Just as
the face of a man is not on the top of his head, but on the front,
so Japan, being in the middle of the top has sun and moon on its
south, which is therefore the front; the north is consequently
behind, the east is the left side and the west the right side.
From which it is perfectly clear that Japan is on the summit
of the terrestrial globe. The objector replied that all countries
which have the sun on their south would have an equal right to
claim the same position. The answer to this is that the position
of Japan is not determined by the fact of the sun and moon
being in front of her, but the manner in which they appear to
her is owing to her position at the top of the earth. Hirata
strengthens the argument by pointing out that Japan altogether
escaped the deluge which took place in China in the reign of
Yaou, and also the Noachian flood which drowned occidental
countries, solely through her elevated situation. China suffered
less than the west, and Korea less again, on account of their
proximity to Japan.

The only mention made of the stars in the ancient
writings is in the *Ni-hon-gi*, where the star-god Kagase-no mimi[39]
is spoken of as being at first unwilling to submit to the fore-

[38] It is hardly necessary to note that this is not warranted by anything in the
ancient records, as the earth was always supposed to be stationary until the Japanese learnt the opposite from Europeans.

[39] Also called Amatsu-mika-boshi and Ama-no-kagase-wo.

runners of Ninigi no mikoto, but nothing is said of the manner in which the stars came into existence. According to a theory proposed by one Satou Nobu-fuchi, which is quoted by Hirata with approval, when the two gods lowered the spear and stirred round the chaotic mass out of which the earth was to be formed the muck which was unfit to enter into the composition of the earth was removed by the action of the spear-point, and scattered lump-wise in all directions throughout space, taking up positions more or less remote. The five planets, the twenty-eight constellations and the host of common stars being thus formed, revolve round the sun together with the earth.[40] Hirata has another view of his own, which is, that as the Thing which formed in space and afterwards developed into the sun and the earth, is said to have resembled a hen's egg in shape, when the Thing separated, its shell must have burst, and the fragments flying off on all sides would begin to revolve round the sun, attracted by the powerful rotatory motion of that body.[41] It is customary to suppose that the stars have no practical purpose; but it is evident that they are intended to guide the course of those barbarian marines, who, if they knew their duty, would bring ships laden with tribute to the Emperor of Japan.

Diagram 6 in the *Tama no Mi-hashira* represents the sun as in the last, with the five black spots which stand for Celestial gods, and the earth is now marked off into Japan, foreign countries variously situated below it, and the sea. The passage from the *Ko-shi* on which this diagram is based narrates what may be euphemistically termed the courtship of Izanagi and Izanami,[42]

---

[40] *Ko-shi Deñ.* vol. ii, f. 36.

[41] Idem, f. 38.

[42] The following is an almost literal translation. Tunc Izanagi quaesivit ab Izanami, "corpus tuum quo in modo factum est?" Et illa, "Corpus meum crescens crevit, sed locus est qui continuus non crevit." "Corpus meum," inquit Izanagi, "crescens crevit, sed locus est qui superfluus crevit. Nunc mihi propositum est, si tibi, videtur, mei corporis eum qui superfluus crevit locum, corporis tui in eum locum inserere qui non continuus crevit, et terram generare." Izanami respondit, "Commodum erit." Tunc Izanagi, "Ego et tu, quin circumeuntes coelestem hanc columnam, thalamo jucunde coimus." Hac pactione facta, "Tu sinistra," inquit Izanagi, "ego autem dextra, circumeuntes occurremus." Hac pactione facta, ubi circumeuntes faciem facei opposuerunt, Izanami primum "O adolescens venuste," deinde Izanagi, "O virgo venusta." Postquam haec locuti sunt, Izanagi, nullo modo gaudens, dixit sorori, "Me decebat primum loqui, quia vir sum; non est foeminae primum verba facere." Sed ubi incipientes (sc. opus procreationis) coierunt in thalamo, artem ignorabant. Tunc advolavit motacilla, qui caput caudamque movebat. Dii hoc imitantes, coitionis viam cognoverunt, et filium hirudini similem pepererunt.

which resulted in a child of so poor a consistency, that he was unable to stand on his legs when he had reached the age of three years. They put him into a boat woven of rushes, which were the only available materials then existing, and abandoned him to his fate on the wide ocean. Another child which they begot, named Aha no shima, was also a failure, and they were driven to ask the advice of the Celestial Gods. The Celestial Gods had recourse to divination, which is explained to be a means of obtaining knowledge or information from divine beings without their being aware of it. It seems strange that the three gods who hold the highest rank among their race should not have been able to give a direct answer without applying to some one else, but Hirata explains this apparent anomaly by the analogy of a prince who charges each of his servants with some branch of affairs, and in answer to a request for information on any point refers the inquirer to the servant who knows all about it. The answer to Izanagi and his consort was that they should try over again, and as they carefully avoided the error which they had committed on the previous occasion, they were very successful. The first of the series of children which they now begot was Oho-yamato Akitsushima, the main island of Japan, and it was born with a caul, which is the present island of Ahaji. Both of the names Yamato and Akitsu-shima originally belonged to the present province of Yamato, the former dating from a late period of the so-called Divine Age, the latter from the reign of Zhiñ-mu Teñ-wau.[43] They were afterwards extended to the whole of the main island, but are no longer so employed. Next were born the islands of Iyo,[44] which had one body and four faces, Tsukushi[45] with one body and five faces, Iki, Tsushima, the triplets of Oki, and Sado. According to a variation of the legend Oki and Sado were twins. Ahaji is added to the others to make up the number of eight, whence the name of *Oho-ya-shima-kuni,* the Country of Eight Islands, applied to the whole

[43] The Chinese posthumous names of the early *mikados* are supposed to have been determined in the reign of Kuwañ-mu (782-806). The earliest case of one being applied was in 758, when the posthumous title of Shiyau-mu was given to the reigning Mikado's predecessor. See *Ke-zhi-ki Deñ,* vol. xviii, f. 3.

[44] That is Shi-koku with its four provinces.

[45] Tsukushi is the ancient name of Kiu-shiu, which was originally divided into five provinces, Tsukushi, Toyo, Hi, Himuka and Kumaso.

empire of Japan. No mention is made of what are now called Kara-futo, or Saghalien and Yezo, which were probably discovered at a much later date than the 8th century, when the *Ko-zhi-ki* and *Ni-hoñ-gi* were committed to writing. The legend also speaks of the birth of other islands, one of which was Kibi no Ko-zhima, now divided into Bi-zeñ, Biñ-go, Bi-chiyuu and Mimasaka, Adzuki-shima in the inland sea, now called Seudzu-shima, Hime-shima off Hizeñ, Chika-shima, supposed to be the Go-tau islands, and the Futago-shima, which cannot be identified. The remaining small islands were formed by condensatioñ of the foam of the sea. After the country had been thus produced, the two gods begot all the gods (*ya-ho yorodzu no kami*) andi bestowed on them all things; and next, seeing that the land was covered with mist, Izanagi produced the two gods of wind, male and female, from his breath.

Hatori has a long note showing that the islands of Japan were begotten in exactly the same manner as human beings and everything else that has life, whether animal or vegetable, and being quite small at their birth, gradually increased in size by the accretion of matter. The result of the birth of Japan was that the sea and land were gradually parted, and the way thus prepared for the formation of foreign countries by the spontaneous condensation of the foam of the sea. Hirata finds this truth concealed in the statement about "the remaining small islands," a not unique example of interpreting ancient records so as to fit in with the progress of modern discovery.

The god of fire was the last child in whose conception the two gods shared. He is called Ho-musubi and also Kagutsuchi, and Hirata thinks he ought to be identified with the element itself. The goddess suffered great pain in bringing him into the world, and from the matter which she vomited forth in her agony originated the god and goddess of metal (*Kane*). Hirata derives the word *kana-yama* (a metalliferous mine), which forms part of the names of these two deities, from a contraction of *kare-nayamashi*, to cause to wither and feel pain. In consequence of Izanagi breaking her injunction not to look upon her face during the period of her retirement, Izanami departed towards the nether region, but bethinking herself that the god of fire, if left uncontrolled in his actions, would bring ruin on the

upper world, she returned for a short time and produced from
her fæces the gods of clay and from her water the god of fresh
water, whom she commissioned to pacify the god of fire whenever
he was inclined to be turbulent. Clay and fresh water were produced at the same moment as the gods which rule them. From
the statement that Izanami forbade the god to look at her during seven days and nights, Hirata argues that day and night
already existed, which supports his view that the sun was already
separated from the earth. As the earth revolved, it was day
when it was opposite to the sun, and night when it was turned
away from the sun. He neglects, however, to explain how the
earth, to the bottom of which the moon was still attached, could
do this, and the expression 'opposite to the sun' is extremely
obscure. It is at least evident that according to this theory of
Japan being on the top of the earth, the 'kingdom of darkness'
must have been illuminated whenever Japan was in the dark.

After the departure of his companion, Izanagi took venge-
ance for her loss upon Kagutsuchi, whom he clove into three
pieces with his sword. From these pieces originated the
god of thunder (*Ikadzuchi*), of mountains (*Oho-yamatsumi*),
and of rain (*Takawo-kami*). The blood which fell from the
edge of his weapon flew up to the sun, and was converted into
unnumbered rocks in the dry bed of the Ama-no-yasu-no-gaha,
and the blood which fell from the guard and point, as well as
that which remained on his hand, spirted on to the rocks thus
formed. Blood and fire being the same thing, the sun thus
became a receptacle of heat.

The next event was the visit of Izanagi to *Yomi,* with the
object of finding Izanami and inducing her to return to the upper
world. No precise information exists with reference to the road
by which he travelled, but it is supposed to have been a hole
through the centre of the earth, the outlet of which is at Ifuya-
zaka (pronounced Yûya-zaka) in Idzumo. "When Izanami no
mikoto came forth from her palace door to meet him, he
addressed her, saying, 'My dear sister, come back again, for the
country which you and I made is not yet finished.' She replied,
'Lamentable indeed that you came not earlier. I have eaten of
the cooking of *Yomi*. Nevertheless, as my brother has graciously
come hither, I would desire to return. To-morrow I will discuss

it fully with the god of *Yomi*. Do not look for me, my brother.'
Saying this she returned within the palace. A long time elapsed,
and he felt impatient; so breaking off the end-tooth of the many-
toothed comb which he wore in the left bunch of his hair, and
lighting it, he entered in to look. He found her over-run with
maggots and in a state of semi-putrefaction." The legend goes
on to relate Izanagi's struggle to escape, during which he created
various gods, one of whom, called Kunado no kami, was produced
from his staff. Another was Chi-gaheshi no kami, the rock with
which he closed up the road. Izanami's reason for not returning was that she had eaten food cooked with unclean fire, and
was defiled thereby. The god of fire hates impurity, and she
was afraid of his wrath. It is well-known that it is impossible to succeed with a casting if the metal has been
melted with fire which is not perfectly pure. As soon
as Izanagi returned to earth he hastened to wash himself
in the sea, at a locality which cannot be precisely determined,
but it appears to have been in either Hiuga or Chiku-zeñ. The
legend says: "The names of the gods whom he produced by
blowing when he plunged into the middle shoal and washed, were
Yoso-Maga-tsu-hi no kami and Oho-Maga-tsu-hi no kami. These
two gods originated from the pollution which affected him when
he went to that region of perpetual foulness. * * The names
of the gods whom he produced by blowing in order to correct
the evil [to be done by the two last] were Kamu-Nahobi no kami
and Oho-Naho-bi no kami. * * The name of the god who
originated subsequently when he washed his left eye was Amaterasu oho-mi-kami, also called Ama-terasu-oho-hiru-me no
mikoto, and the name of the god who originated when he washed
his right eye was Tsuku-yomi no mikoto, also called Take-haya-
Susa-no-wo no mikoto. Then Izanagi no kami rejoiced greatly,
and said, "I have begotten Child upon Child, and at the end of
my begetting, I have begotten me two rare Children." Now the
brightness of the Person of Ama-terasu oho-mi-kami was beautiful, and shone through heaven and earth. Izanagi no kami
spake, and said, "Though my children are many, none of them
is like this miraculous Child. She is not to be kept in this
region." Then taking the necklace of precious stones from his
neck, and rattling it, he gave it to Ama-terasu oho-mi-kami, and

spake, commanding her in these words, "Rule thou over Takama no hara." As the distance between the sun and earth was not great at this period, he sent her up by the *Ame-no-mi-hashira,* * * Next he spake unto Take-haya-Susa-no-wo no mikoto, and commanded him, saying, "Rule thou over Awo-una-bara, and the multitudinous salt water." * *

The statement that Take-haya-Susa-no-wo is another name of Tsuku-yomi is not to be found in any of the ancient texts, and is an emendation of Hirata's founded upon the grounds already noticed for supposing the two gods to be in reality one. The Ame no mi-hashira was supposed by Mabuchi to be one of the gods of wind, but Hirata explains it to be one of the *hashi-date* of which mention has already been made. In the *Ko-shi Deñ* he makes Yaso-maga-tsu-hi and Kamu-nabo-bi to be simply alternative names of Oho-maga-tsu-hi and Oho-naho-bi. The birth of the first was intended as a mark that Izanagi had purified his body from the pollution which he had brought back with him from *Yomi,* and he sprang from Izanagi's strong resolve to get rid of those pollutions. Hence this god utterly detests defilement of whatever kind, and becomes violent in his conduct whenever any unclean thing is done. His name is derived from the calamities (*maga*) which he causes. Motowori's view that this god was actually produced from the filth of *Yomi,* and is therefore an evil god, is wrong. Apart from the wrath which he manifests on certain occasions, he is disposed to do good, as is evidenced by his having planted the whole of Japan with trees, the seeds of which be brought down from heaven. Naho-bi no kami was similarly produced by the earnest desire of Izanagi to remedy the evils which might be produced by the zeal of Maga-tsu-hi no kami. Both gods and human beings have in them the spirit of these two gods, wherefore they are angry with whatever is foul and wicked, and are tempted to act violently. It is Naho-bi no kami's spirit which moderates their wrath and disposes them to mercy.

Hirata endeavours to prove that *awo-una-bara* means the whole earth, and that the phrase "multitudinous salt-water" is only added for the sake of emphasis. He derives *umi* (of which *una* is only another form) from *umu,* to beget, to bear, and interprets *una-bara* to mean the 'just born plain.' *Awo* is green, applied either in the sense of young, or because the earth seemed to be of a green colour when viewed by the celestial gods from above. It will be remembered that Izanagi and Izanami dipped the spear into *awo-una-bara*, and separated the dry land from the sea, so that if Hirata's etymology were correct, the name would be no longer applicable when Tsuku-yomi was invested with his kingdom. The safest opinion is that *awo-una-bara* means simply the 'blue waste of sea,' and that the ancient inhabitants of Japan, amongst whom these different legends sprang up, never thought of trying to make them consistent with each other. Hirata's theory seems to have been invented to prove that Susa-no-wo was first made ruler over the earth, but preferred to go to his mother in the moon, thus leaving the earth vacant for Ninigi no mikoto, who, being in a certain sense the joint offspring of Susa-no-wo and the sun-goddess, united in his person all the rights of Izanagi and Izanami. The rest of the *Tama no Mi-hashira* is occupied by the legends relating to Oho-kuni-nushi's first occupation of Japan and the descent of Ninigi no mikoto which have already been briefly summarized in a former part of this paper. The separation of the moon from the earth, which is figured by him in his tenth and last diagram, is supposed to have taken place after the visit of Oho-kuni-nushi to the lower world. Hatori agrees with him on this point, but supposes Oho-kuni-nushi to have gone to the moon after his surrender of the Empire to Ninigi no mikoto, whereas Hirata maintains that he rules over the Hidden World, which is on the earth.

In the year 1813 Hirata wrote the *Nifu-gaku Mon-dafu*, a short work on the elements of the ancient way, intended for beginners. It is an excellent introduction to his other works on Shiñ-tau, and may be recommended to those who do not care to gain more than a general view of his opinions. At the end of the volume is an useful bibliographical list of all his acknowledged works, compiled by some of his disciples. Two years later he completed the *Ama-tsu Norito Kau*, a commentary on a *norito* which is not contained in the *Yen-gi Shiki*, but which, if genuine, supplies a lacuna in the *Oho-barahi no kotoba*, and serves to clear up a point therein which had considerably puzzled all preceding commentators. During this period he was busily working at the *Ko-shi Den*, which he did not live to complete.

Besides this, he completed a new edition of Hatori's *San-dai-kau,* an account of a curious stone found by him in Kadzusa, which he christened Ama-no-Iha-buye, and the *Ko-shi-chiyau Kai-dai-ki;* began a new edition of the *Zhin-mei Shiki,* or list of Shiñ-tau temples and gods given in the *Yen-gi Shiki,* drafted the *Morokoshi Tai-ko Den,* a work on the ancient traditions of China, of which only the text and about one-fourth of the commentary have yet appeared, began the *Indo Zau-shi,* which is said to have been intended for a complete treatise on Buddhism, and printed a short life of Sugahara Michizane under the title of *Tenman-gu Go-den-ki.* In the year 1819 he completed the draft of his work on the *Zhin-dai no Mozhi,* or so-called native Japanese alphabet of the pre-historic age. This consists of two volumes entitled *Zhin-zhi Hi-fumi Den* and one entitled *Gi-zhi Hen.* The first contain some thirteen or fourteen tables of square and cursive characters; the latter is a collection of a number of specimens of widely different appearance, all of which are asserted to be native Japanese characters, but concerning whose genuineness Hirata does not venture to pronounce an opinion. The first thing that will strike any one who examines the square characters given in volume I. is their unmistakable identity with the Korean alphabet, the sole difference being that the Korean letters are combined so as to form the forty-seven syllables used in spelling Japanese words. The cursive forms, however, bear scarcely the remotest resemblance to the square, and it is difficult to suppose that they have a common origin. Having devoted several pages of Volume I. of the *Kai-dai-ki* to the discussion of the evidence for the existence of an indigenous method of writing in pre-historic times, and having decided the question in the affirmative, Hirata does not think it worth while to entertain the suspicion that these so-called *Zhin-dai no Mo-zhi* have been copied from the Korean alphabet, but on the contrary maintains that the Koreans made their alphabet out of the *Zhin-dai no Mo-zhi,* and arbitrarily invented a number of additional signs to meet their own wants. He supposes that the *Zhin-dai no Mozhi* must have been carried to Korea after its conquest by Zhiñ-gou-kuwau-gou (200 A.D.), and have been preserved there in some mysterious manner, until in the beginning of the 15th century they were utilized to form an alphabet, for which the

Sanskrit alphabet was taken as a model. From a Korean work written in the Chinese language, quoted by Itou Nagatane in the *San-kan Ki-riaku*, the Korean alphabet appears to have been invented by a King of Korea who began to reign 1419. But if a Japanese alphabet ever existed, it had been entirely forgotten by the Japanese centuries before this date, and it is difficult to suppose that it should have been preserved by the Koreans in such a manner that they were still able, after so long an interval, to assign what Hirata acknowledges to be very nearly the correct pronunciation to each letter. An alternative supposition of course, is that those of the so-called *Zhin-dai no Mozhi*, which are identical with combinations of the Korean letters, were copied from that alphabet in comparatively modern times, and if we could obtain a sight of the original manuscripts said to be preserved at various Shiñ-tau temples in Japan, of which Hirata himself only had seen copies, it is probable that such conclusions might be drawn as to the age of the material on which they are written, as would serve to determine their value as authentic documents. Apart from these considerations it would hardly seem probable, arguing à *prior*, that the *Zhin-dai no Mo-zhi*, which must have been alphabetic, should only be preserved in a syllabic form, as is the case with the specimens we speak of, or that the Japanese, if they had ever possessed such a treasure as an alphabet capable of expressing all the sounds of their language, should have abandoned it for the cumbrous method of ideographic writing which they afterwards learnt from the Chinese. The question is of some importance; for if it were decided in favour of Hirata's views, we should be compelled to allow a greater degree of credibility to the earlier historical records of Japan than there seems at present reason to attribute to them.

Hitherto the teaching of Hirata had not appeared to differ much in principle from that of his predecessors, whose object was to preserve from oblivion the ancient monuments of Japanese literature and history, and to disprove the accusation that before the introduction of Chinese philosophy the Japanese were a nation of savages without any rule of conduct. But we shall see that the real goal to which his efforts were directed was the establishment of a religion on a Shiñ-tau basis, before which both Buddhism and Confucianism should disappear. It is this endeavour which has caused him to be regarded in a certain sense as the founder of a new school, although on a close examination of his system it would no doubt be found that he was actually indebted to the Chinese philosophy for the moral code which he attempted to derive from Shiñ-tau, and that the latter possesses only those characteristics of a religion which belong to theological dogma.

The *Tama-dasuki* has already been mentioned as one of the works which Hirata wrote in the year 1811. It appears to have been originally composed in a very colloquial style; but in 1824 he completely rewrote the first nine volumes, and gave to them a shape more worthy of the subject. It is a commentary on certain prayers which he had drawn up for the use of his pupils, and contains, half buried in a mass of irrelevant matter, his views of Shiñ-tau as a religion, and the biographies of Kada, Mabuchi and Motowori, which have been utilized in the foregoing part of this paper. The first five volumes were printed in 1829, the next four some time after his death, and the tenth, which contains his teaching as to the worship of ancestors and his life by his adopted son Kanetane, was published in 1874.

As Hirata observes, the celebration of rites in honour of the gods was considered in ancient times to be the chief function of the Mikados. When Ninigi no mikoto descended from heaven, his divine progenitors taught him how he was to rule the country, and their teaching consisted in this: 'Everything in the world depends on the spirit of the gods of heaven and earth, and therefore the worship of the gods is a matter of primary importance. The gods who do harm are to be appeased, so that they may not punish those who have offended them, and all the gods are to be worshipped, so that they may be induced to increase their favours. To compel obedience from human beings and to love them, was all the sovereign had to do, and there was no necessity for teaching them vain doctrines such as are preached in other countries. Hence the art of Government is called *Matsuri-goto*, which literally means "worshipping." Accordingly the early sovereigns worshipped the gods in person, and prayed that their people might enjoy a sufficiency of food, clothing and shelter from the elements, and twice a year, in the

6th and 12th months, they celebrated the festival of the General Purification,[46] by which the whole nation was purged of calamities, offences and pollutions.

'Although in later ages many foreign customs were adopted, we find that the religious rites of Shiñ-tau always occupied the first place in the books wherein are recorded the rules and ceremonies of the court. For instance, the first book of the ten which are called *Riyau no Gi-ge*,[47] is occupied with the rules of the Department of Religion (*Zhin-gi Riyau*). Of the fifty volumes of the *Yen-gi Shiki*[48] the first ten are devoted to Shiñ-tau matters. The *norito* (liturgies) contained in the 8th volume are not the private prayers of the Mikado, but are those used at the festivals which he celebrated on behalf of the whole people. The 9th and 10th volumes contain the names of 3132 gods in 2861 temples at which the Court worshipped (either personally or by special envoys). In the *Shiyoku-gen-seu* (1431) of Takabatake Chikafusa the constitution of the Department of Religion is described even before that of the Council of State. In the reign of Kautokou (645-654), in answer to an inqury as to how the people were to be ruled, all the ministers of the Mikado replied to him, "First serve the gods, and afterwards deliberate on matters of Government." But the successors of this Mikado neglected the worship of the gods for that of Buddha, and the consequence was the decline of their authority. An effort to reform the practice of the Court was made by the emperor Zhiyuñ-toku (b. 1197, d. 1242), who in his *Kin-pi Mi-seu* says: "The rule of the Forbidden Precinct is that the worship of the gods come first, and other matters afterwards. At morning and evening the wise resolve to do honour to the gods is carried out with diligence. Even in the slightest matters the *Zhin-guu*[49]

---

[46] The *oho-barahi* was one of the most characteristic of all Shiñ-tau festivals. The liturgy used in celebrating it has been made the subject of numerous commentaries besides those of Mabuchi and Motowori. It is still observed in the present day.

[47] The text, called *Riyau*, dates from the year 718, and the commentary *Gi-ge* from 833. Hirata is incorrect in saying that the *Jiñ-gi-Riyau* comes first; it is in reality preceded by five other sections, forming Book I.

[48] The preface of the *Yeñ-gi Shiki* is dated 927.

[49] The *Zhiñ-guu* are the two temples where Amaterasu, the Mikado's ancestress and the goddess of food Uke-mochi no kami are worshipped. In the Nai-shi-Dokoro, a building within the palace, were kept the copies of the sacred mirror of Ise and the sword of Atsuta, which have been already mentioned as being among the divine treasures received by Ninigi when he descended from heaven.

(of Ise) and the *Nai-shi-dokoro* are not to be placed after the emperor. According as the things arrive at maturity, they shall be offered up first (to the gods); but things presented by Buddhist monks and nuns, and from all persons who are under an interdict, these shall not be presented." As it is the duty of subjects to imitate the practice of the incarnate god (*ara-hito-gami*) who is their sovereign, the necessity of worshipping his ancestors and the gods from whom they spring is to be enjoined upon all every man.

'As the number of the gods who possess different functions is so great, it will be convenient to worship by name only the most important, and to include the rest in a general petition. Those whose daily affairs are so multitudinous that they have not time to go through the whole of the following morning prayers, may content themselves with adoring the residence of the Emperor,[50] the domestic *kami-dana,* the spirits of their ancestors, their local patron god, and the deity of their particular calling in life.

'In praying to the gods the blessings which each has it in his power to bestow are to be mentioned in a few words, and they are not to be annoyed with greedy petitions; for the Mikado in his place offers us petitions daily on behalf of his people, which are far more effectual than those of his subjects.

'Rising early in the morning, wash your face and hands, rinse out the mouth and cleanse the body. Then turn towards the province of Yamato, strike the palms of the hands together twice, and worship,[51] bowing the head to the ground. The proper posture is that of kneeling on the heels, which is ordinarily assumed in saluting a superior.'

[50] Adoration of the Mikado's residence is not mentioned in the *Tama-dasuki,* but is enjoined by the last edition (published in 1873) of the *Mai-tefu-zhiñ-pai Shiki* (form of morning prayer). As no form of words is given, it is impossible to say what the character of this prayer should be. The same book contains three other prayers not given in the *Tama-dasuki,* namely to the three primeval gods, to Ninigi no mikoto, and to Zhiñ-mu Ten-wau, while it omits the prayer to Adzumaterasu oho-kami (Tou-seu-guu of Iheyasu commonly called Goñ-geñ Sama).

[51] The word rendered here 'worship' is *wogamu,* which Hirata derives from *wori-kagamu,* a compound verb signifying 'to bend.' If this etymology is correct, 'bow down' would be a closer rendering.

PRAYER.

"From a distance I reverently worship with awe before Ame no Mi-hashira and Kuni no Mi-hasira, also called Shiratsu-hiko no Kami and Shinatsu hime no Kami, to whom is consecrated the Palace built with stout pillars at Tatsuta no Tachinu in the department of Heguri in the province of Yamato.

"I say with awe, deign to bless me by correcting the unwitting faults which, seen and heard by you, I have committed, by blowing off and clearing away the calamities which evil gods might inflict, by causing me to live long like the hard and lasting rock, and by repeating to the gods of heavenly origin and to the gods of earthly origin the petitions which I present every day, along with your breath, that they may hear with the sharpearedness of the forth-galloping colt."

The two deities who are here addressed are the god and goddess of wind. Their first names mean Pillar of Heaven and Pillar of Earth, and are given because the wind prevades the space between Heaven and Earth, and supports the former as a pillar supports the roof of a house. *Shina* in the alternate names means 'long breath'[52] 'Evil acts and words are of two kinds, those of which we are ourselves conscious, and those of which we are not conscious. Every one is certain to commit accidental offences, however careful he may be, and hence the practice of our ancient tongue was to say "deign to correct those failings of which I may have been guilty." But it is better to assume that we have committed such unconscious offences. If we pray that such as we have committed may be corrected, the gods are willing to pardon them. By "evil gods" are meant bad deities and demons who work harm to society and to individuals. They originated from the impurities contracted by Izanagi during his visit to the nether world, and cast off by him during the process of purification. They subsequently increased in number, especially after the introduction of Buddhism. The two deities of wind can of course blow away anything it pleases them to get rid of, and among other things the calamities which evil gods endeavour to inflict. As man is dependent on them for the breath

[52] *Tsu* is the generic particle, and *hiko* and *hime* might be translated lord and lady. Hime is still used in the latter sense.

which enables him to live, it is right to pray to them to give long life. This is also the reason why they are besought to carry our prayers to the gods of heavenly origin and to the gods of earthy origin.' As an illustration of the efficacy of prayer, Hirata gives a long account of a boy who was carried off in the year 1806 by goblins, and afterwards restored to his father, who had earnestly besought the intercession of Shinatsu-hiko and Shinatsu-hime with the other gods.

The next prayer is addressed to Amaterasu and the other gods who dwell in the sun, and consists simply in calling on them by name. The common belief of the lower classes appears to be that the sun is actually a god, and they may often be seen to worship on rising in the morning, by turning towards it, placing their hands together, and reciting prayers. The third prayer is addressed to Izanami and the other gods who dwell in the moon. Hirata says that although the *Man-yefu-shifu* contains verses about the moon, it was generally considered unlucky to admire it, the reason of which is explained by a verse in the *Ise Monogatari* to be that "man grows old by accumulating moons"; but on the 15th day of the 8th month it is customary to make offerings to the moon, because of her great brilliancy at that season of the year. This however may be a practice derived from the Chinese.

The fourth prayer is addressed to the gods of Ise, namely Amaterasu and Toyo-uke-bime no kami, with a certain number of subordinate deities in adjacent shrines.[53] Toyo-uke-bime was the daughter of Waka-musubi, who was the joint offspring of the god of Fire and the goddess of Soil. She has at least eight other names, all of which express the fact of her being the goddess of food, both vegetable, fish and flesh. Here we meet with a curious Shiñ-tau doctrine, according to which a divine being throws off portions of itself by a process of fissure, thus producing what are called *waki-mi-tama*, Parted-Spirits, with separate functions. Two of the parted spirits of Toyo-uke-bime thus formed are Kukunochi no kami, the producer of all trees, and Kayanu-hime no kami, the parent of all grasses. As rice and

---

[53] A detailed account of the legends relating to these goddesses has already been given in a paper on "The Shrines of Ise" published in the Journal of the Asiatic Society of Japan, vol. ii. [First Series].

other seeds, cattle and the silkworm were produced from the dead body of Toyo-uke bime, it is to this goddess and to the action of her 'Parted Spirits' above mentioned that mankind owes the blessings of food, clothing and lodgment. It was an ancient custom therefore to worship this goddess on moving into a new house, built of the wood and thatched with the grass of which she was the first cause. In one of the *norito* entitled·*Ohotono hogahi,* a service of this kind performed twice annually at the Mikado's court, this goddess is besought to protect his Palace from harm.

She is also worshipped under the name of Uka-no-mi-tama no Mikoto, along with two other gods, at the great temple Inari between Kiyauto and Fushimi. Temples consecrated to "Inari sama" are common all over Japan, and it is usually supposed that Inari is the name of a god; the mistake arises from the common Japanese practice of calling persons, and gods also, by the name of the place where they reside. Another erroneous belief is that Inari sama is a fox, and many temples originally dedicated to foxes are consequently mis-called temples of Inari. One origin assigned for the error is the use of a Chinese character which means 'fox' in writing down phonetically Miketsu kami, which is an alternative name of Toyo-uke-bime. The truth is that the fox is the messenger of this goddess, and images of the animal are placed in front of her temples, which may have aided in confirming the error.

The worshipper is next directed to turn in the direction of the province of Hitachi, and bowing down as before, to repeat the following prayer:—

"From a distance I reverently worship with awe before Take-mika-dzuchi no kami, Futsu-nushi no kami and Funado no kami, to whom are consecrated the Palace of Kagushima[54] in the department of Kagushima in the province of Hitachi, the palace of Kadori in the department of Kadori in the province of Shimo-tsu-fusa, and the temple of Ikisu in the province of Hitachi, which are reverently styled the three temples of Adzuma."

Take-mika-dzuchi and Futsu-nushi have already been men-

---

[54] Kagushima and Shimo-tsu-fusa are the archaic spelling of Kashima and Shimofusa. The first-named two temples have been described by Mr. C. W. Lawrence in a paper published in the Transactions of the Asiatic Society of Japan for 1874.

tioned as the two gods who descended from heaven to conquer the country for Ninigi no mikoto, and Funado no kami acted as their guide. After persuading Oho-kuni-nushi to surrender the sovereignty of Japan, they slew or expelled all the evil gods 'who glittered like fire-flies or were disorderly as May-flies, banished to foreign countries all the demons who made rocks, stumps of trees, leaves of plants and the foam of the green waters to speak, and then ascended to heaven from the province of Hitachi on a white cloud. The evil gods originated from the pollution contracted by Izanagi during his visit to the nether world, and having greatly increased in numbers, began to behave in a disorderly manner when Susanowo no mikoto showed them a bad example. Take-mika-dzuchi and Futsu-nushi drove them into Hitachi, whence they expelled them from Japanese soil. The two gods left their Parted-Spirits here, in the temples which were built in their honour.'

Hirata says that these two gods are an example of Duality in Unity, of which many other similar cases exist. The gods of Wind and Metal are in pairs, male and female, but each pair is counted as a single deity; while Oho-wata-tsumi no kami, the god of the sea, is a Trinity in Unity. He remarks that these truths 'have a profound and mysterious signification,' but omits to give any explanation of the mystery, probably because no explanation is possible.

The sixth prayer is addressed to Oho-kuni-nushi, 'who rules the Unseen, and to his consort Suseri-bime, to whom is dedicated the ancient temple of Oho-yashiro in Idzumo. By the term "Unseen" (kakuri-goto) are meant peace or disturbance in the empire, its prosperity and adversity, the life and death, good and bad fortune of human beings, in fine, every supernatural event which cannot be ascribed to a definite author. The most fearful crimes which a man commits go unpunished by society so long as they are undiscovered, but they draw down on him the hatred of the invisible gods. The attainment of happiness by performing good acts is regulated by the same law. Even if the gods do not punish secret sins by the usual penalties of the law, such as strangulation, decapitation and transfixion on the cross, they inflict diseases, misfortunes, short life and extermination of the race. Sometimes they even cause a clue to be given by which

secret crime is made known to the authorities who have power
to punish. The gods bestow happiness and blessings on those
who practise good, as effectually as if they were to manifest
themselves to our sight and give treasures, and even if the good
do not obtain material rewards, they enjoy exemption from disease, good luck and long life; and prosperity is granted to their
descendants. Never mind the praise or blame of fellow-men,
but act so that you need not be ashamed before the gods of the
Unseen. If you desire to practise true virtue, learn to stand in
awe of the Unseen, and that will prevent you from doing wrong.
Make a vow to the god who rules over the Unseen, and cultivate
the conscience (ma-go-koro) implanted in you, and then you will
never wander from the way. You cannot hope to live more
than a hundred years under the most favourable circumstances,
but as you will go to the Unseen Realm of Oho-kuni-nushi after
death, and be subject to his rule, learn betimes to bow down
before him.' In the *Tama no Mihashira* Hirata says that the
spirits of the dead continue to exist in the unseen world, which
is everywhere about us, and that they all become gods, of varying character and degrees of influence. Some reside in temples
built in their honour, others hover near their tombs, and they
continue to render services to their prince, parents, wife and
children as when in the body. Besides praying to the primary
spirit Oho-kuni-nushi, Hirata enjoins on his followers the necessity of addressing themselves also to his "Rough Spirit," worshipped in Yamato under the name of Oho-kuni-mitama, his
"Gentle Spirit," the god of the famous temple of Miwa in the
same province, and his son Kotoshiro-nushi, the god of truth.
The dogma here implied must not be confounded with that before alluded to in speaking of "Parted-Spirits." "Rough Spirit"
(*ara mi-tama*) denotes a god in his character as a punisher of
the wicked, while as a "Gentle Spirit" (*nigi mi tama*) he pardons
the penitent. There is a third character called *saki mi tama*
in which a god confers blessings. Human beings are also said
to possess the rough spirit and the gentle spirit, which are explained to be the powerful excitement of the soul separating from
the body, and acting independently. Thus the feeling of hatred
is capable of avenging injuries, a notable case of which
is the death of unfaithful lovers caused by the indignation of

the women whom they have wronged and deserted. Frequently the indignation puts on the form of the injured person, and appears to the doer of the wrong, without the knowledge of the injured person. A well-authenticated case of a Gentle Spirit appearing to its correlative Rough Spirit is mentioned in the *Ni-hon-gi,* where it is stated that when Oho-kuni-nushi was walking on the sea-shore, and lamenting that the departure of Sukuna-bikona had left him without a coadjutor in the task of civilizing the country, a god came towards him from the sea, and proffered his help. Oho-kuni-nushi did not recognize his other half, and asked his name, on which he received the answer, "I am thy *saki tama.*"

The ninth prayer is addressed to Iha-naga-hime, the goddess of long life. The legend says that Ninigi no mikoto, while making an excursion in the neighbourhood of his palace, fell in with a beautiful young girl. On his inquiring her name, she said that it was Ko-no-hana-Saku-ya-hime, daughter of Oho-yama-tsu-mi, the god of mountains, and that she had an elder sister named Iha-naga-hime. The young god-prince fell in love with her and demanded her in marriage from her father. Oho-yama-tsu-mi thereupon despatched the two sisters to him, but as the elder sister was very ugly, Ninigi no mikoto was frightened and sent her back. Upon this the father said, "My reason for offering both my daughters, was that if you had taken Iha-naga-hime into your service, the lives of the descendants of the heavenly gods would have been eternal, and if you had made use of Ko-no-hana-Saku-ya-hime, they would have been as beautiful as the flowers of the cherry-tree. But now that you have rejected the one and kept the other, they will be as frail as the blossoms, and the anger of Iha-naga-hime will shorten human life." This story presents all the characteristics of the myth. The name of the ugly daughter is a compound of iha, "rock," and naga, "long," and is symbolical of longevity; while the name of the other is explained to mean 'the blossoming of the flowers of trees,' and signifies perishable beauty. The ancient text from which the legend is quoted says "this was the cause of the short lives of the men of the present day," and Hirata takes advantage of the occasion to remark that while it is very natural for a man "to prefer a beautiful wife, as the object of marriage is to beget children, he is far wiser who chooses his wife on account of her virtues." He says that although the son of Ninigi no mikoto lived 580 years at his Palace of Takachiho, that was a short life compared with the lives of those who had lived before him, and the lives of some of the early emperors from Jimmu, which extended over more than a century, were of course still shorter. In fact from the time of Ninigi no mikoto the years of the Mikado and his people continued to grow always fewer, for although it might be supposed that the consequences of Ninigi no mikoto's act would only affect his own immediate descendants, the Mikado's subjects were naturally bound not to live longer than their sovereign. He concludes by the safe opinion that those who wish to live long should constantly take care of their health, and at the same time pray to this goddess for her bessing.

Another of the prayers is to be addressed to the *ichi no miya*, or chief temple of the province in which the worshipper lives. It is not known with exactness at what period certain temples came to have this designation, but at all events it is not to be found in any document older than the 12th century. Nevertheless, Hirata is of opinion that the practice of making such a distinction cannot be wrong, since it has existed for so long a period that it must be supposed to have the sanction of the gods. Besides the *ichi no miya*, there exist in certain provinces temples called *Kuni-tama no yashiro*, which Motowori thinks are probably dedicated to persons who first settled there and cultivated the land, and also a third class called *Sou-shiya*. The origin of the latter term, which means general temple, is supposed to be that some of the ancient governors (*koku-shi*), whose duty it was on arriving in their provinces, to make a tour for the purpose of worshipping at all the Shiñ-tau temples within their jurisdiction, compounded by worshipping only at the *ichi no miya*, if there happened to be one at the provincial capital, or built a new temple to which they gave the name of 'general temple.' Another suggestion is that it was at the *ichi-no-miya* that the governor began his round of worshipping, and that the name is derived from this circumstance. Kanetane, the editor of the *Tama-dasuki*, quotes a passage from the *Teu-ya Gun-sai*, which shows that the new governor had to perform these religious rites before entering upon his administrative duties.

Amongst the ancient Shiñ-tau practices which have descended to the present day is that of presenting new-born infants to the local deity, in order to place them under his protection. This god is commonly called the *uji-gami* (family god), and the inhabitants of the district over which he is supposed to extend his favours stand to him in the relation of *uji-ko*, or children of the family. In Satsuma, Akita, and in some other provinces it is also the custom before starting on a journey to proceed to the temple of this god, and to beseech his protection until the person shall return home again. The priest gives him a paper charm to protect him from harm on the road, and he procures also a little sand from the site of the temple, to be mixed in small quantities with water, and drunk whenever he feels uncomfortable during the journey. Whatever remains of this sand has to be returned to the temple when the traveller reaches home again, and he has of course to give thanks for the protection which he has enjoyed.

The local deity ought correctly to be called *Ubu-suna no kami*, the god of the native earth (or sand), and this term is found in ancient writings. *Uji-gami* should only be applied to the common ancestor of a number of persons who bear the same family name, or if not to an ancestor, to some one who has merited equivalent honours by acquiring a title to their gratitude. The word *uji* being originally the same as *uchi*, 'within,' *uji-gami* must mean the deity who is most closely connected by ties of worship with the persons comprehended 'within' a family or a community. The *Zhin-mei Shiki* contains the name of some *uji-gami* who were simply ancestral gods; but on the other hand the Fujiwara family, which was descended from Ame-no-koya-ne no mikoto, worshipped Take-mika-dzuchi and Futsu-nushi as their *uji-gami*. The importance attached in ancient time to the worship of the *uji-gami* is shown by grants of rice and immunities with respect to passports being given by the Mikado to nobles, in order that they might perform these duties. A regulation of the year 895, after stating that the *uji-gami* are mostly located in the Five Home Provinces,[55] says that any one who asks for leave in the second, fourth and eleventh months

---

[55] *Ki-nai*, that is Yamashiro, Yamato, Idzumi, Set-tsu and Kahachi.

for the purpose of worshipping his ancestors, is to obtain it at once. It would appear from this order that the term had not at that time lost its original meaning. Hirata thinks that the confusion arose from the fact that the *uji-gami*, or ancestral gods, of the hereditary local chiefs called *Kuni-no-miya-tsu-ko* were at the same time the patron gods of the locality. Their subjects would naturally use both terms as synonymous, and as the one fell out of use, the other would come to be employed for the local god, whether he were ancestor or not.

It is suggested by the author of the *Matsu no Ochi-ba* that what is now called the *Uji-gami* of a village was originally the collective name under which the inhabitants worshipped their respective ancestors in a single temple, and that this family-god eventually came to be looked on as the patron-god of the locality. Or perhaps, when there was already a temple to the local god, they worshipped their ancestors in the same building for convenience sake, and thus the two were in the end confounded in one. Hirata does not approve this conjecture, but it certainly seems as probable as his own view, which indeed it appears to supplement. A third supposition is that *uji-gami* is a corruption of *uchi no kami*, the god of a family or community, and that *ubu-suna no kami* is an alternative name for the *uji-gami* taken in the latter sense; so that the supposed confusion would be no confusion at all.

Hirata quotes another author, who remarks that the character of the patron-god affects the people, the animals, and the plants of the locality, which fact accounts for the local differences found to exist between individuals of one species taken from various parts of the country. All the *uji-gami* are under the orders of Oho-kuni-nushi, and acting as his agents, they rule the fortunes of human beings before their birth, during their lifetime, and after their death. Consequently when a person removes his residence, his original *uji-gami* has to make arrangements with the *uji-gami* of the place whither he transfers his abode. On such occasions it is proper to take leave of the old god, and to pay a visit to the temple of the new god as soon as possible after coming within his jurisdiction. The apparent reasons which a man imagines have induced him to change his abode may be many, but the real reasons cannot be other than that, either

he has offended his *uji-gami*, and is therefore expelled, or that
the *uji-gami* of another place has negotiated his transfer. As
the *uji-gami* has such influence over the welfare of his *protégés*,
it is of the highest importance to stand well with him, and to
enforce this argument Hirata narrates several stories of persons
who were punished for neglecting their *uji-gami*.

Next to the *uji-gami* comes the *kami-dana* or shrine in which
are worshipped the Penates. Every Japanese, with the exception
of the more bigoted members of the Buddhist sects called Nichi-
reñ-shiu and Itsu-kau-shiu, possesses such a shrine in his house.
It contains various tablets covered with paper called *o-harahi* and
o-fuda, on which are printed the titles of the gods of Ise and
other gods in whom the householder places his trust. Before
these tablets are offered up on certain occasions, as the New
Year, and the 2nd, 15th and 28th days of the month, *sake* (called
for this purpose *mi ki*), rice, and the leafy twigs of the *sakaki*
(Cleyera japonica). The practice of different families with
respect to offerings is not perfectly uniform, either as to the
articles offered, or the days on which this is done, but no one
omits the *sake*. Every evening, too, a lighted wick floating in
a saucer of oil is placed in the *kami-dana*.

Hirata would add to the *o-harahi* of the two gods of Ise and
the *fuda* of the other gods worshipped in this way an image of
Sohodo no kami, the scare-crow. Concerning this god he says:
'Sohodo no kami, also called Kuye-biko, is the scare-crow placed
in the fields to frighten away birds and animals, and though it
is a very ugly and miserable creature, the divine books say of
it "this is a god which knows everything in the empire, although
his legs are unable to walk." As the spirits of all the gods have
recourse to it, and perform wonders, it is a very dreadful deity,
and therefore an image of it should be placed before the door of
the shrine for the spirits of the gods who are bidden thither
to rest upon.' The ancient legend says that, as Oho-kuni-nushi
was walking along the shore, he saw a tiny god coming towards
him on the crests of the waves, in a boat made of the milkweed
shell, and dressed in the skin of a wren. When asked his name,
he was silent, and none of the gods who were in Oho-kuni-nushi's

following could tell. Then the *taniguku*[56] spoke, and said, "Kuye-biko will know." So they called Kuye-biko, who replied on being asked, "This is Sukuna-bikona, the child of the Musubi no kami."

The following prayer is to be addressed to the *kami-dana*:—

"Reverently adoring the great god of the two palaces of Ise in the first place, the eight hundred myriads of celestial gods, the eight hundred myriads of terrestrial gods, all the fifteen hundred myriads[57] of gods to whom are consecrated the great and small temples in all provinces, all islands and all places of the Great Land of Eight Islands, the fifteen hundreds of myriads of gods whom they cause to serve them, and the gods of branch-palaces and branch-temples, and Sohodo no kami, whom I have invited to the shrine set up on this divine shelf, and to whom I offer praises day by day, I pray with awe that they will deign to correct the unwitting faults which, heard and seen by them, I have committed, and blessing and favouring me according to the Powers which they severally wield, cause me to follow the divine example, and to perform good-works in the Way."

Hirata recounts several miracles worked by *o-harahi* of the Nai-kuu, which I am unfortunately obliged to omit for want of space, and gives a long explanation of the reason why Amaterasu, who detested Buddhism, allowed it to spread throughout the country. His arguments resemble in logical form very closely those by which the origin of evil is accounted for by theologians.

The fifteenth of the prayers is to be offered to what are called the *harahi-do no kami*, gods whose office it is to free the suppliant from evils, sins and pollutions of all kinds. Then follow prayers to the gods who keep off pestilence, to Ame-no-koya-ne no mikoto, who is regarded as the god of wisdom, to Ame-no-uzume no mikoto, the goddess of happiness, Toyo-uke-bime in her capacity as the protector of the abodes of men, the gods of the harvest, of the gate and the front court, of the kitchen fire-place (commonly called Kuwau-zhiñ-sama), of the well, of the privy, and of learning. Amongst the gods of learning he places Kada, Mabuchi and Motowori.

Last of all comes a prayer to the shrine, commonly called *butsu-dan*, in which are deposited the monumental tablets of

---

[56] Either the toad or the bull-frog.
[57] These numbers are merely figurative expressions.

ancestors and deceased members of the family, who are supposed
to become *hotoke* or perfect Buddhas immediately after their
death.   Usually the *butsu-dan* contains an image of the chief
Buddhist god of the sect to which the family belongs placed in
the centre, the monumental tablets being on either side.   Fresh
flowers are offered up as often as they are needed, and the first
portion of the rice boiled for the daily food of the household,
besides a first portion of any fruit or cooked food which the
deceased are known to be fond of.   Part of these practices, which
are corruptions introduced into the native ancestor-worship by
the Buddhist priests, should in Hirata's opinion be abandoned,
and the name of the wooden cupboard in which the tablets are
kept should be changed from *butsu-dan* (Buddhist altar) to
tama-ya (spirit house).   Water and sprigs of the Cleyera should
be offered up every day, and there is no objection to using
flowers as a decoration, but incense (joss-stick) is an abomina-
tion.   Amongst other observances which are in vogue, that of
visiting the tomb of a parent or other member of the family on
that day in each month which corresponds to the day of his death
should be kept up, for this is not a Buddhist custom, and although
the home of the spirits of the dead is in the *tama-ya*, they are
present wherever they are worshipped, being gods and therefore
ubiquitous.   The festival in honour of departed spirits, which is
celebrated on the 14th and 15th days of the 7th month, called
Bon,[58] being of Buddhist origin, ought to be abolished, and the
ancient rule of holding the festival in the 2nd, 4th and 11th
months be reverted to.

The origin of the worship of ancestors, says Hirata, dates
from the descent of Ninigi no Mikoto, who was instructed by the
creator and creatrix that the worship of the celestial and terrestrial gods was the most important part of Government.   They
taught Ama-no-koya-ne and Ama-no-futo-dama how to perform
the rites, and attached them to his person.   Zhiñ-mu Teñ-wau,
after his victories, worshipped his ancestral gods on a mountain.
It is equally the duty of a subject to be diligent in worshipping
his ancestors, whose minister he should consider himself to be.
The custom of adoption arose from the natural desire of having

[58] See Eitel's Handbook of Chinese Buddhism; Art. Ulamba..

some one to perform sacrifices, and this desire ought not to be rendered of no avail by neglect. Devotion to the memory of ancestors is the mainspring of all virtues. No one who discharges his duty to them will ever be disrespectful to the gods, or to his living parents. Such a man will also be faithful to his prince, loyal to his friends, and kind and gentle with his wife and children. For the essence of this devotion is in truth filial piety. These truths are confirmed also by the books of the Chinese, who say that "the loyal subject issues from the gate of the pious son," and again, "filial piety is the basis of all actions."

Hirata began to attract the notice of influential personages in 1822, when he was requested by the Abbot of Uheno, who was a Prince of the Blood, to present him with copies of his chief works on Shiñ-tau. In the following year he quitted the service of the *daimiyau* Itakura, and made a journey to Kiyauto, where he obtained introductions to nobles of the Court, who brought his writings to the notice of the retired Mikado Kuwau-kaku. On returning to Yedo, he devoted himself again to his studies, and during the next fifteen years produced a considerable number of works on Shiñ-tau and various other subjects. In 1836 he printed a book called the *Dai-Fu-sau-koku Kau,* which drew forth warm praises from the Mikado and the Kuwañ-baku,[59] and gave great offence to the Shiyauguñ's government, who ordered it to be suppressed, on the ground, it is said, that it contained detailed information about Japan, and might perhaps get into the hands of foreigners. In 1838 he entered the service of the *daimiyau* of Akita. From the time when he quitted the Itakura family in 1823 he had received many favours from the princes of Mito, Tayasu and Wohari, the latter of whom granted him an allowance of rice.

In 1840 he had a dispute with the government almanac makers about one of his works named *Ten-teu Mu-kiu Reki* upon the native chronology, and his opponents had sufficient influence to get him banished to Akita, with an order to publish nothing more. He left Yedo ten days after the issue of the decree, and died at Kubota in 1843, being over sixty-seven years of age.

---

[59] The Mikado's prime minister, then merely a nominal office.

His son Kanetane, in the biographical notice which forms part of the last volume of the *Tama-dasuki*, says that the number of pupils who entered his school was altogether five hundred and fifty-three. His acknowledged works amount to over one hundred, besides those which he never published. A list of the most important is to be found at the end of the *Nifu-gaku Mon-dafu*, and the biographical notice just referred to contains the dates at which each of them was begun and completed.

Hirata's works are composed in two styles, the one almost entirely colloquial, the other formed on the model of the ancient prose-writers, and crowded with obsolete words which add considerably to the difficulties of the student. His graver writings fall far short of those of Motowori in point of clearness for this reason. His scholarship appears to have been very extensive, and without a wide acquaintance with ancient Chinese literature and Buddhism it would be impossible to follow him into the remote regions whither his researches sometimes carry him. He speaks so frequently of analogies between the native traditions, and those of the Buddhists and ancient Chinese, which he interprets by the theory that the latter borrowed from the Japanese, that it is a matter of regret not to be able to test his statements; since if the supposed analogies really exist, they would be of considerable use in tracing the relationship of the Japanese to the races of the Asiatic Continent.

The object of this paper being merely to give some account of the views entertained by a school of modern writers on Shiñtau, no attempt has been made to determine which of their opinions are in accordance, and which at variance, with the real nature of this religion. It is, however, manifest that such of their conclusions as are founded on the alleged infallibility of the ancient records or on any premises which involve the miraculous or supernatural must for those very reasons be discredited; and the real nature and origin of Shiñ-tau must be decided by the usual canons of historical criticism. The most effectual means of conducting the investigation would be a comparison of the legends in the *Ko-zhi-ki* and the *Ni-hon-gi*, and the rites and ceremonies concerning which the *Norito* and other parts of the *Yen-gi Shiki* afford so much information, with what is known of other ancient religions. A correct interpretation of the extant text is the first requisite, and in arriving at this the philological labours of Mabuchi, Motowori and Hirata, imperfect as their results must naturally be, will be of immense assistance. At the same time, in order to estimate the exact value of these results, the safest method would be to follow the order proposed by Motowori for studying the old literature, and to begin by a careful analysis of the language of the *Gen-zhi* and other *Monogatari*, which form the key to the *Man-yefu-shifu;* for without an accurate knowledge of the latter, the proper reading of the Chinese characters in which the *Ko-zhi-ki, Ni-hon-gi* and *Norito* have been written down cannot be known with any degree of certainty. By carrying out this programme, and following in the footsteps of the native scholars, it would be alone possible to check their work and at the same to arrive at correct conclusions, for it is very clear that the last word has yet to be said on the subject of Shin-tau.

FINIS.